Lecture Notes in Computer Science   15550

Founding Editors

Gerhard Goos
Juris Hartmanis

The series Lecture Notes in Computer Science (LNCS), including its subseries Lecture Notes in Artificial Intelligence (LNAI) and Lecture Notes in Bioinformatics (LNBI), has established itself as a medium for the publication of new developments in computer science and information technology research, teaching, and education.

LNCS enjoys close cooperation with the computer science R & D community, the series counts many renowned academics among its volume editors and paper authors, and collaborates with prestigious societies. Its mission is to serve this international community by providing an invaluable service, mainly focused on the publication of conference and workshop proceedings and postproceedings. LNCS commenced publication in 1973.

Michael Hartisch · Chu-Hsuan Hsueh ·
Jonathan Schaeffer

Editors

Computers and Games

12th International Conference, CG 2024
Virtual Event, November 25–29, 2024
Revised Selected Papers

 Springer

Editors
Michael Hartisch
University of Passau
Passau, Germany

Chu-Hsuan Hsueh
Japan Advanced Institute of Science
and Technology
Nomi, Japan

Jonathan Schaeffer
University of Alberta
Edmonton, AB, Canada

ISSN 0302-9743   ISSN 1611-3349 (electronic)
Lecture Notes in Computer Science
ISBN 978-3-031-86584-8   ISBN 978-3-031-86585-5 (eBook)
https://doi.org/10.1007/978-3-031-86585-5

This Springer imprint is published by the registered company Springer Nature Switzerland AG
The registered company address is: Gewerbestrasse 11, 6330 Cham, Switzerland

If disposing of this product, please recycle the paper.

Preface

This volume collects the papers presented at the 12th *Computers and Games* conference (CG 2024), which took place during 25–29 November 2024. The conference was held under the auspices of the International Computer Games Association, ICGA[1]. It was conducted online and coordinated between the University of Passau (Germany), Japan Advanced Institute of Science and Technology (Japan), Maastricht University (the Netherlands), the University of Alberta (Canada), and NVIDIA (Japan).

The biennial *Computers and Games* conference (alternating with the *Advances in Computer Games* conference) is a major international forum for researchers and developers interested in all aspects of computer games. Topics of interest include game-playing programs, artificial intelligence for games, theoretical advancements, algorithmic search, mathematical insights, and social aspects of (computer) games.

The first *Computers and Games* conference took place in Japan in 1998. Since then, the conference has traveled internationally, with events held in Canada (2002), Israel (2004), Italy (2006), China (2008), the Netherlands (2016), and Taiwan (2018). It has also returned to Japan multiple times, in 2000, 2010, and 2013. In 2020 the conference had to be canceled due to the COVID epidemic and returned as an online event in 2022. The organizers opted to maintain the online format also in 2024 to capitalize on its benefits, including free registration for attendees, enhanced accessibility, and a significantly broader audience. However, logistical challenges remained, particularly in creating a schedule that accommodated attendees across diverse time zones while ensuring suitable timeslots for each presenter.

The Program Committee (PC) received 40 submissions, one of which was desk-rejected by the chairs. The remaining 39 papers underwent a single-blind review process, with each paper initially assigned to three referees. Reviewers were selected based on a bidding process to ensure expertise in the relevant subject areas. In cases of conflicting reviews, an additional referee was consulted. Of these 39 submissions, 2 were withdrawn prior to the final decision. Ultimately, with the support of numerous referees, the PC accepted 17 papers for presentation at the conference and subsequent publication.

The CG 2024 program consisted of four keynote talks and five regular paper sessions, as listed below. All presentations were recorded using the Zoom infrastructure provided by the University of Alberta, which hosted the conference. The recorded videos are available online[2].

Session 1: Chess and Optimal Play

The first paper session, chaired by Martin Müller, explored advancements in computer chess, innovative rating estimation, and novel methods for game-solving and strategy

---

[1] icga.org.

[2] icga.org/?page_id=3907.

analysis. The papers presented were "Convolutional Neural Networks with Specific Kernels for Computer Chess" by Olivier Goudet, Bhaskar Joshi, and Tristan Cazenave, "Chess Rating Estimation from Moves and Clock Times Using a CNN-LSTM" by Michael Omori and Prasad Tadepalli, "Compressed Game Solving" by Jeffrey Considine, and "Optimal Play of the All Yellow Zombie Dice Game" by Todd W. Neller, John C. Llano, Minh Q. Vu Dinh, and Clifton G.M. Presser.

Keynote: Craig Sherstan GT SOPHY – *Building an AI Racing Agent that's Fun for Everyone!*

The first keynote speaker was Craig Sherstan from Sony AI. He was introduced by one of his former PhD advisors, Patrick Pilarski. Craig is a research scientist specializing in reinforcement learning, known for his contributions to developing AI systems capable of mastering complex control tasks. At Sony AI, Craig has been instrumental in the development of GT SOPHY, a racing agent that has achieved superhuman performance in Gran Turismo. In the first part of his talk, Craig detailed the challenges and solutions involved in creating AI that can outperform top human players. He then discussed the importance of human-like behaviors for AI agents, exploring methods for making the agent adaptable to different difficulty levels, cars, and tires to provide a more engaging and enjoyable experience for players. His talk highlighted the dual goals of technical excellence and player satisfaction in designing AI for games.

Session 2: Go and NoGo

The second paper session, chaired by Kokolo Ikeda, delved into advanced analyses and solving techniques for Go and its variants, NoGo and Killall-Go. Topics included comparative evaluations of AI against perfect play, combinatorial game theory approaches for solving NoGo, and innovative methods for improving efficiency in Killall-Go solutions. The session contained presentations on "Analysing KataGo: A Comparative Evaluation Against Perfect Play in the Game of Go" by Asmaul Husna and Martin Müller, "Solving Linear NoGo with Combinatorial Game Theory" by Haoyu Du and Martin Müller, and "Solving 7×7 Killall-Go with Seki Database" by Yun-Jui Tsai, Ting Han Wei, Chi-Huang Lin, Chung-Chin Shih, Hung Guei, I-Chen Wu, and Ti-Rong Wu.

Keynote: Jonathan Schaeffer *Computer (and Human) Perfection at Checkers*

The second keynote speech was delivered by Jonathan Schaeffer (University of Alberta), introduced by Chu-Hsuan Hsueh. Jonathan graciously stepped in as a keynote speaker on very short notice due to the unexpected illness of the originally designated speaker, Hiroki Takizawa, who had planned to discuss his journey in solving the game of Othello. Jonathan, who is well known for leading the development of CHINOOK—the first computer program to win a human world championship in any game—provided fascinating insights into the methods and challenges of achieving perfection in the game of checkers. He discussed the use of endgame databases and how they were critical to the performance of proof-number search. Jonathan also highlighted unexpected obstacles in the process, such as frequent disk I/O operations and network failures, which posed challenges to the efficiency of the solving process. His talk captured the intricate balance between theoretical strategies and practical implementation in game-solving research.

Session 3: Search Algorithms

Ti-Rong Wu chaired Session 3, which focused on search algorithms. The session showcased diverse advancements in solving, generating, and optimizing strategies for puzzles and games. This session featured the following papers: "Solving Nonograms: A Constraint Satisfaction Approach" by Abik Aramian and Varduhi Yeghiazaryan, "Generating Difficult and Fun Nonograms" by Milo Roucairol and Tristan Cazenave, "Monte Carlo Search Algorithms Discovering Monte Carlo Tree Search Exploration Terms" by Tristan Cazenave, "Zweistein: A Dynamic Programming Evaluation Function for Einstein Würfelt Nicht! " by Wei-Lin Hsueh and Tsan-sheng Hsu, and "Chinese Chess EGTB with Perpetual Check-Chase Rules" by Nguyen Pham.

Keynote: I-Chen Wu *Research Journey on Deep Reinforcement Learning: From Computer Games and Beyond*

For the third keynote, Tristan Cazenave introduced I-Chen Wu, a Distinguished Professor at National Yang Ming Chiao Tung University. In his talk, I-Chen provided a comprehensive overview of the field, reflecting on key milestones in AI and games, such as IBM's DEEP BLUE and DeepMind's ALPHAGO, as pivotal moments that have shaped the field. He discussed applications of reinforcement learning in various domains, including computer games like 2048 and Go, robotics, autonomous driving, chip design, and large language models. His presentation also covered recent advancements, such as multilabeled value networks for Go and methods for accelerating ALPHAZERO. I-Chen concluded by addressing current challenges in the field, including the need for explainable AI and the reduction of computational resources in reinforcement learning applications.

Session 4: Social Aspects of Games

The fourth session, chaired by Ting Han Wei, focused on the interplay between gaming and social dynamics, exploring how games affect and are influenced by human interactions. Among the contributions were "Now You See Me: Recognizing the Player's Arousal Changes in the Game through Game Footage Videos and Game Context Features" by Yi Xia, Xiaoxu Li, Siyuan Chen, and Ruck Thawonmas, and "Sexual Harassment in Valorant and Overwatch Voice Chats" by Daniel Görlich, Max Wagner, and Markus Breuer.

Session 5: Randomness in Games and Search

The last paper session was chaired by Jean-Noël Vittaut. This session had a focus on innovative approaches to handling randomness and uncertainty in games and search strategies. The papers included "Anytime Sequential Halving in Monte-Carlo Tree Search" by

Dominic Sagers, Mark H. M. Winands, and Dennis J. N. J. Soemers, "Belief Stochastic Game: A Model for Imperfect-Information Games with Known Positions" by Achille Morenville and Éric Piette, and "A Mathematical Analysis of PlaceIt: a Game of Perfect Online Sorting" by Pablo Ruiz Cuevas, Casey Chock, and Bernardo Subercaseaux.

Keynote: Jaap van den Herik *Our Aim: Solving Chess*

The fourth and final keynote speaker was Jaap van den Herik (Leiden University), introduced by Jonathan Schaeffer. Jaap is renowned for his significant contributions to artificial intelligence, particularly in computer chess and game research. In his talk, Jaap reflected on ongoing efforts to solve chess, referencing successes in games like Connect Four, Qubic, and Checkers. He discussed the immense complexity of chess, with an estimated 10^{43} positions, and predicted it could be weakly solved before 2035. He highlighted the challenges of chess, such as its long game length, and the breakthroughs needed, including better hardware and neural networks or quantum computing. Despite current limitations, he underscored the potential of ongoing research to push the boundaries toward solving chess in the future.

Acknowledgements

The successful organization of CG 2024 was made possible by the invaluable contributions of the authors, reviewers, session chairs, and keynote speakers. We also extend our gratitude to the University of Alberta for providing the online technology that supported the event. Finally, we sincerely thank all who registered for and attended CG 2024—your participation was essential to the success of the conference.

November 2024

Michael Hartisch
Chu-Hsuan Hsueh
Jonathan Schaeffer

Organization

Organizing Committee

Michael Hartisch	University of Passau, Germany
Chu-Hsuan Hsueh	Japan Advanced Institute of Science and Technology, Japan
Jonathan Schaeffer	University of Alberta, Canada

Advisory Committee

Cameron Browne	Maastricht University, The Netherlands
Akihiro Kishimoto	NVIDIA, Japan

ICGA Executive

Tristan Cazenave	LAMSADE Université Paris Dauphine PSL CNRS, France
Hiroyuki Iida	Japan Advanced Institute of Science and Technology, Japan
Mark Lefler	Independent, USA
David Levy	Independent, UK
Jonathan Schaeffer	University of Alberta, Canada
Jaap van den Herik	University of Leiden, The Netherlands
Mark Winands	Maastricht University, The Netherlands
I-Chen Wu	National Yang Ming Chiao Tung University, Taiwan

Program Committee

Yngvi Björnsson	Reykjavik University, Iceland
Bruno Bouzy	Université Paris Cité, France
Cameron Browne	Maastricht University, The Netherlands
Paolo Burelli	IT University of Copenhagen, Denmark
Tristan Cazenave	LAMSADE Université Paris Dauphine PSL CNRS, France

Hung-Jui Chang	National Dong Hwa University, Taiwan
Jr-Chang Chen	National Taipei University, Taiwan
Lung-Pin Chen	Tunghai University, Taiwan
Hsin-Hung Chou	National Chi Nan University, Taiwan
Reijer Grimbergen	Tokyo University of Technology, Japan
Hung Guei	Academia Sinica, Taiwan
Matej Guid	University of Ljubljana, Slovenia
Michael Hartisch	University of Passau, Germany
Tsuyoshi Hashimoto	National Institute of Technology, Matsue College, Japan
Ryan Hayward	University of Alberta, Canada
Chu-Hsuan Hsueh	Japan Advanced Institute of Science and Technology, Japan
Kuo-Chan Huang	National Taichung University of Education, Taiwan
Hiroyuki Iida	Japan Advanced Institute of Science and Technology, Japan
Nicolas Jouandeau	Paris8 University, France
Tomoyuki Kaneko	University of Tokyo, Japan
Akihiro Kishimoto	NVIDIA, Japan
Jakub Kowalski	University of Wrocław, Poland
Sylvain Lagrue	Université de Technologie de Compiégne, France
Kiminori Matsuzaki	Kochi University of Technology, Japan
Martin Müller	University of Alberta, Canada
Todd Neller	Gettysburg College, USA
Diego Perez Liebana	Queen Mary University of London, UK
Éric Piette	Université catholique de Louvain, Belgium
Spyridon Samothrakis	University of Essex, UK
Jonathan Schaeffer	University of Alberta, Canada
Dennis Soemers	Maastricht University, The Netherlands
Matthew Stephenson	Flinders University, Australia
Shogo Takeuchi	Kochi University of Technology, Japan
Ruck Thawonmas	Ritsumeikan University, Japan
Michael Thielscher	University of New South Wales, Australia
Jaco van de Pol	Aarhus University, Denmark
Jonathan Vis	Leiden University Medical Center, The Netherlands
Jean-Noël Vittaut	Sorbonne Université, France
Ting Han Wei	Kochi University of Technology, Japan
Mark Winands	Maastricht University, The Netherlands
I-Chen Wu	National Yang Ming Chiao Tung University, Taiwan

Ti-Rong Wu	Academia Sinica, Taiwan
Shi-Jim Yen	National Dong Hwa University, Taiwan
Kazuki Yoshizoe	Kyushu University, Japan

Contents

Nonograms

Social Aspects of Games

Games with Uncertainty

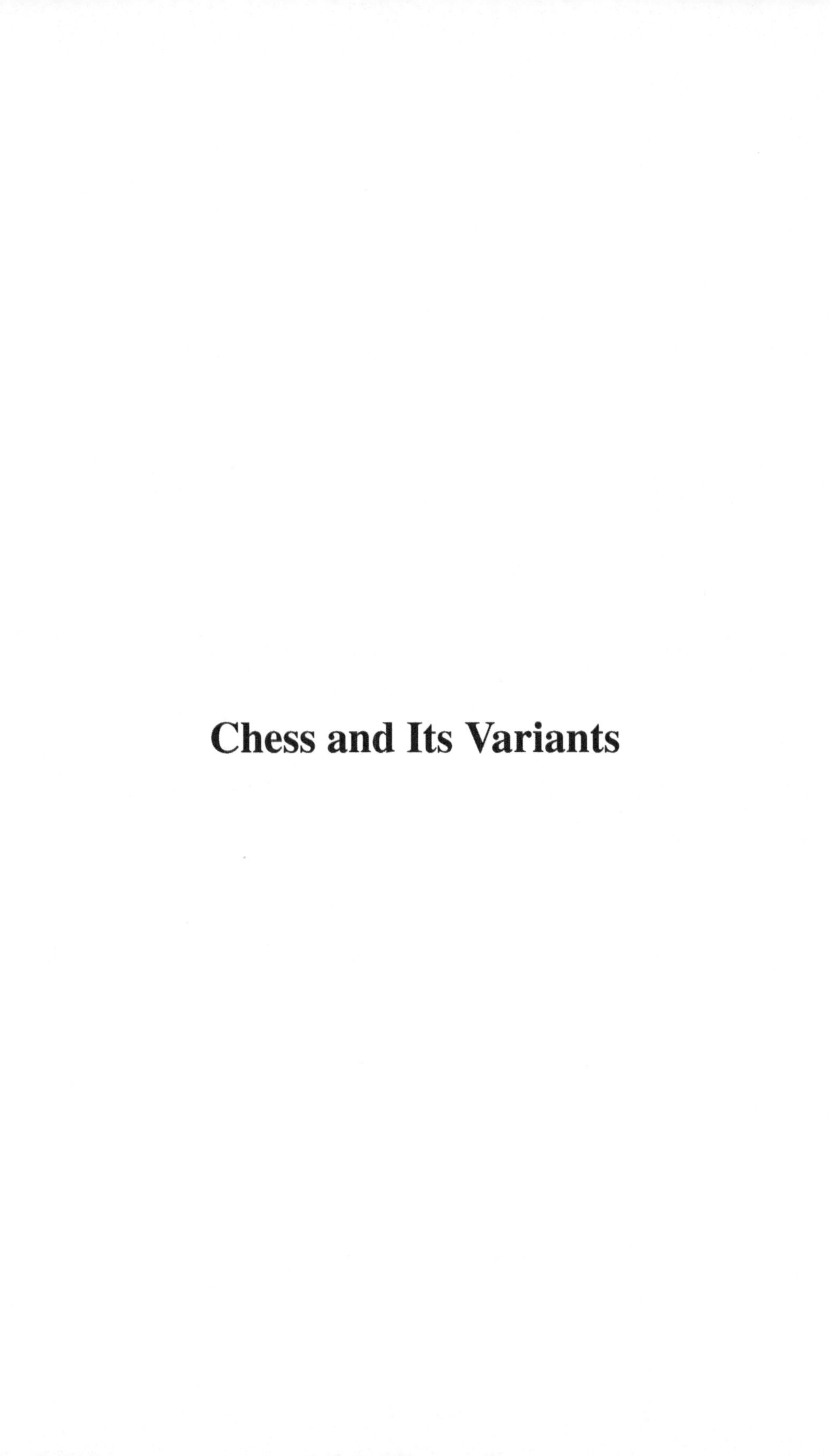

Chess and Its Variants

Chess Rating Estimation from Moves and Clock Times Using a CNN-LSTM

Michael Omori[(✉)] and Prasad Tadepalli

Oregon State University, Corvallis, OR, USA
`{omorim,prasad.tadepalli}@oregonstate.edu`

Abstract. Current chess rating systems update ratings incrementally and may not always accurately reflect a player's true strength at all times, especially for rapidly improving players or very rusty players. To overcome this, we explore a method to estimate player ratings directly from game moves and clock times. We compiled a benchmark dataset from Lichess with over one million games, encompassing various time controls and including move sequences and clock times. Our model architecture comprises a CNN to learn positional features, which are then integrated with clock-time data into a Bidirectional LSTM, predicting player ratings after each move. The model achieved an MAE of 182 rating points on the test data. Additionally, we applied our model to the 2024 IEEE Big Data Cup Chess Puzzle Difficulty Competition dataset, predicted puzzle ratings and achieved competitive results. This model is the first to use no hand-crafted features to estimate chess ratings and also the first to output a rating prediction after each move. Our method highlights the potential of using move-based rating estimation for enhancing rating systems and potentially other applications such as cheating detection.

Keywords: Chess · Rating Estimation · Cheating Detection

1 Introduction

Traditional rating systems like Elo [6] and Glicko [7], though effective, often require many games to accurately reflect the true level of skill of a player, leading to potential mismatches and inaccuracies, especially for new accounts or rapidly improving players. This delay in accurate rating adjustment can skew competitive fairness and hinder effective matchmaking. For example, lower-rated players were shown to have longer winning streaks than higher-rated players on average, suggesting that their rating may be less accurate compared to higher-rated players [3]. This could occur if a person creates a new account and is either an experienced chess player who made a second private account or a new player who transferred skills from other board games. In both cases, their initial rating starts lower on sites such as lichess [16] and chess.com [2], but their performance could be much higher.

To overcome these limitations, we propose a novel method that estimates player ratings directly from game moves and clock times, aiming to provide

M. Hartisch et al. (Eds.): CG 2024, LNCS 15550, pp. 3–13, 2025.
https://doi.org/10.1007/978-3-031-86585-5_1

accurate ratings after each game. Our dataset comes from Lichess, encompasses 1.2 million games from April 2021 to July 2024 (inclusive), covers various time controls and includes detailed move sequences and clock times. Chess streamers like GothamChess [23] have attempted this on their own (without computer aid) by using their chess knowledge to look at games and "guess the elo" and it is quite challenging to be consistently accurate.

Our method is a neural network architecture that combines a four-layer Convolutional Neural Network (CNN) and a Bidirectional Long Short-Term Memory (LSTM) network. The CNN extracts positional features from the chessboard, which are then integrated with clock time data by the LSTM to predict player ratings move-by-move. This approach allows the model to consider both spatial and temporal dimensions of the game, leading to more precise rating predictions. The model achieved a mean absolute error (MAE) of 183 rating points in the test data, demonstrating the effectiveness of the overall approach.

Ablation studies confirm that the inclusion of clock time data improves the model performance. Additionally, the same model is tested on the 2024 IEEE Big Data Cup Chess Puzzle Difficulty Competition dataset, where it predicts puzzle ratings competitively, indicating the model's versatility and robustness.

An additional application of the rating estimate for each move is to check for anomalous behavior. For example, a 1300 rated player that is playing like a 2600 in half their games, but 1300 in the other half may be considered an anomaly. A CNN was [20] trained on Lichess games but only achieved marginally better results than random guessing for classifying cheaters. Lichess itself has software called Kaladin for detecting cheaters [14]. It uses a CNN and also utilizes chess insights, which includes metrics such as average centipawn loss and number of moves. One downside to this approach is that it can only do as well as the people who labeled the data.

Our main contribution is creating the first neural network that predicts chess rating move by move without hand-crafted features. This is unlike the rating players normally get after playing an entire game, which is based off their current rating, the game result, and the opponent's rating. Second, we collated a benchmark from Lichess data for evaluation and finally demonstrated the utility of the amount of clock time remaining after each move in estimating player rating.

In conclusion, this method presents an advancement in chess rating estimation by leveraging deep learning techniques to analyze in-game moves and clock times. The promising results and potential applications highlight the importance of this method, paving the way for more dynamic and fair rating systems in competitive chess.

2   Background

There are various rating systems to estimate a player's skill, such as FIDE's Elo and Lichess's Glicko 2. Elo uses expected scores and a K-factor for rating updates, while Glicko incorporates rating deviation (RD) and volatility for more accurate adjustments. We will briefly explain Glicko2 since that is the rating system that we are trying to estimate through moves.

2.1 Glicko-2 Rating System

Glicko-2 incorporates volatility to indicate how consistent a player plays, along with a rating and a rating deviation for each player. A collection of games like in a tournament is used to update these values and is treated to have occurred simultaneously with the same ratings μ, volatility, and deviation ϕ for each game. The rating deviation is manually set for each player to a specified amount such as between 0.3 and 1.2.

First, the variance v is calculated based on the outcomes of the game for each opponent with the rating μ_j.

$$v = \left[\sum_{j=1}^{m} g(\phi_j)^2 E(\mu, \mu_j, \phi_j) \left\{ 1 - E(\mu, \mu_j, \phi_j) \right\} \right]^{-1} \tag{1}$$

where

$$g(\phi) = \frac{1}{\sqrt{1 + 3\phi^2/\pi^2}} \tag{2}$$

$$E(\mu, \mu_j, \phi_j) = \frac{1}{1 + \exp(-g(\phi_j)(\mu - \mu_j))} \tag{3}$$

The change in rating Δ is then calculated by comparing the actual outcome of the game (win 1, draw 0.5, loss 0) with the expected result based on the logistic formula in Eq. 3. Note that $g(\phi_J)$ and v are directly proportional to the step size of the rating change.

$$\Delta = v \sum_{j=1}^{m} g(\phi_j) \left(s_j - E(\mu, \mu_j, \phi_j) \right) \tag{4}$$

The new volatility is calculated using the Illinois algorithm [27], based on Δ, ϕ, and v. A more detailed explanation can be found in the paper by Mark Glickman [7]. The final step involves updating both the rating deviation and the player ratings to μ' and ϕ'.

$$\phi^* = \sqrt{\phi^2 + \sigma'^2} \tag{5}$$

$$\phi' = \frac{1}{\sqrt{\frac{1}{\phi^{*2}} + \frac{1}{v}}} \tag{6}$$

$$\mu' = \mu + \phi'^2 \sum_{j=1}^{m} g(\phi_j) \left(s_j - E(\mu, \mu_j, \phi_j) \right) \tag{7}$$

Overall, the Glicko-2 rating update is applied after each game, while our work tackles the challenge of rating updates after each move within a game.

3   Related Works

One of the first works on modeling chess player skill used Rybka 3 [31] evaluations to model player moves based off rating [22]. Later, 30 hand-crafted features were fed into random forests [1] and support vector machines [4] to predict ratings on players binned by rating into 10 different splits [28]. Rather than focusing the problem as a classification problem with limited bins, we choose to frame it as a regression problem, as this gives us more flexibility and precision in rating players. Also, the data from the previous rating estimation paper is not publicly available, so we compiled our own open source dataset from Lichess for this task.

The recent popularity of word prediction has permeated its way into the chess field as move prediction. Maia [17] adapted AlphaZero's residual Convolutional Neural Network (CNN) [26], removed the search algorithm to predict moves based on rating bins, and improved the accuracy over a depth-limited Stockfish. Stockfish is currently the strongest chess engine [29] and the original Leela Zero was an open source clone of it, although it has since migrated to a transformer architecture [19]. The Maia model was then fine-tuned to predict specific player moves [18]. GPT-2 was fine-tuned on 2.8 million chess games, demonstrating strategic understanding without directly obtaining a rating. Another transformer model achieved a 2895 Lichess Blitz rating through supervised learning on Stockfish evaluations from 10 million games [24].

Further classification of chess games has been explored through a binary classifier for detecting cheaters, using the Euclidean distance to compare player features such as move accuracy and response time [12]. One paper showed that the winning likelihood strongly correlates with the remaining time in rapid chess games, essentially less time lowers chances of winning [25]. Multi-class classification of chess games, predicting outcomes such as win/draw/loss based on moves and ratings with an LSTM, has also been attempted [21]. Another study predicted the brilliance of moves (a binary classification) using features from chess engine analysis [33]. While these approaches are similar to ours, they focus on classification tasks, whereas our model predicts a continuous value.

Rating prediction has been conducted in other gaming domains, such as Massive Online Battle Arena (MOBA) games. In one case, a transformer was trained to predict player ratings for matchmaking using descriptive features like kills and deaths recorded in three-minute intervals [34]. The predicted rating showed a higher correlation with the win rate than the existing rating system, particularly for players with fewer than 15 games.

4   Dataset

1.2 million Lichess games from April 2021 to July 2024 are used in the dataset, with 30,000 games from each month.[1] Lichess is a chess website chosen because it is open source and contains the largest publicly available database of games

---

[1] Games are taken after March 2021 because of some incorrect results that month in the Lichess database due to a datacenter fire.

for free use. The data is split randomly with 80% used for the training set and 20% used for the test set. Other available input features include the amount of clock time remaining after each move. The outputs to be estimated are the ratings of both players for a single game.

Moreover, we applied the same model architecture to the 2024 IEEE Big Data 2024 Cup Chess Puzzle Difficulty Competition [11]. This data contains a Forsyth-Edwards Notation (FEN) [5] string representation of the starting position, along with the moves in Universal Chess Interface (UCI) [10] notation for the solution.

4.1 Time Controls

Lichess time controls are less than 29 s for UltraBullet, 179 for Bullet, 479 for Blitz, 1499 for Rapid, else Classical. Games with increment add 40 times the increment to the total time [15]. A time control of "5+3", which is 5 min per side with an additional 3 s for each move, becomes 5 x 60 + 40 x 3 = 420 s. 420 s is less than 479 and is considered blitz. 40 comes from an approximation of the average number of moves in a game.

4.2 Metrics

The Mean Absolute Error (MAE) is used to provide an intuitive metric to understand the performance of models. The MAE is given for the pre-standardized rating to allow for a more interpretable loss. The test data is split up by time control to see how model performance varies between time controls. The metric used for the Chess Puzzle Competition is the mean squared error (MSE). We also provide the MSE for the game ratings.

5 Method

5.1 Input Features

We use a similar input representation as AlphaZero, with one plane for each piece-color combination, totaling 12 planes [26]. Each square contains a 1 if the corresponding piece is present; otherwise, it includes a 0. For example, the plane for black pawns contains 1 s in the seventh row and 0 s everywhere else. Following [25], the remaining clock-time is included as a feature. That paper showed a strong correlation between winning likelihood, remaining time, and position evaluation in 3-minute chess games. The remaining clock-time feature is standardized by subtracting the mean and dividing by the standard deviation. The same standardization process is applied to the ratings for more stable learning. The mean rating is 1514, with a standard deviation of 366. The same input is used for the puzzle competition, except it does not have clock time features because they were unavailable. FEN string representations were converted to the array representation.

5.2 Model Architecture

The architecture, which we will refer to as RatingNet, is a CNN that takes in each board state and passes this into a Bidirectional Long Short Term Memory Neural Network (LSTM) to predict both player ratings for the game after each move. CNNs have demonstrated success in various computer vision tasks, having been initially applied to document recognition [13]. LSTMs have also been proven to be successful in modeling long-term dependencies [9]. A four-layer CNN is used with batch normalization and mean pooling after each layer. The CNN is kept shallow to mitigate overfitting without having to train on a lot of data. The output of the CNN is concatenated with the amount of clock time spent for that corresponding move. This is then fed through the LSTM, which has two fully connected layers on top to output the ratings for the players of that game. The LSTM takes in the hidden state representation at the previous move and clock usage as input. One dropout layer is used after the first fully connected linear layer. Leaky ReLU activations are employed [32]. A simple baseline for predicting the mean chess rating is also shown for comparison.

RatingNet does not use one player's rating as input to predict the other player's rating. The reason is to focus the network on understanding chess rather than just predicting a rating close to the other player's rating. This is to mitigate potential problems when the rating difference is significant, one player's rating is provisional, or when a player is playing on an alternate account (Fig. 1).

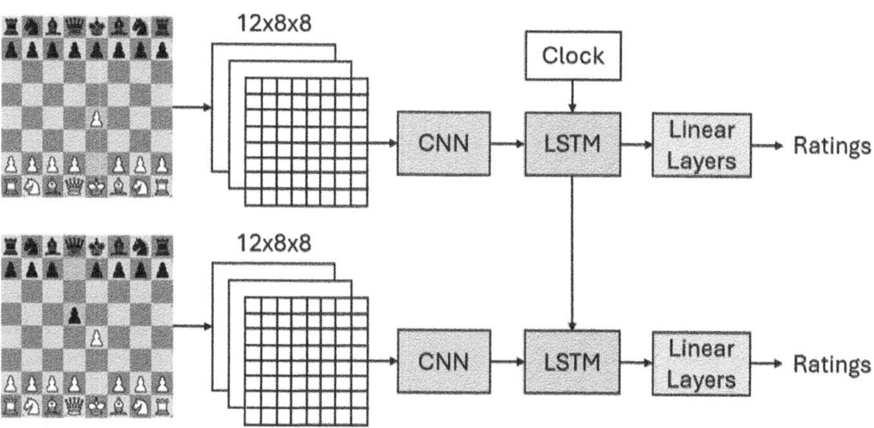

Fig. 1. The model architecture used to predict chess ratings after each move using a CNN and LSTM taking in the remaining clock time feature. This shows the first two time steps of a sample game.

6 Results

Table 1. MAE of Different Methods Across Various Chess Time Controls

Time Control	RatingNet	RatingNetNoClock	Mean
Average Test Loss	182	239	346
Ultrabullet Loss	186	269	250
Bullet Loss	182	274	340
Blitz Loss	183	244	378
Rapid Loss	182	207	305
Classical Loss	151	185	246

Table 2. MSE of Different Methods Across Various Chess Time Controls

Time Control	RatingNet	RatingNetNoClock	Mean
Average Test Loss	56,618	91,619	183,538
Ultrabullet Loss	56,927	115,833	95,459
Bullet Loss	57,569	117,776	176,296
Blitz Loss	57,330	94,048	216,803
Rapid Loss	56,433	71,215	141,016
Classical Loss	38,491	56,032	94,304

The average MAE across the time controls is 182 for RatingNet. This is reasonable given that some chess categories, such as the United States Chess Federation (USCF), are 200 points per class [30]. The loss for longer-time controls is lower. The most likely reason for this is that the range of ratings decreases as the time control increases, partially because faster time controls are more popular. In addition, faster time controls may have a bit more randomness because players have less time to think, making it harder to estimate the skill levels (Tables 1 and 2).

The results may need to be taken with a grain of salt however because the percentage of times that the white player won with a higher rating and when the black player won with a higher rating was calculated only to be 53% in the training data. Such rating problems also appear in over-the-board chess games and possible factors for this center on the fact that rating systems are often overoptimistic for players with higher ratings due to the simplicity of their model [8]. Another consideration is that there is no rating label for each move, but only for the player after having played a certain number of games. The rating outputs after each move is modeling the rating estimate of the player after having seen that move and all the previous moves made by the players in that game.

We additionally report the MSE on the test set of the IEEE Big Data 2024 Cup Chess Puzzle Difficulty Competition. On the public leaderboard, the MSE was 82,049. The score is comparable to the MSE for RatingNetNoClock on estimating rating in games.

7   Clock Ablation

Because faster time controls have less time for thinking and are closer to random play than longer time controls, our hypothesis was that the correlation between move quality and chess rating may weaken, thus having additional information such as the amount of time spent on each move could be useful. To test this, an ablation experiment was performed to determine the usefulness of the clock time feature. Without the clock time feature (setting the clock input to a constant stream of 0 s), the model does slightly worse; specifically, the addition of clock information reduces the MAE by 57 points, a 24% improvement. Notably, the clock feature helps significantly at faster speeds, such as bullets, with a 92-point reduction in error, or a 34% improvement. When the time control is longer, for example, in classical, the error is the lowest, with a 151 MAE for RatingNet. Overall, the network is able to utilize the time spent per move as an effective feature for skill estimation.

8   Game Analysis

A couple of sample games are investigated to determine how different types of moves affect the rating estimation of the model. We sample a game shown in Fig. 2 in which the model performs well. It correctly lowered the rating estimate of the player of the white pieces after the move Nf5, which allows the knight to be taken by the opponent's bishop. The full game is shown in the appendix as game 1. We also analyze a game with high loss, shown in the appendix as game 2. This bullet game was played between a white rating of 2922 and a black rating of 3163. The final predicted rating for white is 1459 and for black it is 1460. Because the average rating is around 1500, we do expect higher ratings to present more difficulties because there are fewer examples of such high rated games. We expect that in some games however, RatingNet would provide more accurate rating estimations than the player's actual rating as players do have off days or games where they play really well. With an accurate enough rating estimation system, one could consider further extending this work to potentially detect engine use or external assistance. For example, if a specific move could be marked as having a much higher rating than what the player's true strength is, further investigation could occur.

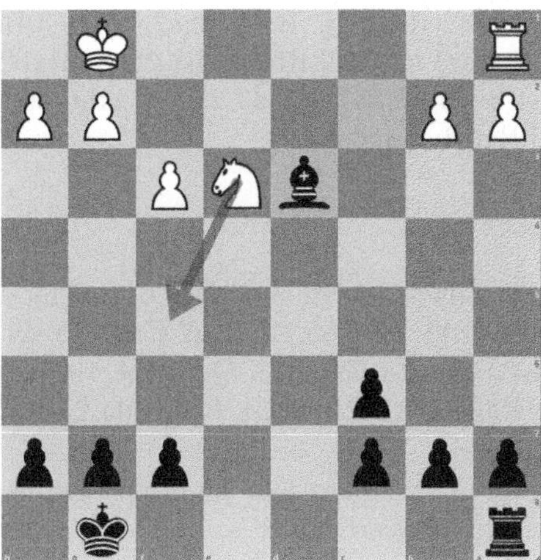

Fig. 2. White plays Nf5, a blunder because black can take it with the bishop on d3. White's estimated rating goes from 1255 to 1241. Their actual Lichess rating in this bullet game is 1224.

9   Conclusion

Our proposed method for online chess rating estimation leverages game moves and clock times without relying on hand-crafted features for a variety of time controls. By integrating a CNN-LSTM architecture, we demonstrated the potential to accurately predict player rating on a move-by-move basis. The performance of the model, with an MAE of 182, shows promise in improving rating systems, providing real-time and dynamic assessments of the player's skills. This novel approach could also serve as a foundation for applications beyond rating estimation, such as anomaly detection in games and paves the way for more granular rating systems in chess

10   Appendix

10.1   Hyperparameters and Code

training batch size: 32, learning rate: 1e−4, weight decay: 1e−5, epochs: 50, learning rate patience: 10, learning rate factor: 0.5, dropout: 0.5.

The model was trained on one A40 gpu and took 12 h to finish training. The code: https://github.com/AstroBoy1/RatingNet

10.2   Game 1

1. e4 e5 2. Nf3 Nc6 3. d4 exd4 4. Nxd4 Nf6 5. Nxc6 dxc6 6. Nc3 Qxd1 7. Nxd1 Bc5 8. Bd3 O-O 9. O-O Re8 10. Be3 Bxe3 11. Nxe3 Nxe4 12. Bxe4 Rxe4 13.

Nd1 Bf5 14. f3 Re2 15. Rf2 Rxc2 16. Rxc2 Bxc2 17. Ne3 Bd3 18. Nf5 Bxf5 19.
g4 Bg6 20. Kf2 Rd8 21. Kg3 Rd2 22. Rb1 Bxb1 23. h4 Rxb2 24. h5 Rxa2 25. g5
Bf5 26. f4 h6 27. Kh4 hxg5 28. Kxg5 Bd3 29. h6 gxh6 30. Kxh6 Rg2 31. f5 f6
32. Kh5 Be2 33. Kh6 Rg5 1/2-1/2

10.3   Game 2

1. e4 g6 2. d4 Bg7 3. Nc3 d6 4. h4 Nf6 5. f3 Nc6 6. Be3 h5 7. Nge2 e5 8. d5 Ne7
9. Qd2 O-O 10. O-O-O a6 11. Bh6 b5 12. Bxg7 Kxg7 13. g4 hxg4 14. fxg4 Bxg4
15. a3 Rb8 16. Bg2 b4 17. axb4 Rxb4 18. Qd3 Qb8 19. b3 a5 20. Kd2 Qb6 21.
Qe3 Bxe2 22. Qxb6 cxb6 23. Kxe2 Rc8 24. Kd3 Rd4 25. Ke2 Rxc3 0-1

Disclosure of Interests. The authors have no competing interests to declare that
are relevant to the content of this article.

References

1. Breiman, L.: Random forests. Mach. Learn. **45**, 5–32 (2001)
2. Chess.com: Chess.com play chess online. https://www.chess.com
3. Chowdhary, S., Iacopini, I., Battiston, F.: Quantifying human performance in chess. Sci. Rep. **13**(1), 2113 (2023)
4. Cortes, C.: Support-vector networks. Machine Learning (1995). https://doi.org/10.1007/BF00994018
5. Edwards, S.: Forsyth-edwards notation. https://www.chessprogramming.org/Forsyth_Edwards_Notation
6. Elo, A.E., Sloan, S.: The rating of chessplayers: past and present. (No Title) (1978)
7. Glickman, M.E.: Example of the Glicko-2 System, vol. 28. Boston University (2012)
8. Glickman, M.E., Jones, A.C.: Rating the chess rating system. Chance-Berlin then New York **12**, 21–28 (1999)
9. Hochreiter, S.: Long short-term memory. Neural Computation. MIT-Press (1997)
10. Huber, R., Meyer-Kahlen, S.: Universal chess interface. https://www.chessprogramming.org/UCI
11. IEEE: Bigdata 2024 cup: predicting chess puzzle difficulty. https://knowledgepit.ml/predicting-chess-puzzle-difficulty/
12. Laarhoven, T., Ponukumati, A.: Towards transparent cheat detection in online chess: An application of human and computer decision-making preferences. In: International Conference on Computers and Games, pp. 163–180. Springer (2022). https://doi.org/10.1007/978-3-031-34017-8_14
13. LeCun, Y., Bottou, L., Bengio, Y., Haffner, P.: Gradient-based learning applied to document recognition. Proc. IEEE **86**(11), 2278–2324 (1998)
14. Lichess: Kaladin: machine learning tool aimed at automating cheat detection using insights data. https://github.com/lichess-org/kaladin
15. Lichess: Lichess faq. https://lichess.org/faq#time-controls
16. Lichess: free online chess server. https://lichess.org
17. McIlroy-Young, R., Sen, S., Kleinberg, J., Anderson, A.: Aligning superhuman AI with human behavior: Chess as a model system. In: Proceedings of the 26th ACM SIGKDD International Conference on Knowledge Discovery & Data Mining, pp. 1677–1687 (2020)

18. McIlroy-Young, R., Wang, R., Sen, S., Kleinberg, J., Anderson, A.: Learning models of individual behavior in chess. In: Proceedings of the 28th ACM SIGKDD Conference on Knowledge Discovery and Data Mining, pp. 1253–1263 (2022)
19. Monroe, D., Team, T.L.C.Z.: Mastering chess with a transformer model. arXiv preprint arXiv:2409.12272 (2024)
20. Patria, R., Favian, S., Caturdewa, A., Suhartono, D.: Cheat detection on online chess games using convolutional and dense neural network. In: 2021 4th International Seminar on Research of Information Technology and Intelligent Systems (ISRITI), pp. 389–395. IEEE (2021)
21. Reddy, K.V., Kumar, B., Kumar, N.P., Parasuraman, T., Balasubramanian, C., Ramakrishnan, R.: Chess match outcome prediction via sequential data analysis with deep learning. In: 2023 International Conference on Sustainable Communication Networks and Application (ICSCNA), pp. 1442–1447. IEEE (2023)
22. Regan, K., Haworth, G.: Intrinsic chess ratings. In: Proceedings of the AAAI Conference on Artificial Intelligence, vol. 25, pp. 834–839 (2011)
23. Rozman, L.: Gothamchess: Chess Youtube channel. https://www.youtube.com/@GothamChess
24. Ruoss, A., et al.: Grandmaster-level chess without search. arXiv preprint arXiv:2402.04494 (2024)
25. Sigman, M., Etchemendy, P., Slezak, D.F., Cecchi, G.A.: Response time distributions in rapid chess: a large-scale decision making experiment. Front. Decis. Neurosci. **4**, 60 (2010)
26. Silver, D., et al.: A general reinforcement learning algorithm that masters chess, shogi, and go through self-play. Science **362**(6419), 1140–1144 (2018)
27. Snyder, J.: Inverse interpolation, a real root of f (x)= 0. Univ. Illinois Digit. Comput. Lab. ILLIAC I Library Routine **H1–71**, 4 (1953)
28. Tijhuis, T., Blom, P.M., Spronck, P.: Predicting chess player rating based on a single game. In: 2023 IEEE Conference on Games (CoG), pp. 1–8. IEEE (2023)
29. Romstad, T., Costalba, M., Kiiski, J., Linscott, G., open source community: Stockfish chess engine. https://stockfishchess.org/
30. United states chess federation: USCF. https://new.uschess.org/
31. Rajlich, V.: Rybka. http://www.rybkachess.com/
32. Xu, J., Li, Z., Du, B., Zhang, M., Liu, J.: Reluplex made more practical: leaky relu. In: 2020 IEEE Symposium on Computers and communications (ISCC), pp. 1–7. IEEE (2020)
33. Zaidi, K., Guerzhoy, M.: Predicting user perception of move brilliance in chess. arXiv preprint arXiv:2406.11895 (2024)
34. Zhang, C., et al.: QuickSkill: novice skill estimation in online multiplayer games. In: Proceedings of the 31st ACM International Conference on Information & Knowledge Management, pp. 3644–3653 (2022)

Convolutional Neural Networks with Specific Kernels for Computer Chess

Olivier Goudet[1(✉)], Bhaskar Joshi[2], and Tristan Cazenave[2]

[1] LERIA, Université d'Angers, 2 Boulevard Lavoisier, Angers 49045, France
`olivier.goudet@univ-angers.fr`
[2] LAMSADE, Université Paris Dauphine - PSL, CNRS, Paris, France

Abstract. We present the use of chess filters for the convolutional layers used in computer chess. We compare different types of blocks with and without chess filters. Our comparison uses the Leela Chess Zero (Lc0) T60 dataset to train the networks with supervised learning.

1 Introduction

The game of chess has long been a benchmark for artificial intelligence (AI), offering a well-defined yet highly complex environment where strategic decision-making is paramount. The advent of computer chess programs marked significant milestones in AI, with early achievements driven by brute-force search algorithms and hand-crafted evaluation functions [8]. However, the limitations of these traditional approaches became evident as the depth of required computations grew exponentially, prompting the exploration of more sophisticated techniques [1].

In recent years, the integration of neural networks into chess engines has revolutionized the field. Notable among these advancements is the development of deep reinforcement learning frameworks, such as AlphaZero, which combine neural networks with Monte Carlo Tree Search (MCTS) to achieve superhuman performance in chess [10,11]. These approaches have demonstrated that neural networks can learn intricate strategies and generalize across a vast array of positions without relying on domain-specific knowledge [7]. The current state-of-the-art in computer chess is to use Residual Networks (ResNets) [2], enabling deep architectures, which have shown remarkable success in improving the accuracy of move predictions and value estimations.

Despite these advances, there remains a need for a comprehensive analysis that compares the performance of different neural network architectures within the domain of computer chess. This study aims to fill this gap by systematically evaluating the effectiveness of various convolutional neural network models, such as ResNets, but also more recent architectures such as MobileNet [6] and ConvNeXt [5] inspired by recent breakthroughs in other AI domains. In this paper, we utilize the T60 dataset, a robust collection of self-play games generated by the Leela Chess Zero (Lc0) chess engine [12], to train and evaluate multiple neural network architectures. We focus on key performance metrics such as latency of network, memory, accuracy and MSE loss to determine which architectures offer the most promise for future developments in computer chess.

The remainder of this paper is structured as follows: Sect. 2 describes the different types of blocks for the trunk of the neural network that we compare, including the specific chess filters that we use in the convolutional layers. Section 3 presents our experimental results, and Sect. 4 concludes the paper with a summary of our contributions and suggestions for future research.

2   Neural Network Architectures

During training and evaluation, we use the *classic encoding* of Lc0. Each chess position is converted into a tensor input for the neural network which consists of 112 planes of size 8×8. As explain more in detail in [4], the first 6 planes encode the position of the pieces of the player whose turn it is (one plane for each type of piece). The next 6 planes encodes the positions of the pieces for the opponent. Plane 12 is set to all 1 if one or more repetitions have taken place. These 13 planes are repeated to encode not only the current position, but also the seven previous chess positions of the game. The last 8 planes encode further information, such as whether each color has the right to castle on queen's or king's side.

After the encoding step, this tensor input for the neural network of size $(112, 8, 8)$ is then processed like an image with 112 color channels by a chain of blocks using convolutional layers in the trunk of the neural network. After these blocks, the output is fed into two heads, called the policy head and the value head (see Sect. 3.2 below).

2.1   Different Type of Blocks for the Trunk

In this subsection, we describe the three types of blocks for the neural network trunk that we have compared in this work: residual block, MobileNet block and ConvNeXt block.

Residual Block. Residual blocks [2] are a widely used architecture in computer chess, due to their ability to train deep networks without suffering from the vanishing gradient problem. Each residual block incorporates two standard convolutional layers for feature extraction, followed by a *squeeze and excitation* (SE) layer [3]. The input is then added back to the output of this SE layer, forming the residual connection.

MobileNet Block. MobileNet neural networks [6] were designed for efficient deep learning models, particularly in resource-constrained environments. This block begins with a pointwise convolutional layer, which increases the size of the number of channels by a factor called *depthwise multiplier*. The next stage is a depthwise convolutional layer, which processes each input channel independently. Each of these two first steps are followed by a batch normalization (BN) layer and the application of a ReLU activation function. Finally, the last layer applies a second pointwise convolution operation that restores the original dimensionality of the output channels, followed by BN and SE layers. Lastly the input is added to the output like in residual blocks.

ConvNeXt Block. ConvNeXt neural networks [5] represent a modern evolution of traditional convolutional neural networks, offering superior performance in certain scenarios. The ConvNeXt block begins with a depthwise convolution layer, which is followed by a normalization layer to ensure stability during training. Next, a pointwise convolutional layer with GELU activation function is applied. It expands the number of channels by a factor of four. A second pointwise convolutional layer (with linear activation) is used to retrieve the number of channels of the input. Finally, the block includes a residual connection as in the other two block types.

2.2 Chess Filters for Convolutional Layers

In this work, we propose some variants of the three types of blocks described in the previous section, using specific chess kernels in the standard and depthwise convolutional layers. The underlying idea is to help the neural network extract relevant patterns in chess positions related to the movement of different types of pieces in the chess game. This idea has certain similarities with the concept of local shape features used for the game of Go in [9], with the difference that in our case, different predefined masks are used to guide the gradient descent towards a better parameterization of the neural network (like a regularization tool), rather than focusing on extracting features that can be directly used at inference time.

Figures 1, 2 and 3 represent three types of masks with 0 and 1 values that can be applied to a convolutional filter of size $(5, 5)$ to retain only those filter parameters corresponding to the most important types of movement in chess: vertical, horizontal, diagonal and knight moves. Any $(5, 5)$ filter parameters that do not correspond to a square with a piece symbol in these masks are set to 0.

Fig. 1. Mask for knight kernel.

Fig. 2. Mask for rook kernel.

Fig. 3. Mask for bishop kernel.

These three types of *chess filters* can be combined together to build new convolutional layers. An example of depthwise convolutional layer with chess filters is depicted in Fig. 4. We see on this figure that the first third of input channels are processed using knight filters, the second third using rook filters and the final third using bishop filters (version called *knight-rook-bishop*). We also introduce an other version with one half of the channels processed by rook filters and the other half by bishop filters (version called *rook-bishop*). We have experimentally observed that using different types of chess kernels combined together instead of a single type of filter in the same convolutional layer yields better results.

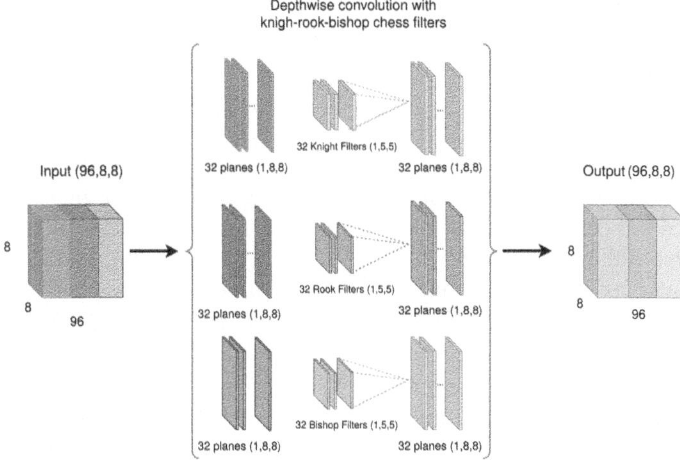

Fig. 4. Depthwise convolution with knight-rook-bishop chess filters applied to input tensor of size $(96, 8, 8)$.

3   Experimental Results

The aim of this section is to answer two questions experimentally. The first concerns the comparison of different block types on neural network performance. The second question concerns the impact of chess filters in combination with each type of block used in the neural network.

3.1   Training and Validation Test Sets

In this paper, we use one million chess games from the T60 dataset[1] which is a classical dataset used to train Lc0 neural networks. Collected over a period

---

[1] https://storage.lczero.org/files/training_data/test60/.

from July 26, 2019, to January 8, 2022, the T60 dataset comprises millions of self-play games generated by Lc0. These games encompass a wide range of board states and movement sequences, providing a varied basis for training and testing various neural network architectures.

From this data set of one million games, we retain 80% for a training dataset and the remaining 20% for the validation dataset. Each game of this dataset is composed of many chess positions, corresponding to the training inputs, that we encode with the *classic encoding* of Lc0 (see Sect. 2).

The training target for each position is a vector of probability of size 1858 corresponding to all the possible moves (source square plus destination square), as well as a vector of probability of size 3, corresponding to the probabilities of losing, winning and drawing the game when in the current position. These probabilities were evaluated with the MCTS during the self-played games performed by Lc0.

3.2 Experimental Settings

The neural networks that we compare in this paper use different type of blocks as described in Sect. 2: residual, MobileNet or ConvNeXt blocks. With each type of block we build architectures with 6, 12 and 18 blocks, using Lc0's open-source training code[2] as a starting point. For each number of blocks, denoted nb_{blocks}, we use $nb_{filters} \in \{96, 192\}$ filters in the trunk. In the MobileNet blocks the *dephtwise multiplier* parameter is set to 6. For all the standard and depthwise convolutional layers used in this work we use kernels of size $(5, 5)$ (with the exception of the pointwise convolutional layers used in the mobile net and ConvNeXt architectures).

On the top of each network trunk, the same two heads are used for each neural network configuration:

- the policy head is the *classical policy head* of Lc0. It consists in a pointwise convolutional layer with 32 output channels, used to convert the output of the trunk of size $(nb_{filters}, 8, 8)$ into a tensor of size $(32, 8, 8)$. This tensor is then flattened and processed with a dense layer with a softmax activation function to obtain a vector of size 1858 corresponding to the probabilities for all the possible moves.
- the value head also consists in a pointwise convolutional layer with 32 output channels, but followed by a first dense layer with 128 neurons and a second dense layer with 3 neurons and softmax activation function. The three outputs model the probability of winning, drawing and losing.

Training of the Networks. For each configuration of the neural network, we launch 5 independent training runs on a V100 Nvidia graphic card with 32 GiB of memory during 100,000 steps of gradient descent with a default batch size of 1,024. We use a reduced batch size of size 512 for the biggest architectures

---

[2] https://github.com/LeelaChessZero/lczero-training.

(when $nb_{filters} = 192$, with $nb_{blocks} = 12$ or $nb_{blocks} = 18$), in order to reduce the memory required on the GPU card during training.

At each training step, a gradient is calculated to minimize the cross-entropy for the policy head in addition to the cross-entropy for the value head (calculated over 3 outputs). In order to calculate the loss for the policy head, a legal mask is first applied to calculate only the cross-entropy for legal moves, as is usually the case when training Lc0 networks.

We use a stepwise decreasing learning rate which is set at the value of 0.02 during the first 30,000 steps, then set at the value of 0.002 until step 60,000, and finally set at the value of 0.0005 for the remaining steps.

Every 2,000 training steps, the neural network is evaluated on the validation set. On all the position extracts from the 200,000 games in the validation set, we calculate two metrics:

- the policy's average precision, which consists in evaluating the percentage of times when the movement associated with the highest probability calculated with the policy head corresponds exactly to the movement with the highest probability in the target (this is the move which was selected during the Lc0 games after applying MCTS).
- the average MSE loss corresponding to the average mean square error loss between the converted z_i output of the value head and the scalar v_i target value for each position of the validation set. For a position i, from the vector of probability $(p_i^{win}, p_i^{draw}, p_i^{loss})$ given by the value head, the scalar value z_i is computed as $z_i = p_i^{win} - p_i^{loss}$.

3.3   Network Features

Table 1 displays different characteristics of the networks we compare in this paper: the number of trainable parameters in millions, the memory required to process a batch of 1024 chess positions (each position is a tensor of size $(112, 8, 8)$ as seen in Sect. 2) and the latency, or time in seconds required to process this batch of size 1024.

We can see from this table that, with the same number of blocks and the same number of filters, the architectures with residual blocks have the highest number of parameters. This high number of parameters comes mainly from the number of weights in the convolutional kernels of size 5 by 5 used in the residual blocks. We see that when applying the chess masks displayed in Figs. 1, 2 and 3, which are broadcast according to the depth of each kernel, that the number of trainable parameters is drastically reduced. Indeed, the application of chess filters reduces the number of parameters in each convolutional kernel with a ratio of 9/25.

Secondly, we observe on this table, that the architectures using the MobileNet blocks with the depthwise convolution operations have less parameters than the architectures with the residual blocks, even when using a depthwise multiplier of 6. This is due to the reduced size of the convolution kernels used in depthwise convolution layers, which have a depth of just one.

Table 1. Number of trainable parameters (in millions), memory (in GiB) and inference time (in seconds) required to process a batch of 1024 chess positions with different neural network architectures.

Residual net

Nb blocks	Nb filters	Nb params (M.)		Memory (GiB)	Latency (s)
		Standard	Chess filters		
6	96	7.195	5.426	2.357	0.0940
12	96	10.046	6.507	2.357	0.108
18	96	12.897	7.589	2.357	0.126
6	192	16.017	8.939	4.405	0.121
12	192	27.414	13.258	4.405	0.165
18	192	38.811	17.578	4.405	0.211

Mobile net

Nb blocks	Nb filters	Nb params (M.)		Memory (GiB)	Latency (s)
		Standard	Chess filters		
6	96	4.921	4.865	3.637	0.103
12	96	5.755	5.645	3.637	0.133
18	96	6.590	6.424	3.637	0.172
6	192	7.265	7.154	6.965	0.144
12	192	10.427	10.206	6.965	0.218
18	192	13.589	13.257	6.965	0.294

ConvNeXt

Nb blocks	Nb filters	Nb params (M.)		Memory (GiB)	Latency (s)
		Standard	Chess filters		
6	96	4.546	4.537	2.639	0.137
12	96	5.006	4.987	2.639	0.203
18	96	5.466	5.438	2.639	0.268
6	192	5.907	5.889	8.007	0.210
12	192	7.712	7.675	8.007	0.344
18	192	9.516	9.460	8.007	0.479

Thirdly, we find that ConvNeXt architectures have the smallest number of parameters. Its latency is high due to the rather slow normalization layer and quadruple expansion of the number of channels with the pointwise convolution used in each block.

3.4   Results on the Validation Set

Figure 5 displays the average evolution (over 5 runs) of the policy accuracy and the MSE loss computed on the validation set every 2,000 steps of training for all the different architectures with 18 blocks and 96 filters in the trunk, with chess filters and without chess filters (versions called "standard"). For residual network architectures, we use the *rook-bishop* version of the chess filters, while for MobileNet and ConvNeXt architectures, we use the *knight-rook-bishop* version. These are the versions that work best for each of these block types, as we will see in more detail in the next subsection. The range of colors around each average curve corresponds to a spread of plus one standard deviation and minus one standard deviation from the average score.

We first see in these figures that for all the architectures there is a huge gap for both metrics when we reach the step 30,000. It corresponds to the first change in learning rate. Next, we observe that the use of chess filters always improves the results for each type of block. This is interesting, as it shows that better results can be obtained with fewer trainable parameters in the various neural networks. (cf. Table 1). It seems that these filters act as a kind of regularizer well suited to chess positions, helping the neural network to extract relevant features related to the movement of the pieces.

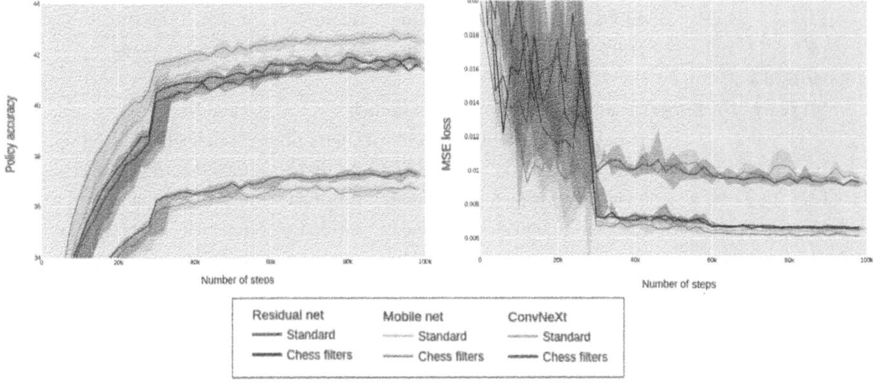

Fig. 5. Policy accuracy and MSE loss on the validation set for architectures with 18 blocks and 96 filters in the trunk.

Table 2 displays a comparison of the average results obtain by the different architectures on the validation set at the end of the training process (after 100,000 steps). From this table we draw the same conclusion regarding the impact of the chess filters. We see that using chess filters almost always improve the results in term of accuracy and MSE loss for each network configuration, but the impact is actually really significant for the network using depthwise convolution operations (MobileNet and ConvNext), or residual nets but with a high number of blocks and high number of filters in the trunk.

3.5   Impact of Different Chess Filters

In this section, we propose a more in-depth analysis of the impact of different versions of chess filters, particularly in comparison with random filters.

Random filters correspond to masks of size $(5, 5)$ randomly constructed for each convolutional layer by randomly selecting 8 squares that are not in the center of the patch and are assigned the value 1, while the other squares remain at value 0. The center of the patch is always set to 1, to be comparable with

Table 2. Average accuracy scores and MSE loss on the validation set obtain after 100,000 training steps for different neural network architectures. The best results are in bold. Significantly better results for a version with chess filters in comparison with the corresponding standard version are indicated with stars. The stars indicate the results of t-tests with p-value 0.05 (*), 0.01 (**) and 0.001 (***).

Accuracy							
Nb blocks	Nb filters	Residual net		Mobile net		ConvNeXt	
		Standard	Chess filters	Standard	Chess filters	Standard	Chess filters
6	96	40.98	41.01	40.90	**41.53****	36.28	37.48***
12	96	41.32	41.60*	41.73	**42.16***	36.54	37.42***
18	96	41.58	41.79	42.07	**42.65***	36.64	37.25***
6	192	42.55	42.74	42.29	**42.87****	37.86	39.38***
12	192	**42.75**	42.42	42.26	42.72**	37.36	38.19***
18	192	41.97	42.54***	42.39	**43.11***	37.54	38.26***

MSE loss							
Nb blocks	Nb filters	Residual net		Mobile net		ConvNeXt	
		Standard	Chess filters	Standard	Chess filters	Standard	Chess filters
6	96	0.00702	0.00705	0.00682	**0.00673**	0.00963	0.00912**
12	96	0.00670	0.00668	0.00657	**0.00631**	0.00952	0.00917***
18	96	0.00665	0.00654	0.00642	**0.00613***	0.00953	0.00927**
6	192	0.00616	0.00607	0.00609	**0.00596***	0.00869	0.00812***
12	192	**0.00591**	0.00620	0.00616	0.00608	0.00898	0.00865**
18	192	0.00625	0.00611*	0.00607	**0.00593***	0.00906	0.00857***

other filter types. Each random filter has the same number of 1's as the chess filters display in Figs. 1, 2 and 3.

Figure 6 on the left displays the average evolution of the policy accuracy on the validation set for the residual networks with always 18 blocks and 96 filters in the trunk, but using different types of filters in the convolutional layers used in the blocks. We compare four different versions with kernels of size $(5, 5)$: the red line corresponds to the standard residual net without filters, the blue line corresponds to the application of random filters, the yellow line to *rook-bishop* chess filters and the green line to *knight-rook-bishop* chess filters.

The graph on the left of Fig. 6 shows that using a combination of rook and bishop filters that take into account only vertical, horizontal and diagonal moves gives better results than other filter types for residual networks. Using the knight filter as a complement to the rook and bishop filters seems to be more useful with the depthwise convolution layer used in MobileNets, as shown in Fig. 6 on the right. As the number of planes in the MobileNet blocks with depthwise multiplier of 6 is really much higher than for residual blocks, and the different planes are processed independently by the different chess filters, this seems to allow a wider variety of filters to be used in combination to improve results.

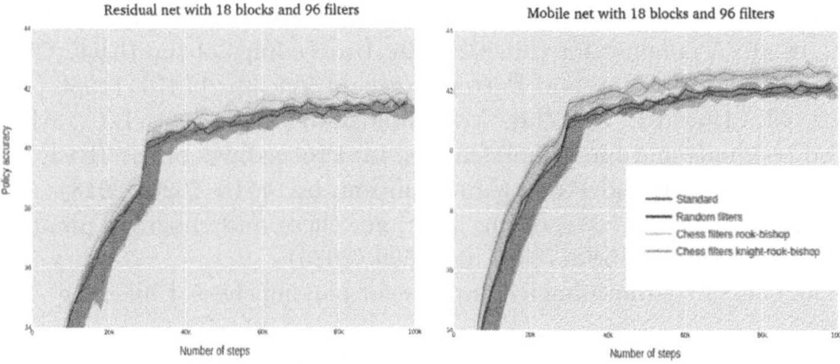

Fig. 6. Evolution of the policy accuracy on the validation set for the residual net (left) and MobileNet (right) with 18 blocks and 96 filters in the trunk and different types of filters.

4   Conclusion

Our study first explores the impact of using different types of blocks for the neural networks used in computer chess engines. We notice that using MobileNet blocks instead of the classical residual blocks can help to improve the results in term of policy accuracy and MSE loss but at the cost of more latency and more memory required for the training and inference steps.

We also find that the use of specific chess filters reduces the number of trainable parameters while improving results for almost all neural network configurations. These chess filters work better than random filters. This means that imposing some kind of structure related the movement of pieces in convolutional layers can be useful for computer chess.

Future work could involve a low-level CUDA or TensorRT implementation of the depthwise convolution layer with chess kernels (without using a mask) that could be optimized for processing 8 by 8 images to reduce the latency. Future work will also involve assessing the impact of these new architectures in terms of ELO, in particular compared to conventional architectures used in Lc0.

Acknowledgment. This work was granted access to the HPC resources of IDRIS (Grant No. AD010611887R1) from GENCI. We are grateful to the reviewers for their comments.

References

1. Campbell, M., Hoane Jr, A.J., Hsu, F.H.: Deep blue. Artif. Intell. **134**(1–2), 57–83 (2002)
2. He, K., Zhang, X., Ren, S., Sun, J.: Deep residual learning for image recognition. In: Proceedings of the IEEE Conference on Computer Vision and Pattern Recognition, pp. 770–778 (2016)
3. Hu, J., Shen, L., Sun, G.: Squeeze-and-excitation networks. In: Proceedings of the IEEE Conference on Computer Vision and Pattern Recognition, pp. 7132–7141 (2018)

4. Klein, D.: Neural networks for chess. arXiv preprint arXiv:2209.01506 (2022)
5. Liu, Z., et al.: A convnet for the 2020s. In: Proceedings of the IEEE/CVF Conference on Computer Vision and Pattern Recognition, pp. 11976–11986 (2022)
6. Sandler, M., Howard, A., Zhu, M., Zhmoginov, A., Chen, L.C.: Mobilenetv2: Inverted residuals and linear bottlenecks. In: Proceedings of the IEEE Conference on Computer Vision and Pattern Recognition, pp. 4510–4520 (2018)
7. Schrittwieser, J., et al.: Mastering atari, go, chess and shogi by planning with a learned model. Nature **588**(7839), 604–609 (2020)
8. Shannon, C.E.: Programming a computer for playing chess. Phil. Mag. **41**, 256–275 (1950)
9. Silver, D.: Reinforcement learning and simulation-based search in computer go (2009)
10. Silver, D., et al. Mastering chess and shogi by self-play with a general reinforcement learning algorithm. arXiv preprint arXiv:1712.01815 (2017)
11. Silver, D., et al.: A general reinforcement learning algorithm that masters chess, shogi, and go through self-play. Science **362**(6419), 1140–1144 (2018)
12. LCZero Development Team. Leela chess zero (lczero) (2018). https://lczero.org

Chinese Chess EGTB with Perpetual Check-Chase Rules

Nguyen Hong Pham[(✉)]

Sydney, Australia
phhnguyen@gmail.com

Abstract. We create algorithms and implement them to completely solve the rules of perpetual check and chase for a Chinese Chess Endgame Tablebase (EGTB) generator. The algorithms are vital for creating endgames when both sides have attackers. The implementation has been published as an open source and it is the first time published ever. The generator can create any endgame for real-life matches.

Keywords: Chinese chess · Xiangqi · endgames · tablebase · EGTB · perpetual check and chase · Asian Xiangqi Federation

1 Introduction

Chinese chess (Xiangqi) is a variant of chess. Besides board size, piece types, and move rules, there is a significant difference in the rules for judging the games when repeating occurs. Whereas in chess those games are judged quickly and simply as draws, in Chinese chess, those games may be judged as draws or losses for violated sides. Those rules are perpetual checks or chases (we use the abbreviation PCC to note them). According to [6], that rule set is long and complicated with multiple ambiguities and it is hard to understand for human players and to program. The PCC may occur in endgames too. Thus, all programs involving Chinese chess EGTBs such as generators, and probe codes should support those rules to ensure their endgames are legal.

In this work, we study how PCC affects endgames and how to support them with practical algorithms and open-source code. There are two PCC rule sets, one is used inside China and the other one (with some small differences) for outside, published by the Asian Xiangqi Federation [1] and we supported the second one.

2 Notations

We use K, A, E, R, C, H, and P for denoting King, Advisor, Elephant, Rook, Cannon, Horse, and Pawn. The main role of Advisors and Elephants pieces is to protect their Kings, they cannot visit nor attack any location in their opposite half-board thus we call them defenders. Other pieces (R, C, H, P) can visit and attack any location on the board thus we call them attackers. A side is called "armed" when it has some attackers and called "armless" if it has no attackers. Based on whether one or both sides are armed, we call an endgame one-sided-armed or two-sided-armed. If both sides are armless their games are always drawn thus we ignore those games.

3   Previous Works

3.1   Algorithms and Implementation of PCC Rules

Nguyen Hong Pham [6] provided theoretical and practical algorithms to fully implement the rules set by the Asian Xiangqi Federation [1], including PCC rules. The algorithms are complicated and slow but workable. They can be used for Chinese chess GUIs (Graphical User Interfaces) and Chinese chess engines[1], running for any period of games, including endgame.

According to [6], two main factors must occur in a PCC 1) a repetition (a loop) and 2) a specific piece being attacked. Within the loop, whenever in turn, a side (suspected of violating the PCC rules) makes moves to set up an attack into a specific piece of the opposite side, whereas, in turn, the opposite side manages to evade that piece from that attack. Any pause of attacking or evading (when in turn) that piece will not be counted as continues as well as a PCC.

In the case of perpetual check, it is simple. The being-attacked piece is a King, causing the state of in-check. The opposite side must evade its King whenever in turn. Any legal move of the King's side is an evasion due to stopping that checking. Since all chess programs must know the state of in-check to generate legal moves, we could verify easily if one side tries to check the opposite King whenever in turn and rule that side as a perpetual check.

In the case of perpetual chase, it is much harder. One side can attack multiple opposite pieces and the opposite side may not evade some of those pieces. We count only the ones as being chased if they keep being attacked by a side and then being evaded by the opponent whenever they are in turn. Other pieces (which are not being attacked or evaded even in one move) are ignored. [6] uses two lists (the main pair) containing pieces attacked from two sides. After each move, it creates two new lists (of being attacked pieces by sides) and then uses the new ones to update the main pair by comparing. Therefore, it could update new locations for moving pieces and remove ones that have not been attacked/evaded. The main lists may be reduced their size from position to position. After processing all positions in the loop, we call the function evaluation() to check for any PCC. That function considers only sides having only one piece left in their lists. Before concluding, it checks some more PCC conditions, for example, the types of attackers and chasers, being protected by other pieces. It may clear a

---

[1] Even though the algorithms are slow, they affect very little the performance of chess engines because they are called rarely when only 0.5% of search nodes involve repetitions. By the way, the games must be ruled legally anyway regardless of the speed.

list if that chase is allowed. After all, based on those lists it will conclude if any side has been doing a perpetual chase. It is complicated and slows in practice because all moves of attacking, evading and protecting should be legal (consider if they cause their King to be checked) and there are multiple involved pieces.

We apply the work [6] to our EGTB generator for Chinese chess. We modify that work by rewriting and packaging all functions into a class ChaseJudger. The original algorithms are called only when there is a repetition and then given all positions in the loop. In contrast, the new one works on the fly when we are going up or down on a searching tree, we continuously add (when visiting a new node) and remove (when going back) positions to and from that class and call the function evaluation() to judge the chase when a repetition is detected.

3.2 Endgames Generating Method

Thompson [10] described the method of generating EGTB for chess using a retro algorithm. We added more details and rewritten it into Algorithm 1. Each position in an endgame could be mapped by an index and vice versa. For each position in an endgame, we store typically only an integer value in a metric, for example, a distance-to-mate (DTM) or a distance-to-convert (DTC). We call EGTB generators with that algorithm "traditional".

When using metrics such as DTM and DTC we all (mentioned in this work: Thompson, Haw-ren Fang, Ren Wu, Wen-Jie Tseng, Nguyen Hong Pham) completely ignore the draw rule 50-move of chess or 60-move (similar one) of Chinese chess.

All PCC positions must be in repetitions [6]. Those repetitions are non-progress ones since with any position in them we cannot find better alternative moves to win or lose. Traditional EGTB generators cannot progress with such non-progress repetitions thus those positions must have the value UNSET before Step 6 and then become DRAW at the end.

Algorithm 1. Generating method

---

1) Initialisation: set UNSET value to all positions
2) Find all positions that are mated in 0 and store MATED IN 0 for them
3) For each position that is MATED IN n, generate retro all moves and all reached positions are MATE IN $n + 1$
4) For each position that is MATE IN n, generate retro all moves then check all reached positions with their children if there are any better results, otherwise, they are filled with MATED IN $n + 1$
5) Repeat 3) and 4) until there is no change
6) All UNSET positions are replaced by DRAW value

3.3 PCC with EGTB

All previous works on Chinese chess EGTBs mentioned their ways of dealing with PCC rules. Haw-ren Fang [2], Ren Wu [8,9] generated only one-sided-armed endgames to avoid those rules completely. Those authors proved that traditional generators can generate one-sided-armed endgames for Chinese chess. Haw-ren Fang [3,4], worked with perpetual check rules but ignored the perpetual chase. Haw-ren Fang [5] abstracted PCC rules for Chinese EGTBs without practical methods. Wen-Jie Tseng [11] said they generated two-sided-armed endgames but their work focused on only merging two EGTB metrics without mentioning the method generating those endgames. None of those works publishes methods or code libraries to create two-sided-armed endgames to use in real-life matches.

4 Probe a Traditional EGTB with PCC Positions

A traditional EGTB is probed by individual positions: give a position to the probe function and get a return score (value of DTM/DTC). The EGTB does not have information about sequences of history moves/positions (all made moves to the given position - we denote *movelist*) and the probe function cannot work with them either. That means the EGTB itself cannot process repetitions in general and PCC in particular. To rule the game with PCC we need some extra information including the history moves as well as some support from coding. On the other hand, a Chinese chess engine or program must implement PCC rules to play Chinese chess accurately [6]. Whenever a repetition occurs, the game is finished at that point (or at the searching branch) and PCC rules are used to judge the result. The engine will not probe the EGTB at that time to guarantee the game is always legitimate. We create Algorithm 2.

Algorithm 2. Probe an EGTB

```
 1: function PROBE_SEARCH(position,movelist)
 2:     if isRepetition(position,movelist) then
 3:         score ← judge_by_PCC_rules(position,movelist)
 4:     else if isHitEGTB(position) then
 5:         score ← probe_endgame(position)
 6:     else
 7:         score ← normal_search(position,movelist)
 8:     end if
 9:     return score
10: end function
```

One interesting idea is that we can solve the PCC issue with a traditional EGTB. In such EGTB, all repetition positions must have the value DRAW, so the same for all PCC positions. We can create a special search with PCC rules to check any DRAW position from the EGTB to see if they are real draws or PCC ones. The advantage is that we can use traditional generators to generate EGTBs for Chinese chess without any code dealing with PCC. However, there are many drawbacks: 1) we need a much more complicated code on engines/programs to check PCC 2) that may take a lot of time to calculate since sometimes the process may go very deep, especially when some pieces can chase others around the whole board 3) it requires to probe multiple times (instead of probing only one) when searching 4) the call of this code may be unnecessarily in high frequencies for many endgames, especially for mostly-draw ones. For example, the endgame KCPAKHAA has 90% of legal positions drawn and the PCC positions take only 0.4% of that draws.

Ideally, we detect all positions involving PCC and store them with special values back into the EGTB. That can help applications be simpler and save a lot of computing time for chess engines.

4.1 Endgames with One-Sided-Armed

Examples of those endgames are KRKA, KHPAKAAEE. The armless side cannot check nor win because it does not have any piece to attack directly the opposite land or opposite King thus it cannot make perpetual checks[2]. Its defenders (Advisors and Elephants) can attack opposite attackers when they come to their land but they cannot chase them due to their move types and opposite attackers' types being too different. Even though the armless Kings can chase any pieces repeatedly that is allowed and not counted as perpetual chases [1]. As the sequence, the armless side cannot make perpetual chases. In contrast, the armed side can perpetually check or chase as typical.

Figure 1a, 1b and 1c are positions with probed scores for the White shown in circles[3]. In Fig. 1a and 1c, the white Rook can move up and down in the top two ranks (8–9) to chase the black King, forming a perpetual check. In Fig. 1b the white Rook moves similarly to chase the black Advisor, creating a perpetual chase. Figure 1a and 1b are wins for White. White has the better moves, for example, to capture the Advisors, instead of checking or chasing repeatedly. The generator can find those mates and make progress and not be stuck, the values of those positions in the endgame are MATE/MATED IN n (not UNSET nor DRAW). With those values when probing, a chess engine can make progress too.

In contrast, the position in Fig. 1c is a draw. White does not have better moves for that position since all moves have the same score of DRAW. When the engine is in that position it can select any moves and it may accidentally check the black King continuously, creating a repetition of checking. However, at

---

[2] There are some special cases where the armless side can win a Horse and 2 Advisors such as the position 4k4/9/9/9/9/9/9/9/4H4/3AKA3 w - - 0 1 but those such positions are so few and not dealing with any perpetual checks or chases. It is safe to ignore them for this work.

[3] Green circles with the character M denoted MATE IN (winning moves), red ones with the character -M denoted MATED IN (losing moves), and yellow ones with the character D denoted DRAW (drawn moves).

the last move before encircling that repetition, based on Algorithm 2, the engine detects that repetition and understands that move as a losing one, so it avoids that move and tries to find alternative ones instead, just for drawing. Luckily, in that case, it has many choices, say, move the white King up (it is a draw move too), to stop the continuousness of checking and avoid being ruled as a loss.

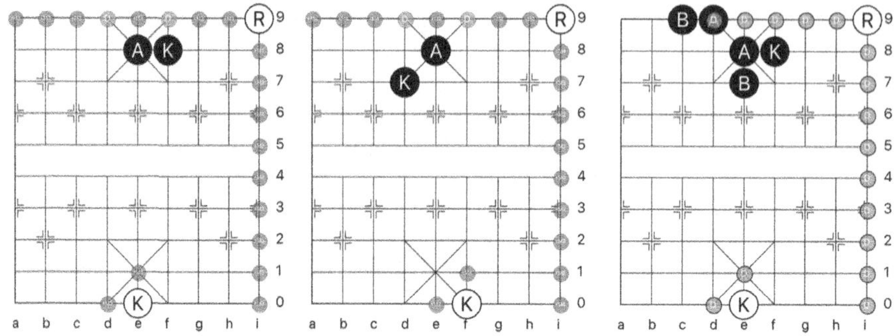

(a) Rook may chase black King

(b) Rook may chase black Advisor

(c) Rook may chase black King

Fig. 1. Rooks may go up and down the top two ranks 8 and 9 to permanently check or chase

We may worry about the case when there is no luck in having a better alternating moves noted as Dilemma 1. Dilemma 1 cannot happen for endgames with an armless side because the opposite (the armless) side cannot win, in the worst-case scenario the armed side can always find alternative moves that are not losses (draws), say, from moving the King or defenders, moving or sacrificing attackers. Consequently, we do not need to do any special treatment for both generators and endgames to work with that class of endgames. Haw-ren Fang [3], Ren Wu [8,9] generated only that endgame class to avoid dealing with PCC issues.

Dilemma 1 (No Better Alternative Moves) *The program may:*

- *accidentally made a sequence of moves forming a perpetual check or chase*
- *be at the last position to enclose the repetition but there is no better alternative move to avoid losing (all alternative moves are losses)*

4.2 Endgames with Two-Sided-Armed

Examples of those endgames are KRAKR, KRAKPA, KRAKHAAE. In Fig. 2a the white Rook tries perpetually checking the black King since those moves have DRAW value (suppose that EGTB is traditional) when all other moves lose. Similarly, in Fig. 2b (the position is from [1], page 16) the white Rook tries perpetually chasing the black Cannon in columns c and h when all other moves lose. Before enclosing repetitions the chess engine tries finding alternative moves to avoid losing. But all other moves are losing too. Both positions Fig. 2a and Fig. 2b are losing for White. The chess engine started following a line in the hope of getting a draw but then it ended up with a loss. Dilemma 1 happens for that endgame class.

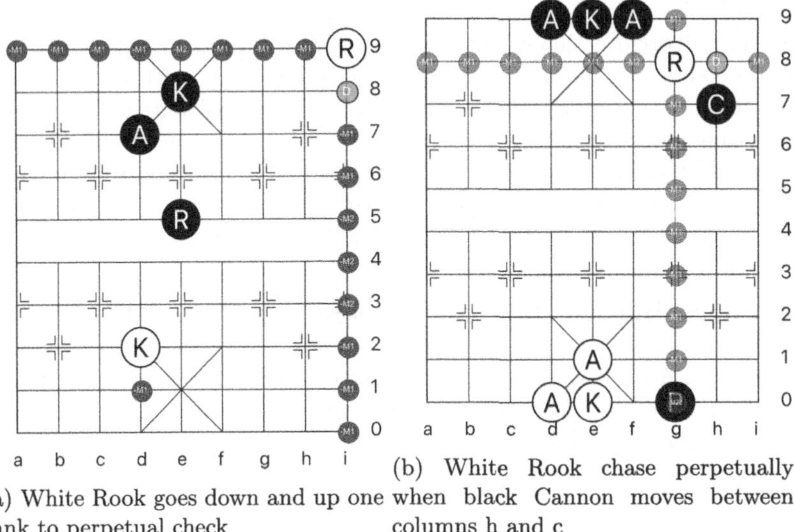

(a) White Rook goes down and up one rank to perpetual check

(b) White Rook chase perpetually when black Cannon moves between columns h and c

Fig. 2. All white draw moves are actually in perpetual checks or chases, all other white moves are losing

4.3   Values for PCC Positions

We need to detect and replace the value of UNSET or DRAW for PCC positions with some special values thus the search could avoid miscalculations. The simplest solution is to use values MATE or MATED IN n when n is an integer number. However, that solution may not work smoothly since PCC positions are not determined, and their lengths to win vary (they all are in repetitions and we do not know the points when the engine starts or ends those repetitions). Any fixed number for n may confuse the chess engine and affect the search progress.

Our solution uses special values, PERPETUAL_CHECK and PERPETUAL_CHASE for perpetual checks (such as Fig. 2a) or chases (Fig. 2b). Ancestor positions that lead toward perpetual ones will have values PERPETUAL_TOWARD n when n is an integer number of steps toward a PCC position. Positive and negative values are winning and losing, respectively.

For comparing values, we suppose perpetual ways to be longer to win or lose than mate or mated (even though that is not always correct because they are undetermined and depend on cases). In practice, we assign a large integer number, say 10000, for MATE 0, and reduce it one by one for longer mates, say, for MATE 1 (9999), MATE 2 (9998)... We assign numbers between DRAW (=0) and MATE 0 (=10000) for PERPETUAL_CHECK (=8199), PERPETUAL_CHASE (=8198), PERPETUAL_TOWARD 0 (=8197), PERPETUAL_TOWARD 1 (=8196)[4]... All make sure we can compare two scores by applying the simple comparison between two integers (e.g., score0 < score1).

We call all the above special values "perpetual". Those values take a large range (they all are over 255 values, and cannot fit into a one-byte integer), located under the DTM metric range. They are separated clearly with DTM values. We named them as Perpetuation metric (PPM). The disadvantage of using PPM is that their endgames must use a two-byte integer per index/position (some endgames may need only 1 byte per index/position if not using PPM). However, that is not a big problem since the majority of two-sided-armed endgames are large ones and need two-byte integers regardless of PCC.

5 Generating Method for Two-Sided-Armed Endgames

The generator needs to detect all PCC positions to fill in the appropriate values. The additional code works with all positions of UNSET value after step 5 of Algorithm 1 (generating EGTB). We insert three more steps 6–8) into Algorithm 1 and create a new Algorithm 3.

Algorithm 3. Generating method for two-sided-armed

---

1) ... 5) are similar to 1)... 5) of Algorithm 1
6) For all positions with UNSET value:
  - if it starts a perpetual check, change its value to -PERPETUAL_CHECK (losing). All involved positions in repetitions will be filled with appropriate perpetual check values
  - if it starts a perpetual chase, change its value to -PERPETUAL_CHASE. All involved positions in repetitions will be filled with appropriate perpetual chase values
7) Propagate of all positions with perpetual values
8) Repeat 6) and 7) until there is no change
9) All UNSET positions will be replaced by DRAW value (similar to step 6 of Algorithm 1

5.1 Detect Perpetual Check, Chase Positions

When starting at a UNSET value position and tracing to other UNSET positions we always can find some repetitions. In other words, that position is always in

---

[4] Chess engines may use directly our score range and they may have a huge range [-8000, 8000] for scoring non-mating evaluation.

at least a loop. We use a simple search with the AlphaBeta-like algorithm to track up repetitions. Each node in the search tree is a position. The search tree will expand on nodes with UNSET values but we should check and consider all their sibling values as conditions of stopping or expanding.

For easy understanding and coding, we separate the search into two main function types based on their plies and work alternatively. They return a result as a set of pairs (index, side) of positions in a PCC repetition. We named that result set *indexSet*.

The first type with the suffix "*Attack*" is used for the suspected side of PCC violation. If there is any better alternative move (drawn or breaking the continuity of checking/chasing) that side will take that move to avoid losing. In that case, the search will terminate and return an empty set. This means that the position is not in a PCC. Otherwise, it returns a non-empty set.

The second type function with the suffix "*Evasion*" is used for the side being checked/chased. The function mainly rescues its pieces from being checked or chased. However, unless there is a clear win/mate, it also tries forcing the rival side to re-check or chase in the next moves, to form perpetual checks/chases because those are winning for that side. It returns an empty set (non-PCC) only if all moves are not being checked/chased.

Evasion functions may call their correspondent Attack functions to expand their search trees. In turn, Attack functions may call Evasion ones too. Those functions work recursively. They may stop in one of two ways: stop at the first non-empty result or exhaust all results. Algorithm 4 we start calling Evasion functions and fill in the results. *xside* is the opposite of a given *side*.

Perpetual Checks. Algorithm 5 shows two functions *checkAttack* and *checkEvasion* to detect perpetual checks. The status of in-check could be verified directly by the chess board or via probed scores (an in-check position always has a valid score for one side and an ILLEGAL value for the other side). Since kings in Chinese chess can move limitedly in tiny areas, the attackers have to move in a very limited range to check those kings. The numbers of their moves are relatively small. In general, those functions are quite simple, straightforward for coding and can run quickly.

Perpetual Chases. Algorithm 6 has two functions Attack-Evasion for detecting perpetual chases. It is based on the work of Nguyen Hong Pham [6] and briefed in Sect. 2. All codes are packed in a class ChaseJudger as mentioned in Sect. 2. The variable chaseJudger of that class is fed by positions when going deeper in the search tree and removed when going back. When adding a position it immediately updates its internal data, verifies and returns false if there is no chase, and true if some pieces are being chased. When a repeat occurs, the function chaseJudge.evaluation() is called to judge if the chase violates or is accepted by PCC rules.

The code for detecting perpetual chases is much more complicated and requires much more computing than the one for checking. If we implement it straightforwardly it may not run in a reasonable time for some endgames when

---

Algorithm 4. Detect perpetual checks or chases

```
 1: function DETECTPCC
 2:     for (position, side) ← all_positions(score : UNSET) do
 3:         perpetual_check ← false
 4:         if in_check(position,xside) then
 5:             indexSet ← checkEvasion(position, xside)
 6:             perpetual_check ← indexSet.isNotEmpty
 7:         end if
 8:         if !perpetual_check then
 9:             indexSet ← chaseEvasion(position, xside)
10:         end if
11:         for (index, index_side) ← indexSet do
12:             if perpetual_check then
13:                 score ← index_side == side ? -PERPETUAL_CHECK : PERPET-
    UAL_CHECK
14:             else
15:                 score ← index_side == side ? -PERPETUAL_CHASE : PERPET-
    UAL_CHASE
16:             end if
17:             save (score, index, index_side)
18:         end for
19:     end for
20: end function
```

---

the search nodes may increase exponentially, say, when a Rook chases a Cannon or a Horse over the whole board. We have to apply many tricks to speed it up, such as marking visited non-chase positions, and applying the rule 60-move (draw rule, similar to rule 50-move of chess) to make the search run in reasonable periods.

5.2 Propagate Perpetual Values

After detecting all PCC positions we will find and fill all their ancestral positions. The new algorithm works somewhat similarly to Algorithm 1 but works with positions of perpetual values and fills their ancestral ones with perpetual values too.

5.3 Verify Generated Endgames

All generated endgames must be verified for their data. We check only the consistency between the score of a node and the score synthesized from all its children's positions. That includes perpetual ones. From a given index and side we could retrieve the correspondent chessboard. All children's scores should be converted into new ones in the view of their parents by the function *convertToParentScore*. Typically we flip their signs and add +/-1 correspondingly since a child's position is one move towards a mate/mated (or a change). However, perpetual

---

Algorithm 5. Functions Attack/Evasion to detect perpetual checks

---

```
 1: function CHECKEVASION(position,side)
 2:     for child_position ← children(position, side) do
 3:         child_score ← probe(child_position)
 4:         if child_score < 0 then                          ▷ /// winning score
 5:             break
 6:         end if
 7:         if child_score == UNSET then
 8:             indexSet ← checkAttack(child_position, side)
 9:         end if
10:         if indexSet.isNotEmpty then return (position_index, side) + indexSet
11:         end if
12:     end forreturn empty
13: end function
14: function CHECKATTACK(position,side)
15:     for child_position ← children(position, side) do
16:         child_score ← probe(child_position)
17:         if !in_check(child_position, side) || child_score == DRAW then return
    empty
18:         end if
19:         if child_score == UNSET then
20:             if isRepetition(child_position) then return (position_index, side)
21:             else
22:                 indexSet2 ← checkAttack(child_position, side)
23:             end if
24:         end if
25:         if indexSet2.isEmpty then return empty
26:         end if
27:     end for
28:     indexSet ← indexSet + (position_index, side) + indexSet2 return indexSet
29: end function
```

---

scores may take some special exceptions: 1) we flip signs only for PERPET-UAL_CHECK/CHASE but do not change their distances, 2) From PERPET-UAL_FORWARD 0 it could jump to any of PERPETUAL_CHECK/CHASE. We create Algorithm 8.

6   Probe New EGTB with PCC Positions

6.1   In the Middle of a Searching Tree

When a chess engine is searching, it may realise the current position is an endgame in an EGTB. The engine will stop at the current branch and probe for the score. Probed scores may be normal or perpetual ones, the engine can compare those scores as usual, regardless of whether perpetual or not, thus it could keep the search progressing.

Algorithm 6. Functions Attack/Evasion to detect perpetual chases

---

```
function CHASEEVASION(position,side)
    if chaseJudger.add(position) == false then return empty
    end if
    for child_position ← children(position, side) do
        child_score ← probe(child_position)
        if child_score < 0 then                              ▷ /// winning score
            indexSet ← empty
            break
        end if
        if child_score == UNSET then
            indexSet2 ← chaseAttack(child_position, xside)
            if indexSet2.isNotEmpty then
                indexSet ← indexSet + (position_index, side) + indexSet2
            end if
        end if
    end for
    chaseJudger.removeLastPosition() return indexSet
end function
function CHASEATTACK(position,side)
    if chaseJudger.add(position) == false then return empty
    end if
    chasing ← true
    for child_position ← children(position, side) do
        child_score ← probe(child_position)
        if child_score == DRAW then
            chasing ← false
            break
        end if
        if child_score == UNSET then
            if isRepetition(child_position) then
                chasing ← chaseJudger.evaluation()
            end if
        end if
        if chasing then
            indexSet ← (position_index, side)
            break
        end if
        indexSet2 ← chaseEvasion(child_position, xside)
        if indexSet2.isEmpty then
            chasing ← false
            break
        end if
        indexSet ← indexSet + (position_index, side) + indexSet2
        break
    end for
    chaseJudger.removeLastPosition() return chasing ? indexSet : empty
end function
```

Algorithm 7. Propagate perpetual values

1) For each position that is perpetual values, generate retro all moves then check all reached positions and probe, if those positions have UNSET value, we probe their children if there are any better scores

2) Repeat 1 until there is no change

Algorithm 8. Verify data consistency

```
 1: for (index, side) ← all_indexes(endgame, sides) do
 2:     score ← probe(endgame, index, side)
 3:     position ← createChessPosition(endgame, index, side)
 4:     bestscore ← -MATE
 5:     for move ← all_legal_moves(position,side) do
 6:         make(position, move)
 7:         child_score ← probe(position, xside)
 8:         child_score ← convertToParentScore(child_score)
 9:         bestscore ← max(child_score, bestscore)
10:         takeback(position, move)
11:     end for
12:     if score != bestscore then
13:         print "endgame data inconsistent at", index, side
14:         break
15:     end if
16: end for
```

6.2 At Root

When the chess engine finds perpetual scores at the root node, it will process similarly to a traditional EGTB: probe all children to find the best one to move. The best score (of the best child) may be:

- $+/-$PERPETUAL_TOWARD n, it is just similar to MATE/MATED IN n. That move is one step towards PCC
- $+/-$PERPETUAL_CHECK/CHASE. The positive score means it is winning, otherwise losing. Sooner or later it will lead to a repetition and finish. However, the number of moves in a repetition may be huge if we move randomly. Thus the search should examine all possible cases until encircling the perpetual check/chase repetitions and take the shortest one. The number of extra moves is counted, say, n, and we can convert the score into MATE or MATED IN n.

7 Experiment

7.1 Felicity EGTB

The project is our experiment EGTB generator and prober (Nguyen Hong Pham [7]. It is an open-source, C++, supports chess, Chinese chess, and Jeiqi, rewritten in April 2024. It can generate any endgame[5] for Chinese chess, including two-sided-armed. It also provides a code library to probe endgames and to search solutions on roots.

7.2 Statistics of Some Endgames

Since the project is still developing and due to weak hardware, we have just created hundreds of small two-sided-armed endgames, mostly for testing and verifying tools before trying to generate bigger ones later (which could take years). Table 1 shows statistics of some endgames. #pos: numbers of legal positions, draw %: numbers of draws and percentages on #pos, #PChecks, #PChases: numbers of perpetual checks/chases. All numbers are counted for both sides. Not every one of those endgames has PCC but they are the major. The proportions of PCC positions are typically small and vary under 10%.

PCC generating consumes time but periods vary much depending on endgames. We observed that it may add extra time from under 1% (almost instantly) to 500% (5 times longer) of traditional generating time.

Table 1. Some endgames with both-side-armed

Endgames	#pos	Draw %	#PChecks	#PChases
KCAAKPA	10540425	5411697, 51%	0	0
KCAKH	2157881	1861077, 86%	4981	0
KRAAKCAA	28296350	13132933, 46%	4110	0
KCAKHP	111042339	45498944, 40%	173403	107
KCPAKH	112554674	45135314, 40%	4709493	33931
KCPAKHAA	850298157	768378743, 90%	2763212	54068
KRAAKCPA	795621683	5347850, 0%	1387319	26780
KRKCH	36856968	817576, 2%	645312	13902

8   Conclusions

Firstly we confirmed that one-sided-armed endgames can work well with traditional EGTB generators (without any implementation of PCC rules for generators or for the data of endgames). A program with a PCC implementation can probe and work legally with those endgames.

Secondly, when both sides of endgames are armed the EGTB generator should implement PCC code to detect all PCC positions and their ancestors and then

---

[5] As usual, the generated endgames are limited by their sizes to fit in hardware and generating time.

store them with corresponding perpetual values. That helps chess engines and other programs speed up probing and work legally.

We developed a full set of algorithms for probers and generators to work with two-sided-armed endgames. Those algorithms have been implemented and published in an open-source project (Felicity EGTB [7]). They could work well with any Chinese chess endgame, from one to two armed sides. The code has been tested to create many endgames that can be used for real-life game matches.

References

1. Asian Xiangqi Federation: Rules of Xiangqi. http://www.asianxiangqi.org/English/AXF_rules_Eng.pdf, Accessed 10 Oct 2024
2. Fang, H.-w., Hsu, T.-s., Hsu,S.-C.: Construction of Chinese chess endgame databases by retrograde analysis. Comput. Games (2000)
3. Fang, H.-r., Hsu, T.-s., Hsu, S.-c.: Indefinite sequence of moves in Chinese chess endgames. In: 3rd International Conference on Computers and Games (2002)
4. Fang, H.-r., Hsu, T.-s., Hsu, S.-C.: Checking indefinitely in Chinese-Chess endgames. ICGA J. **27**(1) (2004)
5. Fang, H.-r.: The nature of retrograde analysis for Chinese Chess. ICGA J. **28**(2) (2005)
6. Pham, N.H.: A completed implementation for Xiangqi rules. ICGA J. **40** (2018)
7. Pham, N.H.: Felicity EGTB GitHub. https://github.com/nguyenpham/FelicityEgtb, Accessed 10 Oct 2024
8. Wu, R., Beal, D.: Fast, memory-efficient retrograde algorithms. ICGA J. **24**(3)(2001)
9. Ren, W., Beal, D.: A memory efficient retrograde algorithm and its application to solve Chinese Chess endgames. More Games of No Chance edited by Richard J, Nowakowski (2002)
10. Ken, T.: Retrograde analysis of certain endgames. ICCA J. **9**(3) (1986)
11. Tseng, W.-J., Chen, J.-C., Wu, I.-C.: Merging metrics of special rules in Chinese chess endgame databases. In: The Conference on Technologies and Applications of Artificial Intelligence TAAI (2019). Kaohsiung, Taiwan (2019)

Go and NoGo

Analysing KATAGO: A Comparative Evaluation Against Perfect Play in the Game of Go

Asmaul Husna[✉] and Martin Müller

University of Alberta, Edmonton, Canada
{asmaul,mmueller}@ualberta.ca

Abstract. Much of the research on board games focuses on strong play and on solving games exactly. Recently, programs such as AlphaZero have reached superhuman level in board games such as chess and Go. We study the gap between such AI systems and perfect play, in order to deepen our understanding of their current strengths and limitations. Our study uses Go endgame puzzles with special combinatorial sum game structure, for which an optimal solver is available. We develop an extended Go endgame dataset labelled with exact scores and optimal moves. We evaluate KATAGO, the strongest open source AlphaZero-derived program for the game of Go, on these puzzles. We study how the training of different neural networks and the amount of search used affect KATAGO's ability to play perfectly. We observe improved move selection with strong policies, and measure the effect of different MCTS search settings, as well as the challenges KATAGO faces in competing against an exact solver. We further analyse move choices in terms of changes of average action value, lower confidence bound, winrate, and number of visited nodes in the MCTS search of KATAGO. On our perfect game dataset, KATAGO achieves a 90.8% success rate in matches against the exact solver.

Keywords: Performance Evaluation · Safety-Critical Systems · AlphaZero · KATAGO · Exact Solver

1 Introduction

DeepMind's AlphaZero (AZ) program [12] has greatly advanced the state of the art in playing two player board games. It convincingly beat top human players and previous programs by learning from scratch. Search methods inspired by AZ have been applied to many problems beyond games [4]. There is much interest in further applications in safety-critical systems, such as autonomous driving, where even a tiny mistake can cause big problems, and having accurate solutions is extremely important. Autonomous driving includes a wide range of tasks, including lane keeping [5], overtaking [6], and making higher-level driving decisions [3].

Can AlphaZero-based algorithms find exact solutions? We explore KATAGO, a strong AlphaZero-derived open source Go program [14]. We test how well

M. Hartisch et al. (Eds.): CG 2024, LNCS 15550, pp. 43–53, 2025.
https://doi.org/10.1007/978-3-031-86585-5_4

this program plays Go endgame puzzles compared to perfect play. We aim to better understand the learning process of KATAGO and its limits. We study its behavior in several scenarios: when using either a strong or a weak neural network, and with different amounts of search as well as without search. We use endgame puzzles from the literature [1,7], and create a larger dataset that is labeled with perfect solutions by using an exact endgame solver [8]. We design a methodology with experiments and analysis in order to investigate the following research questions:

- What are the differences in move selection between stronger and weaker neural networks?
- How does the addition of a small MCTS search enhance move selection compared to using only a neural network?
- What is the impact of increasing the search budget on the overall performance?
- How good is KATAGO at finding a best incentive move in the sense of combinatorial game theory, compared to "just" finding a minimax optimal move?
- How often can KATAGO win games against an exact solver in matches from endgame starting positions?
- Are there any cases where using deeper search adversely affects move selection compared to using a small search?

2   Related Work

Comparing a heuristic search-based algorithm against a perfect solution offers important insights into its quality. In related games research, Haque et al. [2] compare Leela Chess Zero (lc0), an open-source chess program derived from AlphaZero, against perfect chess endgame play. They find that more training and deeper search are both very effective for increasing the number of optimal moves found. However, they also identify some cases where a neural network suggests the correct move, but a small search using MCTS (Monte Carlo Tree Search) switches to the wrong move. They also find that some difficult 5-piece endgames are far beyond the current abilities of even the strongest available network combined with deep search. Sadmine et al. [11] extend this study by comparing lc0 and Stockfish, another strong open source chess engine which uses a very different neural network architecture. They use an Average Centipawn Loss (ACPL) measure to quantify how much value is lost by wrong moves, and focus on difficult situations where errors are more common, which include imbalanced positions with one extra black pawn against a stronger extra white piece.

Romein and Bal [10] analyse the game of Awari using a perfect-play database. They find that the top programs MARVIN and SOFTWARI, which were previously assumed to be almost perfect, played a correct move in only 82% and 87% of the cases, respectively.

Wang et al. [13] train adversarial policies which can exploit specific weaknesses in KataGo and win over 99% of games against KataGo using no search, and more than 97% against KataGo with some search.

3 Background

3.1 Solving Go Endgame Puzzles

Solving a game means finding an optimal strategy that guarantees the game-theoretical best outcome, such as a win or a draw for a player, no matter how the opponent plays. In two-player games of perfect information, all of the game state is known to both players. However, many game positions are too complex to be solved in practice. In Go endgame puzzles, most of the board has already been secured by one of the players, and they focus on small but crucial battles on the rest of the board, in order to increase their territory and reduce their opponent's. Figure 1 shows the safe stones and territories of a Go endgame position.

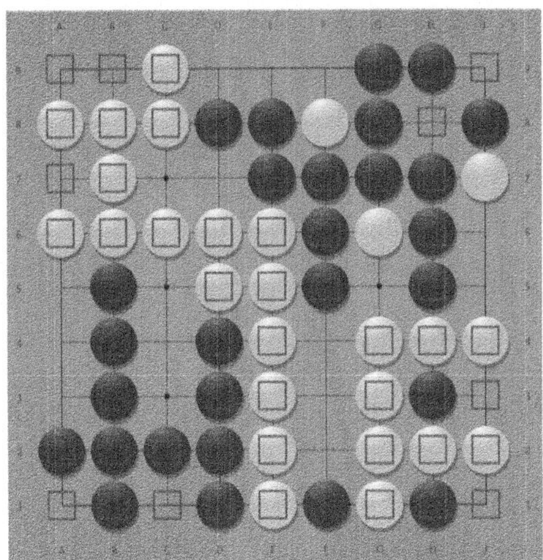

Fig. 1. Safe stones and territories of a Go endgame position.

3.2 Exact Solver for Go

An exact solver for Go can find the best moves and outcomes for a given Go position. Due to the game's complexity and large number of possible moves, such solvers only exist for special cases: small boards, and endgame puzzles with extra structure such as the one in Fig. 1. In our work, we use a solver [7] that can handle endgame puzzles with solution lengths exceeding 60 moves. It uses a technique called decomposition search [8] to find the outcome and the best moves. The solver first finds safe stones and territories, then identifies independent local subgames, and performs local combinatorial game search (LCGS) in each subgame. Next, the algorithm evaluates the combinatorial game value for each subgame, and tries to find a move with the highest incentive overall. **Incentive** is a combinatorial game concept that measures the improvement to a game position made by a move. Incentives are only partially ordered. If one incentive dominates all others, as often happens in Go endgames, then a move with this incentive is optimal and can be played without further search. If several incentives are incomparable in the partial order, then an optimised **minimax search** among the corresponding candidate moves is used to find their minimax score, and a minimax-optimal move. In our experiment, we study both cases: positions where a unique **best incentive** exists, and those with two or more nondominated incentives. We study minimax-optimal play, as well as whether a policy network can identify best incentive moves and separate them from locally weaker ones.

3.3 KataGo

KataGo [14] is an open-source Go program that implements and extends the AlphaZero algorithm. It learns from scratch through self-play. Unlike AlphaZero, it includes domain-specific features to boost learning. Its key contributions include general purpose improvements over AlphaZero, such as better data balance, focused training, and enhanced neural networks with global pooling layers. Go-specific improvements include extra input features to improve learning, and helpful auxiliary targets such as as predicting point ownership and the final score.

KataGo is the strongest open-source Go program, and is very widely used as a study tool in the Go community, by amateurs and professionals alike. Therefore a study of its limitations is directly relevant for this audience.

4 Dataset and Evaluation Method

4.1 Original and Modified Dataset

We used the 22 endgame problems labeled $C.1, C.2, ..., C.22$ from Berlekamp and Wolfe's "Mathematical Go: Chilling Gets the Last Point" [1]. We refer to these as the **original problems**. We also used the **modified problems** from [8]. These modified versions are equivalent in terms of local endgame values, but clearly separate endgame areas by safe stones and territories. This allows the exact solver to analyse each small area separately, and solve the overall problem. In each problem, white is to play, and if both players play perfectly, then white wins by 0.5 points.

4.2 Extended Datasets

We use the exact solver to generate an extended dataset by playing perfect games starting from different states in the modified endgame problems. As each game progresses, we adjust the komi when stones are captured. We then play matches between the exact solver and KataGo from these starting positions. If KataGo suggests a move that is not winning as indicated by the solver, then we verify that it leads to KataGo losing the game. We expand our dataset for each endgame position as follows:

– Find the winning move of that board position using the exact solver
– Play the winning move on the board and get the next starting position
– Adjust the komi if stones were captured
– Repeat until the end of the game

To expand the dataset, we use the modified problems $C.1, C.2, C.3, C.6, C.7,$ $C.8, C.9, C.10,$ and $C.21$. We name this collection of data **perfect games**. To add more 19×19 endgames to our dataset, we use an extension of the subsets of $C.11$ from [9]. From these subsets, we generate additional data and name these endgames **C.11 subsets**. All these endgame problems are stored in Smart Game Format (SGF), a popular file format.

4.3   Splitting the Dataset by Existence of a Dominating Incentive

We divide our dataset of perfect games and C.11 subsets into two categories to evaluate KataGo's decision-making ability. For positions in category **DI**, a single dominating incentive exists. The **no-DI** positions do not have a single dominating incentive. Among the set of moves with two or more non-dominating incentives, the best ones must be determined by minimax search.

4.4   Engine Settings

We used KataGo version v1.12.4 to analyse our endgame dataset. We also used two different KataGo neural networks. For the best performance, we chose a strong network called "kata1-b18c384nbt-s5832081920-d3223508649" with 18 blocks and 384 channels. Its self-play Elo rating is 13488.6 ± 14.1. Our weaker option is a smaller network, "kata1-b6c96-s37368064-d5536083" with 6 blocks and 96 channels, and a 7098.1 ± 19.0 elo rating.

For computational resources, we used one CPU core to process datasets and OpenCL GPU to run KataGo. For example, the strong network took 64.1 s to process 126 endgames with 100 search nodes each. The weak network did the same task in 1.2 s. Analysing all perfect games with the strong network and 102,400 search nodes took nearly 5 h.

5   Experiments and Analysis

5.1   Evaluating KataGo with Basic Settings

To evaluate KataGo's performance, we run two types of tests: one uses only a neural network policy, without search, while the other test applies the network during search as usual. In both types of tests we try the weak and the strong version of the network. In each endgame position, we count a KATAGO move as correct if it is one of the known set of optimal moves. We consider both notions of optimality, incentive optimal and minimax optimal. We measure the number and percentage of correct moves among all generated moves. Since KATAGO's results can change between runs, we run each experiment five times and average the results. Table 1 summarises the average performance of KATAGO for each of the four test sets, in four scenarios: using the weak and the strong policy without search, and using both policies with a search with a limit of 100 node visits.

Table 1. Total number of correct moves along with average success rate by the weak and strong policy, and policies with 100 visits search.

Dataset	Test Cases	Average Total Number of Correct Moves and Success Rate (%)			
		Policy		Search, 100 visits	
		Weak	Strong	Weak	Strong
Original	22	8.8(40%)	12.8(58.2%)	9.6(43.6%)	16.2(73.6%)
Modified	22	7.8(35.5%)	13.6(61.8%)	9(40.9%)	16.8(77.3%)
Perfect games	126	98.8(78.4%)	118.8(94.3%)	105.8(84%)	123.8(98.3%)
C.11 subsets	371	355.6(95.8%)	369.6(99.6%)	361.4(97.4%)	370(99.7%)

As expected, in general the strong policy outperforms the weak one in all settings and across all datasets. Among datasets, the success is higher in perfect games and C.11 subsets, likely because many of these endgames offer more winning moves (4 to 10) compared to the challenging other sets with only one or two correct moves. Furthermore, when playing out perfect games, the endgame size is gradually reduced, with fewer contested points, often leading to progressively easier to solve positions. The results also show that adding a small search to the weak net does not improve results much for the challenging original and modified problems. Many of these problems remain out of reach. In contrast, the more focused searches using the strong network shows more improvement.

Scaling the Search. We increase the search amount by ten successive doublings from 100 to 102,400 maximum visits for all test cases. Figure 2 shows the average success rate while using the weak and strong policies in these settings. In Fig. 2 (a), the success rate of the weak policy steadily rises for original, modified, and perfect games. However, this combination still struggles with original and modified problems, reaching only about 60% accuracy with 102,400 visit searches. The scaling results for the strong policy in Fig. 2 (b) are surprising. Initially, the success rate increases, but then it starts to deteriorate. This suggests that in several endgame scenarios, picking a correct move is more due to chance, even at this level of search. For C.11 subsets, we focus on one endgame unsolved by the strong policy with 100 visits in Table 1. It still cannot be solved by either policy with any amount of search that we tried.

5.2   Evaluating KataGo's Incentive- and Minimax-optimal Play

In Subsect. 4.3 we split our datasets into DI, the positions where a dominating incentive exists, and no-DI, where it does not. In all cases, we evaluate whether KataGo's move is minimax optimal. For test set DI, we additionally check if KataGo's move is incentive-optimal. In each position, the set of incentive-optimal moves is a subset of the minimax-optimal ones. The sets can be equal, and always contain at least one move. Table 2 shows the average results for DI with weak and strong policies, and for the same policies with a 100 node search. We use the datasets perfect games and C.11 subsets, because for these sets, both incentive and minimax-optimal moves are available from the exact solver. From the results of Table 2, we find that KataGo struggles more to identify best incentive moves compared to minimax ones. This shows in the success rates of finding incentive and minimax optimal moves. We see a large difference, ranging from 10 to 40 percent. It appears that KataGo focuses more on finding any win, rather than relying on the policy learning the small differences in move strength. We only show the results for the DI test set here, as our no-DI set is too small to analyze the results in a meaningful way.

Table 2. Total number of correct moves and average success rate for weak and strong policy, and with 100-visit search, for the DI test set.

Name of Dataset	Number of Endgames	Total Number of Correct Moves with Avg Success Rate (%)			
		Weak policy		Strong Policy	
		Incentive optimal	Minimax optimal	Incentive optimal	Minimax Optimal
Perfect games	125	70.8(56.6%)	96.8(77.8%)	103(82.4%)	115.8(92.6%)
C.11 subsets	345	190(55.1%)	328.8(95.3%)	251.6(72.8%)	345(100%)
		Weak policy + 100 visit search		Strong Policy + 100 visit search	
		Incentive optimal	Minimax optimal	Incentive optimal	Minimax Optimal
Perfect games	125	89.2(71.4%)	106.2(85%)	106.2(85%)	122(97.6%)
C.11 subsets	345	235(68.1%)	333.8(96.8%)	254.6(73.8%)	345(100%)

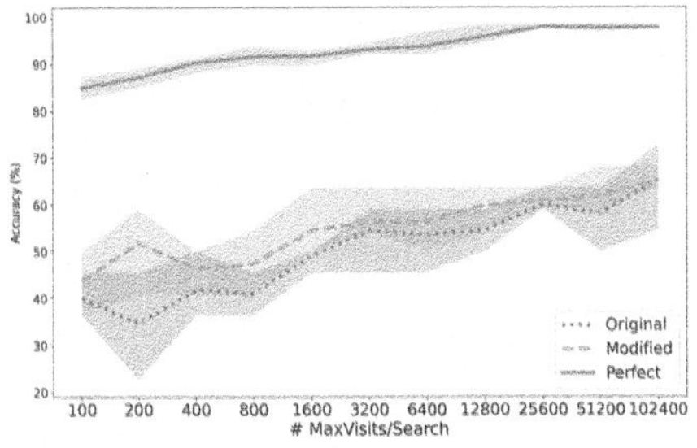
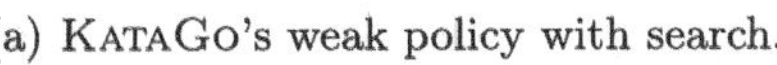

(a) KataGo's weak policy with search.

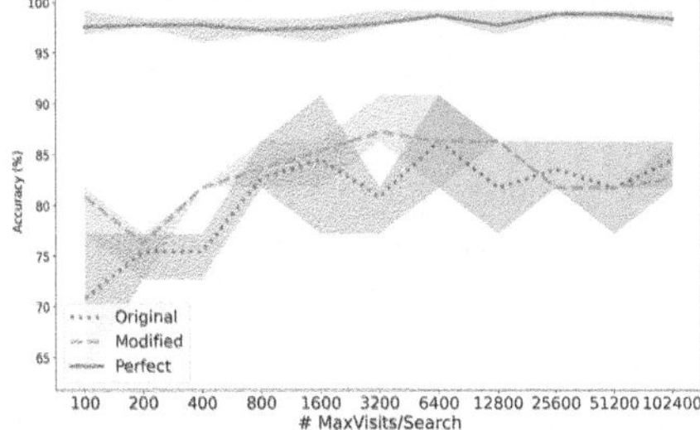

(b) KataGo's strong policy with search.

Fig. 2. Average, minimum and maximum success rate of KataGo's weak and strong policy with different amounts of search.

5.3   Playing Matches Between the Exact Solver and KataGo

Matches between the exact solver and KataGo show the importance of perfect play. We use the strong policy with 500 visit search. Since the exact solver can solve every position in the perfect games and C.11 subsets, we use these two sets for our experiment. KataGo preserves the win in 90.8% of the perfect games and wins 100% of the matches starting from the C.11 subsets. In Sect. 5.1, we identified an endgame in the C.11 subsets that KataGo is never able to solve. However, this position doesn't affect the win rate here, as Black (the losing side) is to play here.

5.4   Case Studies of Interesting Mistakes

Figure 2 shows that the number of mistakes fluctuates with larger searches. Several endgames remain unsolved even with our deepest search. For further analysis, we run selected endgames with more than 200k search visits and observe the changes of utility (action value), lower confidence bound (lcb), winrate, and number of visited nodes explored during the search process. Two examples discussed below are shown in Fig. 3.

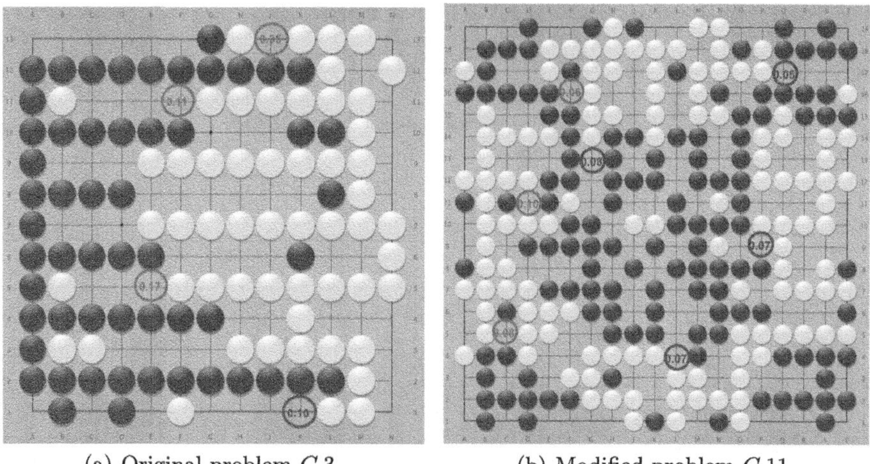

<table>
<tr><td>(a) Original problem C.3.</td><td>(b) Modified problem C.11.</td></tr>
</table>

Fig. 3. Examples for two types of interesting mistakes. KataGo's suggested moves are shown as red circles, and winning moves as blue circles. The number inside each circle is the policy probability for that move. (Color figure online)

The original problem C.3 in Fig. 3(a) is not solved by KataGo even with deep search. In different searches, KataGo suggests three different moves: $J13$, $E5$, and $F11$, while the only winning move is $K1$. Figure 4(a-d), shows the changes of winrate, lcb, utility and the number of visited nodes during the search. $J13$ has high prior probability in Fig. 3(a), but as the search progresses, it drops. Move

$F11$ starts out with a low prior, but with more search it becomes KataGo's preferred move. The optimal move $K1$ goes up, then down again. The win rate

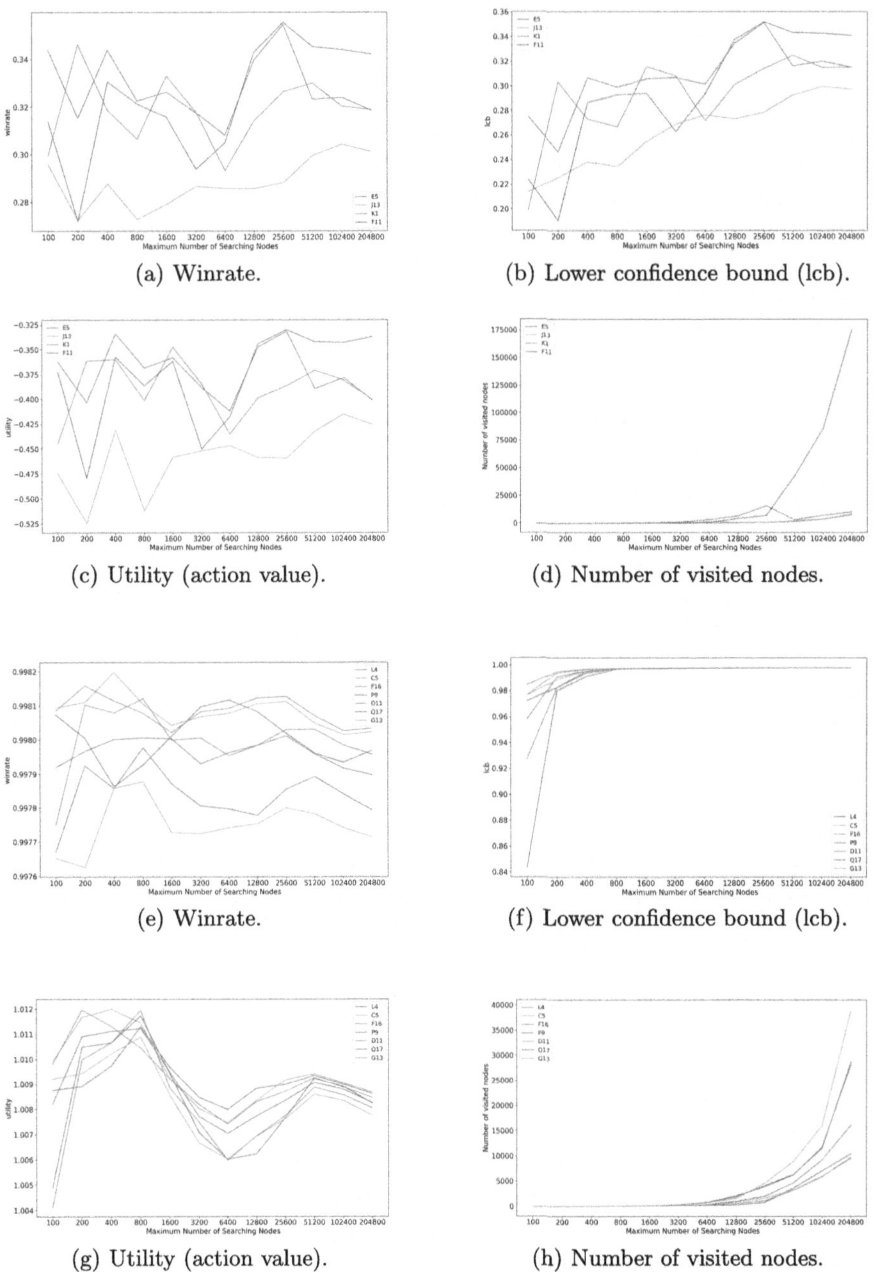

(a) Winrate.

(b) Lower confidence bound (lcb).

(c) Utility (action value).

(d) Number of visited nodes.

(e) Winrate.

(f) Lower confidence bound (lcb).

(g) Utility (action value).

(h) Number of visited nodes.

Fig. 4. The changes of winrate, lcb, utility, and number of visited node during the search.

and lcb of all moves in Fig. 4(a and b), remain below 0.4. KATAGO completely fails to recognize that $K1$ wins. Figure 4(d) shows that after 25,600 visits, almost all visits go to $F11$, a losing move.

Small Search Correct but Longer Search Wrong. In modified problem $C.11$ shown in Fig. 3(b), KATAGO correctly identifies winning moves with a small search but switches to a wrong move after a longer search. The winning moves of this position are $G13$, $L4$, $P9$, and $Q17$. However, KATAGO also suggests the losing moves $D11$, $F16$, and $C5$ in different searches.

The changes of winrate, lcb, utility and the number of node visits in Fig. 4(e-h) show that initially, the winning moves are visited less often. After 1600 visits, there is a significant improvement for $P9$, and KATAGO starts selecting this winning move. However, with deeper search the value of $P9$ decreases again, and the losing move $C5$ becomes KATAGO's preferred move. The main issue here is that KATAGO cannot distinguish at all between winning and losing moves. The win rate, utility, and lcb of all losing moves in Fig. 4(e-g) remain high. In Fig. 4 (h), KATAGO explores $C5$ more in larger searches.

6   Limitations and Future Work

We explored some key questions of move selection, the role of search, and the performance across several Go endgame datasets. The difference between weak and strong neural networks was large. Adding even a small amount of search greatly improved both. In matches against an exact solver, KATAGO did well but made mistakes in some simple endgames, particularly those with long corridors of similar values. The network has not learned the correct relative values of those moves, and often prefers a simple capture of slightly lesser value. Larger searches generally boosted KATAGO's performance but did not solve all these puzzles.

Limitations. We do not have a large enough set of complex endgames, such as no-DI. Our perfect game and C.11 subsets are relatively much easier to solve than the original and modified Berlekamp/Wolfe problems. We did not run detailed enough experiments to fully understand why KATAGO struggles to find the best incentive moves.

Future Work. One interesting future topic is to measure KATAGO's winrate errors separately for winning and losing moves. In theory, all winning moves should approach a winrate of 1, and all losing moves should be close to 0. A similar winrate for both winning and losing moves indicates a poor understanding of the position. We can evaluate problem difficulty more clearly by looking at additional factors such as number of winning moves. We could also add more challenging 19×19 test sets by following a narrow winning line from C.11 instead of just removing subgames as in prior work, which tends to make the problems much easier.

References

1. Berlekamp, E., Wolfe, D.: Mathematical Go: Chilling Gets the Last Point. CRC Press (1994)
2. Haque, R., Wei, T.H., Müller, M.: On the road to perfection? Evaluating Leela Chess Zero against endgame tablebases. In: Advances in Computer Games, pp. 142–152. Springer (2022). https://doi.org/10.1007/978-3-031-11488-5_13
3. Hoel, C.J., Driggs-Campbell, K., Wolff, K., Laine, L., Kochenderfer, M.J.: Combining planning and deep reinforcement learning in tactical decision making for autonomous driving. IEEE Trans. Intell. Veh. **5**(2), 294–305 (2019)
4. Kemmerling, M., Lütticke, D., Schmitt, R.H.: Beyond games: a systematic review of neural Monte Carlo tree search applications. Appl. Intell. **54**(1), 1020–1046 (2024)
5. Kővári, B., Hegedüs, F., Bécsi, T.: Design of a reinforcement learning-based lane keeping planning agent for automated vehicles. Appl. Sci. **10**(20), 7171 (2020)
6. Mo, S., Pei, X., Wu, C.: Safe reinforcement learning for autonomous vehicle using Monte Carlo tree search. IEEE Trans. Intell. Transp. Syst. **23**(7), 6766–6773 (2021)
7. Müller, M.: Computer Go as a sum of local games: an application of combinatorial game theory. Ph.D. thesis, ETH Zurich (1995)
8. Müller, M.: Decomposition search: a combinatorial games approach to game tree search, with applications to solving Go endgames. In: IJCAI, pp. 578–583 (1999)
9. Müller, M.: Not like other games - why tree search in Go is different. In: Proceedings of Fifth Joint Conference on Information Sciences (JCIS 2000), pp. 974–977 (2000)
10. Romein, J.W., Bal, H.E.: Awari is solved. ICGA J. **25**(3), 162–165 (2002)
11. Sadmine, Q.A., Husna, A., Müller, M.: Stockfish or Leela Chess Zero? A comparison against endgame tablebases. In: Advances in Computer Games, pp. 26–35. Springer (2023). https://doi.org/10.1007/978-3-031-54968-7_3
12. Silver, D., et al.: A general reinforcement learning algorithm that masters chess, shogi, and Go through self-play. Science **362**(6419), 1140–1144 (2018)
13. Wang, T.T., et al.: Adversarial policies beat superhuman Go AIs. In: ICML 23, vol. 1484, pp. 35655 – 35739 (2023)
14. Wu, D.J.: Accelerating self-play learning in Go. In: AAAI-20 Workshop on Reinforcement Learning in Games (2020)

Solving Linear NoGo with Combinatorial Game Theory

Haoyu Du$^{(\boxtimes)}$ ⓘ and Martin Müller ⓘ

University of Alberta, Edmonton, Canada
`{du2,mmueller}@ualberta.ca`

Abstract. NoGo is a version of Go where stones are never removed from the board, once played. Strong computer players have been created for NoGo. However, the game properties and optimal play strategies are not well studied. We introduce CGTSolver, a search algorithm that applies concepts from combinatorial game theory (CGT) in order to solve Linear NoGo. We develop several decomposition strategies and simplification rules for this game. Our results show that CGTSolver is much more efficient than previous solvers, and as the board size increases, the performance gap widens. With this new approach we solved all NoGo boards up to 1×39—twelve boards more than in previous work.

Keywords: NoGo · Combinatorial Games · Minimax Search

1 Introduction

NoGo, or *Anti-Atari Go* [1], is a variant of the well-known game of Go. NoGo shares the basic mechanisms and concepts of Go, but with different rules of play:

- Capturing and suicide are both forbidden.
- Passing is forbidden.
- When a player cannot make a move, the game ends and the player loses.

With just a simple twist to the rules, NoGo becomes a very different game strategically. Linear NoGo or $1 \times n$ NoGo[1] refers to NoGo games played on a one-dimensional board, a $1 \times n$ strip consisting of n *points* which are initially empty. In Sect. 2, we review NoGo rules and previous work on this game. In Sect. 3, we briefly introduce our notation and the relevant combinatorial game theory (CGT) concepts. Starting in Sect. 4, we analyze and solve Linear NoGo by search. We represent a board as a sum of independent subgames in the sense of CGT [15]. We develop rules for board simplification, decomposition, and reduction. These rules allow us to replace a position by simpler sum games with equal outcome. In Sect. 5, we discuss the structure of reduced Linear NoGo positions, and construct a database of all such games with up to 15 empty points. We

---

[1] We use the terms Linear NoGo and $1 \times n$ NoGo interchangeably.

M. Hartisch et al. (Eds.): CG 2024, LNCS 15550, pp. 54–65, 2025.
https://doi.org/10.1007/978-3-031-86585-5_5

design a static evaluation function based on sum game properties in Sect. 6, and in Sect. 7 we implement the new NoGo solver *CGTSolver* based on Negamax search with many CGT-related improvements. In the experiments in Sect. 8, we analyze the performance of CGTSolver and solve boards up to 1×39, greatly surpassing the previous state of the art.

2   The NoGo Game and Previous Work

NoGo is a relatively young game with few human players. It is a two-player perfect information game played on a graph, usually a grid. We study Linear NoGo on a one-dimensional strip. Each point on the board except the two endpoints has two neighbors. Following standard Go notation, a maximal set of adjacent stones of the same color is called a *block*. In Linear NoGo, each block has either one or two adjacent empty points, which are called its *liberties*. In contrast to Go, it is illegal to *capture*—to remove the last liberty of an opponent's block. It is also illegal to play a *suicide* move, which removes the last liberty of a player's own block.

NoGo is less studied than popular board games, and few useful heuristics are known for playing it. Previous research mainly focused on creating strong computer agents for game playing [3,6,13]. She [13] solved NoGo on the 5×5 board; Cazenave [2] provided an incomplete table of winners for boards up to 25 points. The most complete computer-proved NoGo results so far, by Du et al., include results for all starting moves on all rectangular boards up to 27 points [4]. They proved by a symmetry argument that the first player, Black, wins all $1 \times n$ NoGo games for odd $n > 1$.

Previous studies that combine search algorithms and CGT to solve games other than NoGo include [8,9,16,17]. Shan [12] used CGT methods to calculate the mean and temperature of many NoGo positions, and proved fundamental theorems about board partitioning into independent subgames.

The best previous computer program to solve NoGo is SBHSolver [4], a Negamax-based solver using a transposition table implemented with Sorted Bucket Hash (SBH), a memory-efficient perfect hashing scheme. SBHSolver also uses the History Heuristic [11] and Enhanced Transposition Cutoff [10]. This program does not use reduced NoGo positions or any CGT concepts. We use it as a baseline for evaluating CGTSolver.

3   Notation and CGT Concepts

We write NoGo positions, and templates for them, as a string with the colors of each point. We use the characters x, o, . to indicate Black, White, and empty points respectively. x^+ and o^+ indicate a string of one or more stones of the same color. <L> and <R> denote arbitrary substrings, of size 0 or longer, of a legal NoGo position, while <L>$^+$ and <R>$^+$ denote substrings of size at least 1. Strings written next to each other are concatenated. For example, the template <L>x.o.x<R> matches positions such as x.o.x, x.o.x., and o.xx.o.x..o, but not the illegal ox.o.x, where the leftmost o has no liberty.

3.1 Notation for Move Restrictions

We use the following notation from [12] to express move restrictions on single points due to NoGo rules. A point on a NoGo board is called a *0-Go* if no one can play there, a *1-Go* if only one player can play, and a *2-Go* if both players can play. The set of 1-Go points can be partitioned into disjoint sets *B-Go* and *W-Go*, where only Black (White) can play.

3.2 Outcome Classes and Search Results

As usual, we identify Black with Left and positive values, and White with Right and negative values. The four possible outcome classes for a game G in CGT [15] correspond directly to the four combined results of two boolean minimax searches of G with alternating play: In outcome class $\mathscr{L}$, **Left** wins both going first and going second; in $\mathscr{R}$, **Right** wins in both searches; in $\mathscr{N}$, the **n**ext player (toPlay) wins both times; and in $\mathscr{P}$, the **p**revious (second) player wins both.

3.3 CGT Concepts

We provide a short review of the most relevant CGT concepts used in this paper. For a thorough introduction, we refer to the literature [15]. A game G is defined recursively as a pair $G = \{G^L | G^R\}$ of left and right options, which are in turn sets of games.

Sum of Games. In a sum of subgames $G_1 + G_2 + \cdots + G_k$, a player must move in exactly one of the components G_i to an option G_i^L or G_i^R, leaving all other subgames unchanged.

Inverse. For a game $G = \{G^L | G^R\}$, its inverse $-G$ is defined recursively by $-G = \{-G^R | -G^L\}$. In NoGo, the inverse of a game can be obtained by swapping the color of all stones from black to white and vice versa.

Equality. Two games G and H are called *equal* if for all games X, the outcome class of $G + X$ is equal to the outcome class of $H + X$. All games of second-player win (in outcome class $\mathscr{P}$) are equal to 0. If $G = H$, then the *difference game* $G - H = 0$ is a second-player win. This fact can be used to simplify games by search.

4   Simplifying and Reducing $1 \times n$ NoGo Games

Theorem 1 (Block Simplification). *In a $1 \times n$ NoGo game, a block of stones of the same color can be replaced by a single stone of that color. The resulting game is equal to the original game. For arbitrary* <L> *and* <R>*,*
<L>x$^+$<R> = <L>x<R> *and* <L>o$^+$<R> = <L>o<R> .

This is clear from the rules, since representing a block by a single stone does not affect its liberties, or the set of legal move sequences of both players. As an example, `.xxx..ooxx..` can be simplified to `.x..ox..` by reducing larger blocks to single stones.

Theorem 2 (xo-Split). *A $1 \times n$ NoGo game can be split into two independent subgames at the boundary between two blocks of opposite colors:* <L>xo<R> = <L>x + o<R> *and* <L>ox<R> = <L>o + x<R> .

Proof. Separating a game G in this way into $G_1 + G_2$ does not affect the liberties of any block, or any future block when the game is continued. A move played on the left side of the boundary in the original game does not affect the liberties, and therefore the set of legal moves, in any continuation on the right, and vice versa. Since the set of legal move sequences does not change for both players, the outcomes $o(G + X) = o(G_1 + G_2 + X)$ are equal for any X, so the games are equal.

For example, `.x..ox..` = `.x..o + x..` is an xo-split.

Definition 1 (Reduced $1 \times n$ NoGo position). *A $1 \times n$ NoGo position is called* reduced *if neither block simplification nor xo-split can be applied.*

Any sum of $1 \times n$ NoGo positions can be simplified into an equal sum of reduced positions.

5   A Pre-computed Database of Reduced NoGo Positions

We study the set of all reduced positions with a given number n of empty points.

Theorem 3. *For all $n > 0$, there are 3^{n+1} distinct reduced positions with n empty points.*

Proof. By definition, a reduced position does not contain adjacent stones of the same color, or adjacent stones of opposite color. So any neighbors of a stone must be empty points. We can build any position with n empty points by starting with those empty points, then optionally adding a single stone at either end and between two empty points. There are $n + 1$ insertion locations with three choices each (Black stone, White stone, and no stone), a total of 3^{n+1} distinct positions.

Consider all reduced positions with $n = 3$. For the empty board `...`, the four possible stone insertion points marked by underscores are `_._._._`, and at each `_` we can insert `x`, `o`, or nothing. Positions `...` and `x..o.x` are two examples.

5.1 The Database

Our pre-computed database contains all reduced $1 \times n$ NoGo positions with up to 15 empty points, and information about their value. With this database, CGTSolver can solve games more efficiently. It can query a game directly in the database, and it can use information about subgames of a sum. Each database entry stores a reduced position, its outcome class, and for parts of the database, a pointer to the simplest equal game. The database is organized in layers, by the number of empty points n in each position. It is built incrementally from $n = 1$ to $n = 15$. The data stored for positions with smaller n is used to speed up the computation of later positions.

The analysis above provides an efficient way of constructing all reduced boards with a fixed number of empty points. To order all reduced positions, we first sort them by the number of empty points, then by a base 3 encoding of the inserted stones. Let $n = n(G)$ be the number of empty points in game G, and $code(G)$ be a $n + 1$ digit base 3 number. Each potential insertion point has code 0 if no stone is inserted, 1 for a black stone, and 2 for a white stone. In the examples above, `code(...)` = `0000` and `code(x..o.x)` = `1021`. The ordering $ord(G)$ is the dictionary ordering of the pairs $(n(G), code(G))$.

5.2 Simplest Equal Game

Given a $1 \times n$ NoGo position, its *simplest equal game* is defined to be the smallest game in the ordering defined above that is equal to this game. During search, we replace each subgame in a sum with its simplest equal game, if known. This reduces the breadth and the depth of the search.

As an example, the game $A = $ `..o.x.o..x` is equal to the game $B = $ `..`, $A = B$, and B is the simplest game equal to A. This is proven when constructing the database by verifying that $A - B = 0$, a second player win, while $A - X \neq 0$ for all games X that are simpler than B. The consequence is that during search, any subgame A can be replaced by the much simpler B.

In general, to add the simplest equal game of game G to the database, we search if $G - H = 0$ for simpler games H with $ord(H) < ord(G)$. We try candidate games H in increasing order in the database.

5.3 Database Statistics

Our database contains all $\sum_{i=1}^{15} 3^{i+1} = 64,570,077$ reduced positions for $n \in \{1, \ldots, 15\}$, and their outcome class. Due to computational limitations, we fully compute simplest equals only for positions up to $n = 8$. The most frequent values of positions with $n \leq 8$ are shown in Fig. 1 and Table 1. For each pair of games G and their inverse $-G$, only one is shown. "idx" in Table 1 corresponds to the

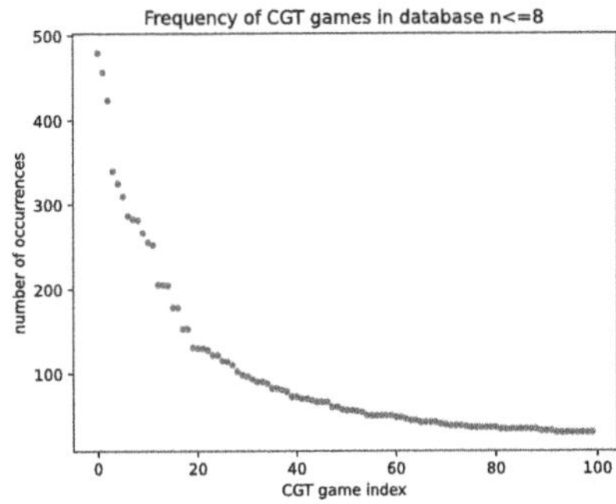

Fig. 1. The number of occurrences of the most frequent simplest equal games in the database.

Table 1. The 11 most frequent simplest equal games in the $n \leq 8$ database.

Idx	board	canonical form	occurrences
0	.x.x.o.	$1*$	481
1	..	$*$	457
2	...	± 1	424
3	...x.o.	$\pm(1*)$	341
4	..x.x.	$\{2|1\}$	326
5	.x.	1	310
6	.x.x.x.	3	287
7	.x.x.x.o.	$2*$	284
8	.	0	282
9	..x.	$\{1|0\}$	268
10	.x.x.	2	256

"CGT game index" in Fig. 1. To limit the precomputation cost, for the larger database entries with $8 < n \leq 13$ we only computed simplest equals from among the 18 games in Table 1 and their inverses.

6 State Representation and Static Evaluation of Sum Games

Much of the power of CGT comes from its representation of a game as the sum of independent subgames, and its rules for simplifying games and determining their outcome class. In CGTSolver, each node in the search tree stores a sum of one or more subgames, plus whose turn it is.

6.1 Static Evaluation

If the outcome classes of all remaining subgames are known from the database, we can sometimes determine the search result of the sum statically [16], and save further search. This is trivially true when a sum consists of a single such subgame only. In larger sums, Black going first wins games $G + H$ with $o(G) = \mathscr{L}$ and $o(H) = \mathscr{N}$, where G itself can be a sum, and similarly white going first wins when $o(G) = \mathscr{R}$.

7 Implementation Details of CGTSolver

In this section, we discuss some implementation details of CGTSolver. The core search engine is Boolean Negamax. In addition to static evaluation, CGTSolver uses CGT-based techniques to simplify and split large games into independent subgames. Pseudocode is provided in Algorithm 1.

Algorithm 1. NEGAMAX for sum games

Require: *games* - a collection of games to evaluate
         player - the color of current player
Return: true if current player wins; **false** otherwise
  result ← TRANSPOSITIONTABLE(*games*, *player*)
  if *result* is valid **then return** *result*
  result ← STATICEVALUATION(*games*, *player*)
  if *result* is valid **then return** *result*
  moves ← GETLEGALMOVES(*games*)
  for *move* in *moves* **do**
    PLAY(*games*, *move*, *player*)
    SIMPLIFY(*games*)
    SPLIT(*games*)
    DATABASELOOKUP(*games*)
    win ← **not** NEGAMAX()
    UNDO(*games*, *move*, *player*)
    if *win* **then return true**
  return false

7.1 Updating Sum Games

In each recursive negamax call, a move is played in one subgame, followed by simplification and split, which changes the sum. To undo a move, the sum is restored to its previous state. The search depth of a NoGo position with n empty points can be up to $n - 1$. CGTSolver uses a *change stack* to track the game history. The stack stores both previous (inactive) and current (active) subgames, in the order of their creation. The stack initially contains only a single active subgame for the starting position. Each move is played on one active subgame G, resulting in zero or more new subgames H_i. G is deactivated, and all H_i are pushed on top of the stack as active games. To undo this move, all H_i are popped from the stack, and G is re-activated.

To play a move in subgame G, the move is first played on a copy of G. The resulting local board is simplified, splits are done, and subgames found in the database are possibly replaced by their simplest equals. Subgames of value 0 are removed. The zero or more new subgames H_i are added to the current sum S. If for a new subgame H_i, its inverse $-H_i$ is also in S, both are deactivated, and this is recorded on the change stack as well.

7.2 Play-in-the-Middle Heuristic

The play-in-the-middle (PITM) heuristic tries moves closer to the middle of a subgame first. It helps to quickly break down a large game into smaller subgames, increasing the chance of database hits.

For global move ordering, active subgames in the stack are processed in order from largest to smallest in length, using PITM in each subgame.

7.3 Global Transposition Table

A transposition table stores the results of previously searched nodes. The table greatly improves a game solver's performance by searching nodes that can be reached via different move sequences only once. The transposition table in CGT-Solver is implemented as a hash table. To efficiently hash a game position that is a sum of subgames, similar to the approach of Folkersen [5] we use a hashing scheme based on sorting to achieve a normal form of a sum, followed by Zobrist Hashing [18].

The board of each subgame is considered as a string, with standard string ordering. The string is replaced by its reverse if it comes first in the order. For the normal form, the strings of all subgames in a sum are sorted in increasing order, and then concatenated as follows: A sum game S is represented by a string of four characters: x, o, ., and a subgame separator symbol |. Sorted subgame strings are concatenated, with | separators in between. The resulting unique string representation of S is then hashed. Given a maximum game length (including separators) of N, a Zobrist hash code is prepared for each location $i \in \{0, \ldots, N-1\}$ and each of the four characters in four random number tables $\mathcal{R}^B$, $\mathcal{R}^W$, $\mathcal{R}^E$, $\mathcal{R}^|$ with the codes for black, white, empty, and separator. The string representation s of S is hashed to $h(s) \doteq \bigoplus_i \mathcal{R}_i^{s_i}$, where s_i is the i-th character in s, $\mathcal{R}_i$ is the i-th entry in a random number table, and $\bigoplus$ is the XOR operator.

8 Results and Performance Analysis

We solve $1 \times n$ NoGo boards for $n = 8$ to $n = 39$. In each case, we pre-play B1, the second point from the end, as a strong first move and prove a win for Black. This confirms previous results up to $n = 27$, and agrees with the general conjecture in [4]. We extend these previous results by computing win/loss for all opening moves up to $n = 33$. New results are shown in Fig. 3.

We compare SBHSolver and CGTSolver in terms of node count and wall-clock time in Fig. 2a and 2b. For larger boards, CGTSolver uses over two orders of magnitude fewer nodes than SBHSolver, and is also faster by a similar ratio[2]. The CGT-based optimizations in CGTSolver do not add much overhead to the main search algorithm.

---

[2] Wall-clock time measured on a single core AMD EPYC 7313.

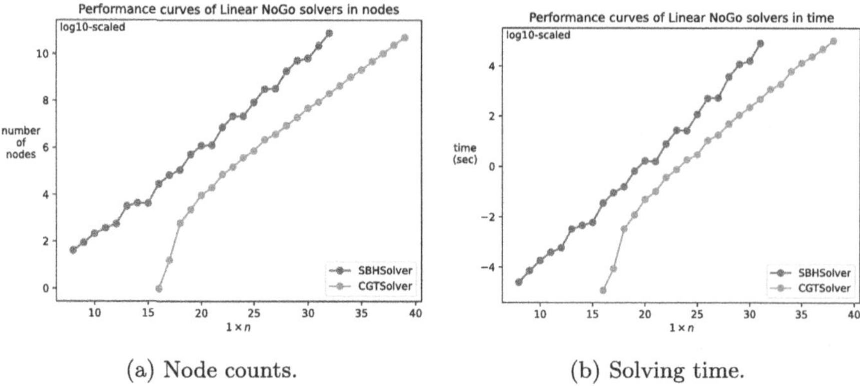

(a) Node counts.   (b) Solving time.

Fig. 2. Performance comparison of SBHSolver and CGTSolver for solving $1 \times n$ NoGo with the B1 opening. The graphs are log10-scaled on the y-axis.

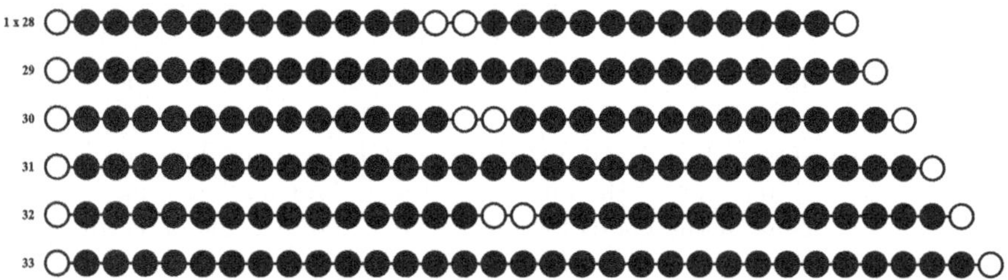

Fig. 3. The opening moves on empty $1 \times n$ NoGo with $28 \leq n \leq 33$. A black (white) stone indicates a winning (losing) opening move.

8.1   Ablation Study

The ablation study shown in Fig. 4 evaluates the effect of omitting one of the CGTSolver components: the PITM heuristic, the replacement scheme of simplest equal games, the static evaluation to catch early wins, and the transposition table. The transposition table most strongly improves the performance, but unexpectedly, the benefit of static evaluation diminishes with increasing board size.

8.2   In-Search Statistics

Figure 5 presents detailed search statistics for solving 1×30 NoGo with B1 preplayed. The shallowest terminal nodes appeared early at a depth of 4. The CGT approach greatly reduces the search depth. The maximum number of subgames in a position was 6. The most common number of subgames was 2. Having more

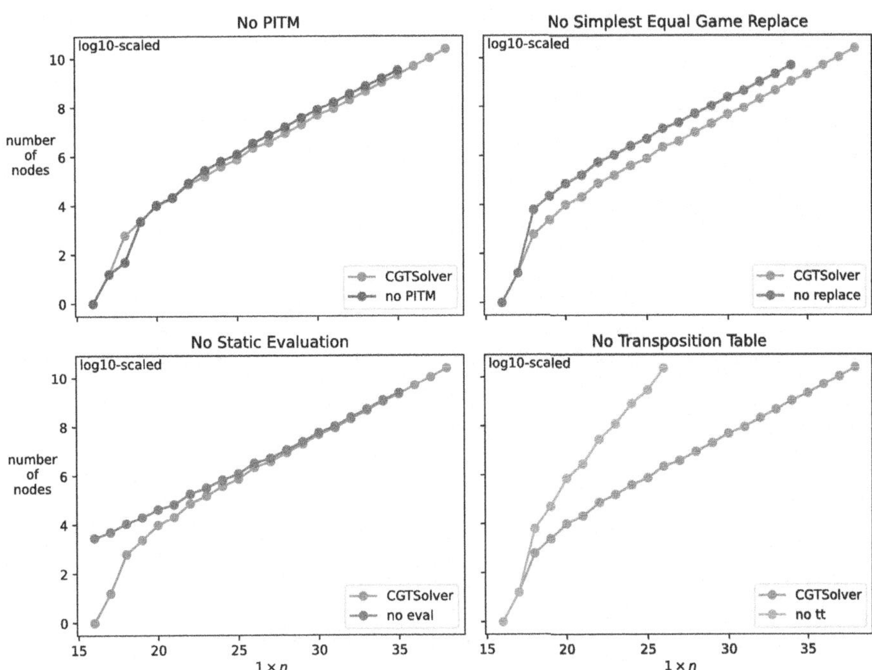

Fig. 4. Ablation on components of CGTSolver: the PITM heuristic, replacement with simplest equal games, static evaluation, and transposition table (TT).

subgames of smaller size increases the likelihood of detecting wins and losses early. A potential improvement would be targeted move ordering heuristics that aim to produce more xo-splits.

8.3 Comparison with CGSuite

Siegel's CGSuite [14] is a very powerful and versatile system that implements many CGT algorithms. This system has been widely used for research in this area. However, it is not an efficient tool for solving $1 \times n$ NoGo due to its dependence on canonical form computations, which can become very complex. We could compute results with CGSuite for boards up to $n = 16$ in several minutes on comparable hardware. The 1×16 board has a massive canonical form with 1201194 stops! Our attempt to compute $n = 17$ resulted in a Java heap space overflow. In contrast, CGTSolver running from scratch, without using its precomputed database, proves the Black win for $n = 16$ in less than 30 milliseconds.

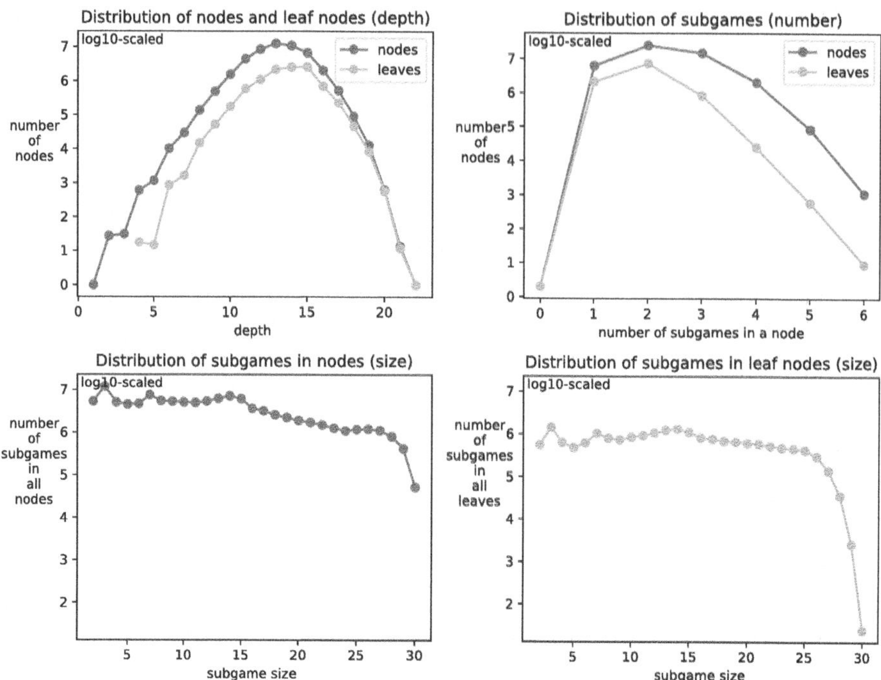

Fig. 5. Statistics in solving 1×30 NoGo with B1 opening: the number of nodes and leaf nodes across depths, the number of nodes and leaf nodes having different numbers of subgames, and the number of subgames of different sizes in all nodes and leaf nodes of the game DAG.

9   Conclusions and Future Work

CGTSolver is a CGT-enhanced Negamax search algorithm that solves $1 \times n$ NoGo positions efficiently. We exploit several game properties in order to solve a position as a simpler sum of subgames, which greatly improves the search. Our experiments show that CGTSolver far surpasses the previous state of the art in terms of node counts, wall-clock time, and new results. We solved boards up to 1×39, including new results on 12 boards of size 28 and larger.

For future work, we would first like to extend our specific techniques to other NoGo boards. Block simplification works on any graph, not just on a one-dimensional strip, by contracting all edges between neighboring stones within the same block. For board decomposition, instead of xo-Split, which relies on the linear board structure, the techniques of Shan [12] can be used.

We believe that similar sum game solving techniques can be applied to a wide class of "short" combinatorial games. Search approaches based on decomposition work well when there are many subgames, as in linear Clobber [5] and Go endgames [7], and even on small Amazons boards, which have very few subgames [16].

References

1. Anti Atari Go. https://senseis.xmp.net/?AntiAtariGo. Accessed 25 Feb 2024
2. Cazenave, T.: Monte carlo game solver. In: Monte Carlo Search, MCS 2020. Communications in Computer and Information Science, vol. 1379, pp. 56–70 (2021)
3. Chou, C.W., Teytaud, O., Yen, S.J.: Revisiting monte-carlo tree search on a normal form game: NoGo. In: Applications of Evolutionary Computation (2011)
4. Du, H., Wei, T.H., Müller, M.: Solving NoGo on small rectangular boards. In: Advances in Computer Games, pp. 39–49 (2024)
5. Folkersen, T.: Linear Clobber solver (2022). Capstone report, University of Alberta
6. Gao, Y., Wu, L.: Efficiently mastering the game of NoGo with deep reinforcement learning supported by domain knowledge. Electronics **10**(13), 1533 (2021)
7. Müller, M.: Decomposition search: A combinatorial games approach to game tree search, with applications to solving Go endgames. In: IJCAI, pp. 578–583 (1999)
8. Müller, M.: Global and local game tree search. Information Sc. **135**, 187–206 (2001)
9. Müller, M., Li, Z.: Locally informed global search for sums of combinatorial games. In: Computers and Games. LNCS, vol. 3846, pp. 273–284 (2006)
10. Plaat, A., Schaeffer, J., Pijls, W., de Bruin, A.: Exploiting graph properties of game trees. In: AAAI/IAAI, vol. 1 (1996)
11. Schaeffer, J.: The history heuristic. ICGA J. **6**(3), 16–19 (1983)
12. Shan, Y.C.: Solving games and improving search performance with embedded combinatorial game knowledge. Ph.D. thesis, National Chiao Tung University (2013)
13. She, P.: The Design and Study of NoGo Program. Master's thesis, National Chiao Tung University (2013)
14. Siegel, A.: CGSuite. A computer algebra system for research in combinatorial game theory (2003–2024). https://www.cgsuite.org
15. Siegel, A.: Combinatorial Game Theory, vol. 146. American Math, Soc (2013)
16. Song, J., Müller, M.: An enhanced solver for the game of Amazons. IEEE Trans. Comput. Intell. AI Games **7**(1), 16–27 (2015). https://doi.org/10.1109/TCIAIG.2014.2309077
17. Uiterwijk, J., Griebel, J.: Combining combinatorial game theory with an α-β solver for clobber: theory and experiments. In: BNAIC 2016 (2017)
18. Zobrist, A.L.: A new hashing method with application for game playing. ICCA J. **13**(2), 69–73 (1990)

Solving 7x7 Killall-Go with Seki Database

Yun-Jui Tsai[1], Ting Han Wei[2], Chi-Huang Lin[1], Chung-Chin Shih[3],
Hung Guei[3], I-Chen Wu[1], and Ti-Rong Wu[3(✉)]

[1] National Yang Ming Chiao Tung University, Hsinchu, Taiwan
[2] Kochi University of Technology, Kami City, Japan
[3] Academia Sinica, Taipei, Taiwan
`tirongwu@iis.sinica.edu.tw`

Abstract. Game solving is the process of finding the theoretical out-come for a game, assuming that all player choices are optimal. This paper focuses on a technique that can reduce the heuristic search space signif-icantly for 7x7 Killall-Go. In Go and Killall-Go, *live* patterns are stones that are protected from opponent capture. Mutual life, also referred to as seki, is when both players' stones achieve life by sharing liberties with their opponent. Whichever player attempts to capture the opponent first will leave their own stones vulnerable. Therefore, it is critical to recog-nize seki patterns to avoid putting oneself in jeopardy. Recognizing seki can reduce the search depth significantly. In this paper, we enumerate all seki patterns up to a predetermined area size, then store these pat-terns into a seki table. This allows us to recognize seki during search, which significantly improves solving efficiency for the game of Killall-Go. Experiments show that a position that could not be solved within a day can be solved in 482 s with the addition of a seki table. For general posi-tions, a 10% to 20% improvement in wall clock time and node count is observed.

Keywords: Game solving · Seki · Endgame database · Killall-Go

1 Introduction

Games solving [14], particularly for the complex game of Go, is one of the most challenging pursuits in artificial intelligence. While AlphaZero [13] has mastered 19x19 Go in game playing, only up to 5x6 Go has been fully solved [15]. One interesting variant of Go is *Killall-Go*, which follows similar rules but with Black aiming to capture all White's stones to win. The game can also be viewed as a whole board *life-and-death* problem in Go, which is a fundamental concept for Go learners. Killall-Go is therefore a valuable test bed for solving larger board sizes in Go, with many attempts to solve the 7x7 version of the game [12,21,22].

In 7x7 Killall-Go, Black plays two consecutive moves first, followed by alter-nating turns between White and Black, as shown in Fig. 1a. There are two ways for White to win: by achieving unconditional life (identifiable via the Benson algorithm [3]), shown in Fig. 1b, or by reaching mutual life with Black, known

M. Hartisch et al. (Eds.): CG 2024, LNCS 15550, pp. 66–76, 2025.
https://doi.org/10.1007/978-3-031-86585-5_6

as *seki*, shown in Fig. 1c. In comparison to knowledge-based analysis for Benson safety, seki requires an exhaustive search to identify. Knowing when to attempt detecting seki to minimize overhead costs is an issue that has yet to be addressed. Additionally, by pre-computing seki information, we can save significant time during the game solving process. For this reason, we propose constructing a seki database, using the detection method proposed by Niu et al. [9], to aid with solving 7x7 Killall-Go. In the best case, when using this seki database, positions that cannot be solved in a day can be solved in just 482 s. Our experiments also show that the addition of the database also improves the overall solving time for general cases, with a 10–20% reduction in search time.

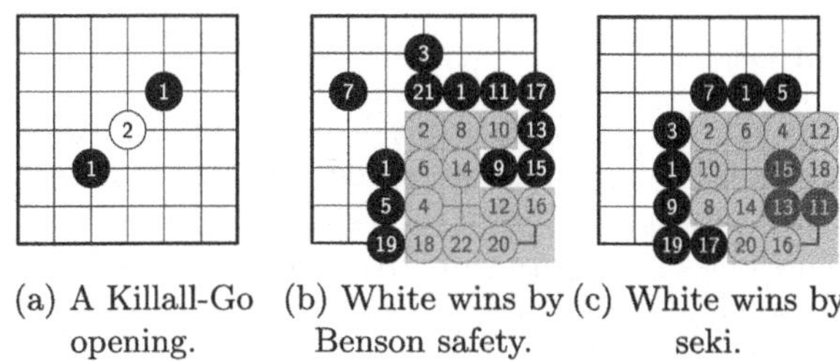

(a) A Killall-Go opening.   (b) White wins by Benson safety.   (c) White wins by seki.

Fig. 1. An illustration of a 7x7 Killall-Go opening with two different winning conditions for White.

2   Background

2.1   Game Solver

A game is considered solved when its game-theoretic value is found, i.e. we know the outcome under optimal play. Since the search space is often extremely large, heuristics are often used to guide the search, minimizing the number of winning moves explored, while simultaneously searching through the shortest game length that leads to a solution. AlphaZero-like algorithms are known for producing strong agents that do not necessarily attempt to finish games as quickly as possible [22], which make them less ideal for game solving. Proof-number search (PNS) [2], depth-first proof number search (DFPN) [7], and threat-space search [1] are some common search algorithms that prune unnecessary branches when solving games, potentially leading to more efficient solutions.

A notable example of a game solved is checkers. Schaeffer et al. [10] used a distributed solving system comprised of a proof-tree manager and numerous workers. The manager breaks the problem down into tasks, consisting of interesting game positions, which are sent to workers. The workers were each an instance of a solver with a strong checkers playing program providing heuristic value. Once a worker finds a solution for a game position, it returns the result to the manager, which uses that information to construct a solution tree. In addition to this process – referred to as the forward search – they also computed a large collection of endgame databases.

We use the online fine-tuning distributed solver [21] in this paper. This system follows the manager-worker paradigm. Each solver is a Monte-Carlo tree search (MCTS) solver [17] that uses a Proof Cost Network (PCN) [22] to provide heuristics, the Benson [3] algorithm to determine terminal conditions, and the Relevance-Zone based search [11,12] to prune irrelevant nodes. During the solving process, the online trainer continuously fine-tunes the deep learning-based heuristic to maintain its accuracy. Additionally, the seki database proposed in this paper can also be thought of as endgame information that can reduce the search space significantly.

2.2 7x7 Killall-Go

Killall-Go is a two-player, zero-sum game like Go. In 7x7 Killall-Go, Black is given a large advantage by placing two stones in their first turn. Accordingly, Black is expected to capture all White stones to win. On the other hand, White only needs to secure one safe area to win. To determine whether an area is secure, Benson [3] proposed an algorithm based on Go rules to determine whether a set of blocks is unconditionally alive (UCA), i.e. the block is guaranteed to be safe from capture, even if the opponent is allowed an unlimited number of consecutive turns. There are two core rules in Go. First, a string of connected stones are called *blocks*, and empty grids that are adjacent to blocks are called *liberties*. A block is captured, with its stones removed from the board, when it no longer has any liberties. Second, neither player is allowed to capture stones of their own. With these two rules in mind, a block is UCA if it has at least two liberties in which their opponent may not play in. Benson's algorithm examines blocks systematically to determine if this is true. It is worth noting that UCA is a strong guarantee. White does not need to achieve UCA to secure a safe area to win in Killall-Go. In fact, Black and White can coexist in the same area, sharing liberties between their stones, unable to capture each other. This situation is referred to as mutual life, or *seki*.

2.3 Seki

In Killall-Go, seki often involves 1) White securing an area; 2) Black occupying the boundary of the White area, while also attempting to capture white stones inside it, as shown in Fig. 1c. In the seki area, neither Black nor White can capture all opponent stones, nor achieve UCA. In fact, whichever player plays inside the seki area renders their stones vulnerable for capture. Thus, players can only move outside the seki area or pass when playing optimally.

A seki situation signifies secure territory, which in turn means White has won. However, if the search cannot recognize seki, White must satisfy the stronger condition of UCA to win. Therefore, the only way to arrive at this conclusion is for Black to play inside the seki area, which might not occur until much deeper in the search because it is a suboptimal move.

In addition to the local seki described above, there are also global seki, where the shared liberty is not enclosed. We focus on local seki in this paper, because global seki are difficult to detect and are much rarer in 7x7 Killall-Go.

Previously, Niu et al. [9] describe the issue of recognizing seki thoroughly and propose algorithms for recognizing global and local seki. Niu's local seki algorithm takes a region as input and generates all legal moves in the region, including passes. The region is searched twice using DFPN, where Black or White play first. Where Black plays first, if the result is a win for Black, the situation is not a seki. Otherwise, if the result is a loss for Black, the situation can either be seki or a White win. The second search assumes White goes first. If the result is a White win, the situation is determined to not be seki. Otherwise, the situation is confirmed to be seki. We omit the more complicated global seki detection method in this paper.

Gol'berg et al. [5] propose projecting the positional information onto a matrix, which is composed of the shared liberties in the seki. They then describe mathematical conditions that need to be satisfied to confirm a seki. Wolf [19] proposes a graph representation that forms a topological description of seki. However, its usage is limited to situations where all blocks have two liberties. Wolf [18] also introduces a computer program called GoTools, which includes life or death analysis, and a large database of single eye patterns. However, to our knowledge, the database and methods from GoTools have not been extended for seki detection nor game solving.

Kishimoto and Müller [6] built the program TSUMEGO EXPLORER to solve life and death problems like GoTools, which can also be used to analyze seki. While they emphasize general methods such as DFPN, they also propose heuristics such as the miai strategy and forced moves. In addition, Müller [8] designed a set of static rules that can be used with a search to recognize safe areas in Go earlier than the Benson algorithm. We do not use these heuristics and static rules in this paper.

Lastly, several efforts were made to classify safe patterns instead of search. Vilá [16] proposes identifying single eye shapes to help with game solving, discussing how different eye shapes affect safety in detail. Cazenave [4] generates a pattern database for Go, focusing on the pattern's external condition. Adding external conditions enables each pattern to capture a wider range of board states without increasing the complexity of the search tree. The motivation is similar to this paper, but the database in this paper does not consider the external conditions of patterns.

3   Method

In this section, we describe how the seki database is created and how it is used. First, we enumerate all potential seki patterns for specific area sizes. Second, each pattern is analyzed via exhaustive search to determine whether they are seki, where valid entries are stored in the database. Lastly, we describe how the seki database is integrated into the search algorithm during game solving.

3.1 Pattern Enumeration

The process of generating a seki database is similar to that of chess endgame tablebases. As mentioned in Subsect. 2.3, we only focus on local seki. For all potential local seki patterns, there are three key components: a black boundary, a white block enclosing a contiguous potential seki area, and interior black stones within the seki area. There are two examples of such patterns on the left hand side of Fig. 2. All potential local seki can be categorized according to the pattern size, just like how chess tablebases are categorized by piece count. In this paper, we enumerate all possible patterns from size 5 to 8. We skip sizes 4 and below since they are too small to form seki patterns.

We begin by generating all possible contiguous shapes of the specified area size n. For each shape, we create a potential pattern in four steps. First, we define the generated shape as the seki area. Next, we surround the area with an enclosing white block. A black boundary is then added to the pattern to deprive the enclosing white block of all external liberties. Lastly, we systematically fill the interior area with black stones until there are only two or three empty grids; this will yield $\binom{n}{2} + \binom{n}{3}$ combinations.

3.2 Seki Verification and Storage

For each generated pattern, we mostly follow Niu et al.'s local seki detection method [9] to determine whether they are seki. As with Niu et al.'s method, we search each pattern twice, where Black and White each play first. All candidate moves need to be within the seki area. Moves played outside of the area have no impact, and therefore can be viewed as equivalent to passing; thus, two consecutive passes no longer ends the game. Following the definition of a seki (see Subsect. 2.3), whoever plays inside the area first loses. For this reason, we prohibit passing as the first move of the search, i.e. the position must change as a result of the first player's first move. To avoid perpetual delays, if the position remains the same due to continual passing from both sides, the first player must play to change the situation. If the pattern inside the area is a seki, the first player is guaranteed to lose. Following Niu et al.'s method, if both Black and White loses as the first player, the area is a local seki. Since the seki database is generated offline, with no time constraints, we simply implemented this verification and-or search with depth-first search, instead of the more efficient but elaborate DFPN algorithm.

Next, patterns that are verified to be seki are stored into the database. Since we focus on local seki, we assume that the enclosing white block has no external liberties and eyes. This means we only have to store the contents of each grid (empty or occupied by Black).

3.3 Using the Seki Database in Solving Killall-Go

In Killall-Go, the winning condition for White simply requires them to hold any amount of territory. This can usually be achieved through UCA, but seki,

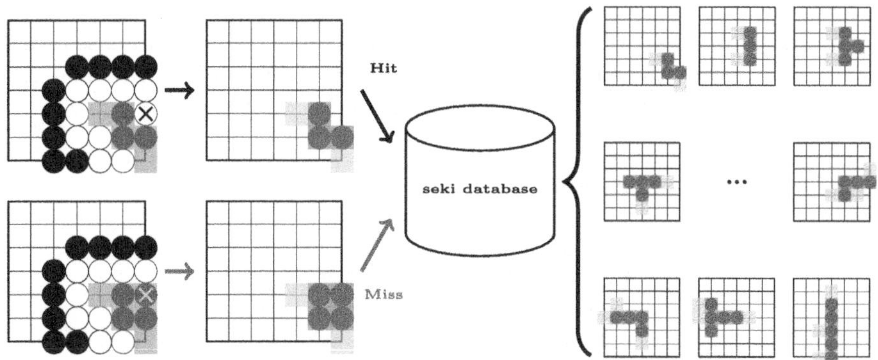

Fig. 2. Querying the seki database. The enclosed area is shaded in gray based on the last played move (marked with a cross). (Color figure online)

while rare, can also guarantee life. Therefore, upon confirmation of either UCA for White or seki, we have reached a terminal position and White's win can be updated accordingly in the and-or tree.

We describe how the seki database is used via Fig. 2. To reduce overhead, we only query the seki database if the most recent move is either part of an enclosing White block (as is the case on the top) or within a White enclosed area (as is on the bottom). The input for the query consists of the shape of the area (represented by their indices, and denoted by the shaded colors) and whether each grid is empty (green) or contains a black stone (blue).

In this illustrated example, we could not find a matching pattern for the bottom case, which means the search must proceed to obtain the correct game outcome. On the other hand, the top case is a hit, which means the enclosing white block must be alive due to seki or UCA. To explain the latter case, keep in mind that we only look for matching patterns inside the enclosed area, which confirms that Black cannot invade successfully. Meanwhile, if White's enclosing block also forms at least one eye, it satisfies the stronger UCA condition. In either case, White has secured territory and won.

It is worth noting that there are edge cases of seki that our generation method does not cover. For example, even in patterns that do not match, an external eye formed by the enclosing white block may form a seki. Nonetheless, for the game of Killall-Go, we can guarantee that the edge cases cause negligible impact to our search performance.

4   Experiments

We perform our experiments on the online fine-tuning solver presented in our previous paper [21], for which the code is based on the MiniZero framework [20], only changing the top-k configuration from 4 to 2. Subsection 4.1 provides statistics related to the generation of the seki database. The online fine-tuning solver is a distributed solver system that has workers analyzing different positions in parallel. Subsections 4.2 and 4.3 both investigate how the seki database affects performance, where the former looks at the whole solving system, from manager to workers, and the latter looks at job statistics (i.e. only workers).

4.1   Database Generation

Table 1. Seki database information.

Area size	# Patterns	# Seki patterns	Seki rate	Time (s)
5	28,432	1,318	4.64%	3
6	133,812	8,208	6.13%	31
7	578,064	51,354	8.88%	946
8	2,315,014	193,462	8.36%	26,716
5-8	3,055,322	254,342	8.32%	27,696

We generate seki patterns between area sizes of 5 to 8 using two E5-2683 v3 CPUs, for a total of 16 threads. Table 1 shows the relevant data for each area size, along with the cumulative statistics. The possible number of patterns roughly increases by four times for each area size increase. Larger area sizes mean larger search spaces, and longer times to generate seki entries. For each increase in area size, the time to generate entries roughly increases 30 fold. The right hand side of Fig. 2 shows eight examples of the patterns stored in the database, two for each area size. Note that size 8 patterns take up the majority of stored entries in the database.

4.2   Solver Performance on Benchmark Openings

We now try to solve a collection of ten openings using our previously presented online fine-tuning solver [21]. The benchmark problems can be separated into three parts. Cases A and B are problems suggested by Go experts, with a high probability of seki occurring. Cases C to H are problems that were collected during self-play training for our deep learning-based heuristic. Lastly, openings 1 and 2 are frequently used opening moves in Killall-Go. In other words, they are typical use cases when trying to solve Killall-Go.

Table 2 shows the results of solving each case. First, when not using the seki database, cases A and B cannot be solved within a day. With the seki database, they can be solved in 482 and 5,719 s, respectively. This demonstrates that when seki is inevitable, it is significantly more costly, even infeasible, to analyze without out some kind of seki detection method. In a distributed game solver (see Subsect. 2.1), the manager sends interesting positions (jobs) to workers to analyze in parallel. In Table 2, the average job time indicates how much time each worker

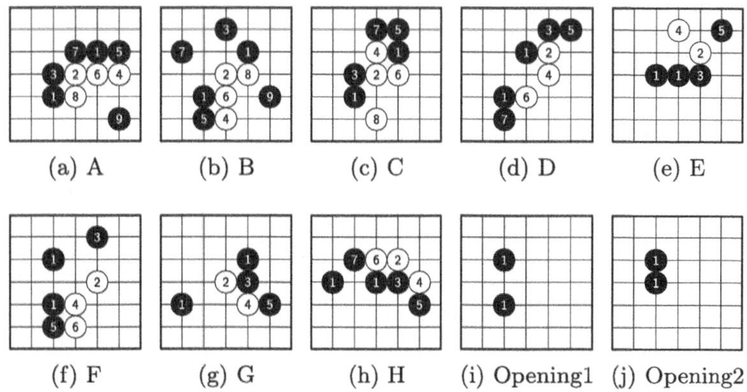

(a) A (b) B (c) C (d) D (e) E

(f) F (g) G (h) H (i) Opening1 (j) Opening2

Fig. 3. The collection of openings used to evaluate the seki database.

Table 2. Solving results for 10 7x7 Killall-Go benchmark openings.

	w/o Seki table			w/ Seki table			Reduction rate(%)	
	Time(s)	# Nodes	Avg. jobs time(s)	Time(s)	# Nodes	Avg. jobs time(s)	Time	Nodes
A	≥86,400	-	246.86	**482**	11,055,902	4.89	-	-
B	≥86,400	-	59.83	**5,719**	284,020,298	24.67	-	-
C	14,100	467,441,600	67.74	**11,257**	581,523,050	38.27	20.16%	-24.41%
D	68,582	3,021,039,537	41.39	**30,660**	1,441,063,897	25.70	55.29%	52.30%
E	710	24,483,162	7.20	**624**	22,256,876	7.07	12.06%	9.09%
F	≥86,400	-	40.65	**33,761**	1,479,511,498	21.04	-	-
G	21,744	1,057,881,380	30.23	**13,288**	706,327,784	27.05	38.89%	33.23%
H	1,223	56,350,104	26.90	**927**	49,982,460	20.87	24.23%	11.30%
Opening1	14,641	767,298,193	25.96	**13,122**	682,063,159	24.84	10.38%	11.10%
Opening2	30,240	1,654,756,361	25.31	**24,683**	1,376,817,358	21.72	18.38%	16.80%

spends analyzing these interesting positions. For case A, the average job time is 246.86 s without seki, but 4.89 s after using the database. Note that unsolved jobs will take roughly 420 s. This implies that workers might be stuck in long sequences of capturing and re-capturing. We perform additional experiments to analyze jobs in Subsect. 4.3.

With the exception of case F, problems C to H are solvable even without the seki database. However, using it yields a 20% to 50% discount on solving time, solving nodes, and jobs average time. Only in case C were there a 24.4% increase in total nodes searched. This was caused by the manager sending more jobs due to a significant discount on the average job time. In addition, we examined the search logs and discovered that a matching pattern could indicate either a seki or the stronger UCA requirement, as explained in Subsect. 3.3. In Killall-Go, both seki and UCA indicates a White win. This allows us to skip the Benson algorithm completely, significantly reducing the time and nodes necessary to solve the position. Similarly, utilizing the seki database for openings 1 and 2 also gives a discount of 10.38% and 18.38% for time, respectively. This shows that the seki database can still be useful when solving typical openings, where seki may or may not be part of the solution.

4.3   The Seki Database's Impact on Job Solve Rates

In Subsect. 4.2, we looked at the seki database's impact on the online fine-tuning solver holistically. In this subsection, we now turn to its impact on individual jobs, categorized by the number of seki encountered during the job. We randomly sampled 10,000 jobs sent from the manager, while not using the seki database when solving opening A, as shown in Fig. 3a. These jobs are then recalculated with and without the seki database, then categorized by the seki database hit rate within each job, where the hit rate is calculated by the number of matching patterns divided by the total number of terminal nodes encountered while analyzing the job. As an extreme example, if the position shown in the upper left corner of Fig. 2 is sent as a job to a worker, it will match an entry in the database, and recognized as a win for White, with a seki hit rate of 100%. Alternatively, if the position in the bottom left is sent as a job, no matches can be found, and the search will proceed as usual. If it is then solved and exactly two positions are matched among 100 terminal nodes, its hit rate is 2%.

Table 3. Solving rate of opening A.

Seki table hit rate	# jobs	w/ Seki table	w/o Seki table
0%	4,580	94.13%	
(0% − 10%)	3,856	85.68%	33.87%
[10% − 50%)	389	91.77%	6.68%
[50% − 100%]	1,175	100.00%	3.40%

In Table 3, jobs with 0 hit rate have a 94.13% solving rate, and the seki database does not improve the solving rate. However, with only 10% hit rate, the solving rate without using the seki database drops drastically to 33.87%. Where the hit rate exceeds 10%, the solving rate without using the seki database drops to less than 6.68%. In contrast, when using the database, the solving rate is higher than 85% in all cases. This shows that when seki are possible, the database can be tremendously helpful.

5   Conclusion

This paper clearly illustrates that attempting to solve 7x7 Killall-Go without seki detection is prohibitively costly even for simple positions that may encounter relatively few seki situations. When encountering positions where seki appears more than 10% of the time, the solving rate drops to lower than 6.68%. In the most extreme case, Subsect. 4.2 demonstrates that previously unsolvable seki positions can now be solved in just 482 s, especially since it avoids exhaustive seki detection algorithms during runtime.

Even for common openings in Killall-Go, seki knowledge also gives a 10-20% discount on solving time and nodes. Other than local seki, we could also extend the database for global seki, edge cases, or relevancy zones [12]. We believe that the underlying concept of endgame databases such as the database presented in this paper can also be applied to other applications.

Acknowledgments. This research is partially supported by the National Science and Technology Council (NSTC) of the Republic of China (Taiwan) under Grant Numbers 111-2222-E-001-001-MY2 and 113-2221-E-001-009-MY3.

References

1. Allis, L., Herik, H., Huntjens, M.: Go-Moku and Threat-Space Search. Comput. Intell. **12**, 1–12 (1994)
2. Allis, L.V., van der Meulen, M., van den Herik, H.J.: Proof-number search. Artif. Intell. **66**(1), 91–124 (1994)
3. Benson, D.B.: Life in the game of Go. Inf. Sci. **10**(2), 17–29 (1976)
4. Cazenave, T.: Generation of patterns with external conditions for the game of Go. In: Advances in Computer Games (2001)
5. Gol'berg, A., Gurvich, V., Andrade, D., Borys, K., Rudolf, G.: Combinatorial games modeling Seki in GO. Discret. Math. **329**, 19–32 (2014)
6. Kishimoto, A., Müller, M.: Search versus knowledge for solving life and death problems in Go. In: Proceedings of the AAAI Conference on Artificial Intelligence (2025)
7. Kishimoto, A., Müller, M.: DF-PN in Go: an application to the one-eye problem. In: IFIP Advances in Information and Communication Technology, vol. 135, pp. 125–142 (2003)
8. Müller, M.: Playing it safe: Recognizing secure territories in computer Go by using static rules and search. In: Game Programming Workshop in Japan, vol. 25, 80–86 (1997)
9. Niu, X., Kishimoto, A., Müller, M.: Recognizing Seki in computer Go. In: van den Herik, H.J., Hsu, S.-C., Hsu, T., Donkers, H.H.L.M.J. (eds.) ACG 2005. LNCS, vol. 4250, pp. 88–103. Springer, Heidelberg (2006). https://doi.org/10.1007/11922155_7
10. Schaeffer, J., et al.: Checkers Is Solved. Science **317**(5844), 1518–1522 (2007)
11. Shih, C.C., Wei, T.H., Wu, T.R., Wu, I.C.: A local-pattern related look-up table. IEEE Trans. Games **16**, 1–10 (2023)
12. Shih, C.C., Wu, T.R., Wei, T.H., Wu, I.C.: A novel approach to solving goal-achieving problems for board games. In: Proceedings of the AAAI Conference on Artificial Intelligence, vol. 36, pp. 10362–10369 (2022)
13. Silver, D., et al.: A general reinforcement learning algorithm that masters chess, shogi, and go through self-play. Science **362**(6419), 1140–1144 (2018)
14. van den Herik, H.J., Uiterwijk, J.W.H.M., van Rijswijck, J.: Games solved: now and in the future. Artif. Intell. **134**(1), 277–311 (2002)
15. van der Werf, E.C., Winands, M.H.: Solving go for rectangular boards. ICGA J. **32**(2), 77–88 (2009)

16. Vilà, R., Cazenave, T.: When one eye is sufficient: a static classification. In: Van Den Herik, H.J., Iida, H., Heinz, E.A. (eds.) Advances in Computer Games. ITIFIP, vol. 135, pp. 109–124. Springer, Boston, MA (2004). https://doi.org/10.1007/978-0-387-35706-5_8
17. Winands, M.H.M., Björnsson, Y., Saito, J.-T.: Monte-Carlo Tree Search Solver. In: van den Herik, H.J., Xu, X., Ma, Z., Winands, M.H.M. (eds.) CG 2008. LNCS, vol. 5131, pp. 25–36. Springer, Heidelberg (2008). https://doi.org/10.1007/978-3-540-87608-3_3
18. Wolf, T.: Two applications of a life & death problem solver in go. J. ÖGAI **26**(2), 11–18 (2007)
19. Wolf, T.: Seki with 2 liberties per chain in the game of go. ICGA J. **39**, 1–20 (2017)
20. Wu, T.R., et al.: MiniZero: comparative analysis of AlphaZero and MuZero on Go, Othello, and Atari Games. IEEE Trans. Games, 1–13 (2024)
21. Wu, T.R., Guei, H., Wei, T.H., Shih, C.C., Chin, J.T., Wu, I.C.: Game solving with online fine-tuning. In: Advances in Neural Information Processing Systems, vol. 36 (2024)
22. Wu, T.R., Shih, C.C., Wei, T.H., Tsai, M.Y., Hsu, W.Y., Wu, I.C.: AlphaZero-based proof cost network to aid game solving. In: International Conference on Learning Representations (2021)

General Approaches for Solving and Playing Games

Compressed Game Solving

Jeffrey Considine(✉) iD

Boston University, Boston, USA
jconsidi@bu.edu

Abstract. We recast move generators for solving board games as operations on compressed sets of strings. We aim for compressed representations with space sublinear in the number of game positions for interesting sets of positions, move generation in time roughly linear in the compressed size and membership tests in constant time. To the extent that we achieve these tradeoffs empirically, we can strongly solve board games in time sublinear in the state space. We demonstrate this concept with the game Breakthrough where we empirically compress relevant sets of n positions to roughly $n^{0.5}$ to $n^{0.7}$ states and solved the 5×6 size.

1 Introduction

Computer game playing has been an interest nearly as long as general purpose computers have existed; Alan Turing's "Proposed Electronic Calculator" report in 1946 predicted that computers "could probably be made to play very good chess" [25]. The idea of methodically solving a game to determine the winner under perfect play goes back farther to Zermelo's theorem in 1913 [22]; previously, it was not even clear that games could be solved in general. The first example of formally solving a game is even older – the game of Nim was strongly solved in 1901 [4]. So what keeps us from solving all the games of interest?

Interesting games tend to have too many positions for our generic techniques to work, so we end up looking for knowledge-based short cuts or investing inordinate amounts of compute power. If the game is too small or a trick is too powerful, we lose interest in the game. For example, Tic-tac-toe is often solved informally by elementary school children, and Nim has a trivial to calculate rule to determine both the winner and ideal moves. Early game solutions such as Qubic [16], Connect 4 [3], and Gomoku [1] were achieved by integrating knowledge into the solving program to significantly reduce the search space.

The earliest non-trivial game solved without a substantial advantage from knowledge is generally held to be Nine Men's Morris which solved by Gasser in 1993 [7]. The solution of Nine Men's Morris comprised of an endgame database of about 10^{10} states solving the midgame and endgame phases and an 18 ply alphabeta search from the beginning of the game to the midgame. At the time, this was a non-trivial amount of resources. Since this first interesting solution, Checkers has also been shown to be a draw through a combination of a ten piece endgame database, and proof number search from the beginning of the game [21].

M. Hartisch et al. (Eds.): CG 2024, LNCS 15550, pp. 79–90, 2025.
https://doi.org/10.1007/978-3-031-86585-5_7

More recently, Othello was also shown to be drawn [24]. Table 1 provides a longer list of games solved with such strategies.

Table 1. Games solved with the help of endgame databases.

Game	Year	State Space	Positions Solved	Solve Strength
Nine Men's Morris	1993 [7]	10^{10}	10^{10}	strong
Awari	2002 [17]	9×10^{11}	9×10^{11}	strong
Checkers	2007 [21]	5×10^{20}	3.9×10^{13}	weak
Fanorona	2008 [19]	10^{21}	6.3×10^{9}	weak
Pentago	2014 [12]	3×10^{15}	3×10^{15}	strong
Othello	2023 [24]	10^{28}	1.5×10^{9}	weak

A strategy shared across these solutions was the identification of a set of intermediate positions whose solution would prune a substantial fraction of a search tree from the beginning of the game. That intermediate set of positions was then solved via a brute force method, and then a search from the root was used to construct a proof solving the starting position of the game. A key design decision is identifying the set of intermediate positions to solve. A smaller set of intermediate positions will require a larger search process, while a larger set of intermediate positions will require more time to solve. In previous work, solving the set of intermediate positions took time at least linear in the size of that set; linear time was required just to write the solutions, and individual positions might need to be processed multiple times to resolve them. The most common strategy, retrograde analysis, solves a set of intermediate positions that is closed under reachability by working from the end of the game, and efficient implementations can meet that linear ideal. Our work aims to break that linear time requirement by compressing the sets of positions into sublinear representations, and performing move generation directly on those compressed sublinear representations.

Our contributions are as follows. We recast the move generation operations of retrograde analysis as set operations, similar to the exposition by Von Neumann and Morgenstern [15], and argue that suitable compressed set representations can radically change the cost of retrograde analysis. We then show how to instantiate this compressed set approach using deterministic finite automata. We demonstrate this approach by solving several new sizes of the game Breakthrough on a single commodity laptop, and share preliminary results for other games.

2   Retrograde Analysis Using Sets

The most common strategy for solving interesting games has been retrograde analysis. Retrograde analysis starts at the end of the game with positions defined as won or lost, and iteratively solves positions that require one more ply (turn) before the winning side can force its win. We will now sketch this process, roughly following Von Neumann and Morgenstern [15] due to their focus on sets.

Let P be the set of all positions of the game and T be the set of terminal positions where the game has ended. Let $W_0 \subseteq T$ be the set of positions where the game has ended and the current player has won, and $L_0 \subseteq T$ be the set of positions where the game has ended and the current player has lost. Descriptions of both W_0 and L_0 will be provided as part of the game definition. For $i > 0$, let W_i and L_i be the sets of positions where a player can force a win within i ply, and the current player respectively will win or lose. Then,

$$W_{i+1} = W_0 \cup \text{reverse}(L_i)$$
$$L_{i+1} = L_0 \cup (\text{inverse}(T) \setminus \text{reverse}(\text{inverse}(W_i)))$$

where

$$\text{inverse}(S) = P \setminus S$$
$$\text{reverse}(S) = \{p \in P \mid \exists p_S \in S \text{ s.t. there is a move from } p \text{ to } p_S\}$$

We can completely solve the game if we compute

$$W_\infty = \lim_{i \to \infty} W_i$$
$$L_\infty = \lim_{i \to \infty} L_i$$

In the terminology of Allis, constructing W_∞ and L_∞ is sufficent to strongly solve the game [2], since we can lookup any position in each set immediately, and if it is in neither, the position is drawn. As long as P is finite, $W_\infty = W_i$ and $L_\infty = L_i$ for some $i \leq |P|$ [15,22], though that i may be exponentially larger than a natural encoding of a position [6].

In previous practice, retrograde analysis worked with individual positions instead of sets. Each time a new losing position p_L is identified, a reverse move generator is used to identify positions p that can move to p_L, and flag those positions p as winning positions. Each time a new winning position p_W is identified, a reverse move generator to identify positions p that can move to p_W, and if p can only move to positions known to be winning, then flag p as losing. Altogether, the total work is linear in the number of positions solved, though there are many systems issues to manage to actually achieve that, particularly when the sets of winning and losing positions do not fit in memory and to avoid repeatedly calling the reverse move generator on the same position. See [20] for details. In contrast to those previous methods, our approach will be focused on set operations, and will not work with individual positions.

3   Meet-in-the Middle Analysis Using Sets

Many previous game solutions using retrograde analysis did not solve all of P. Instead, these "weak" solutions [2] only target solving the initial position of the game and any positions necessary to support that solution. While small games such as 3×3 Tic-Tac-Toe can be solved with pure search, larger games such as Nine Men's Morris [7], Checkers [21], and Fanorama [19] used a meet-in-the-middle approach using more sophisticated proof search techniques pruned when they reached positions solved by retrograde analysis. For "converging" games [2], such as when captures irreversibly decrease the number of pieces on the board, this strategy can be particularly effective. Such proof search techniques will work just as well whether the retrograde analysis was computed with individual positions or sets. In contrast to proof search techniques which rely heavily on pruning, our set-based approach to meet-in-the-middle analysis starts with constructing sets reachable at a given number of ply from the beginning of the game.

$$R_0 = \{p \in P \mid \text{s.t. } p \text{ is the initial position}\}$$
$$R_{i+1} = \text{forward}(R_i)$$

Define $RW_{i,j}$ to be the set of positions reachable in i ply that will win within another j ply, and $RL_{i,j}$ to be the set of positions reachable in i ply that will lose within another j ply. Then define $RU_{i,j}$ as the set of positions reachable in i ply that do not have a win or loss forced within another j ply. By those definitions,

$$RW_{i,j} = R_i \cap W_j$$
$$RL_{i,j} = R_i \cap L_j$$
$$RU_{i,j} = R_i \setminus (RW_{i,j} \cup RL_{i,j})$$

We can also write recursive versions of these equations.

$$RW_{i,j+1} = R_i \cap (W_0 \cup \text{reverse}(RL_{i+1,j}))$$
$$RL_{i,j+1} = R_i \cap (L_0 \cup (R_i \setminus \text{reverse}(\text{inverse}(RW_{i+1,j}))))$$

There, the recursive equations tradeoff the forward ply i and backward ply $j+1$ to forward ply $i+1$ and backward ply j. That recursion can be stopped at whatever number of backward ply j has W_j and L_j computed via retrograde analysis. And if $RU_{i+1,j} = \emptyset$, then all of R_{i+1} was solved within an additional j ply, so all of R_i will be solved with an additional $j+1$ ply and we can compute $RL_{i,j+1}$ more simply via set difference.

$$RL_{i,j+1} = R_i \setminus RW_{i,j+1}$$

Thus, if for some $i' > 0$ we can completely solve $R_{i'}$, then we can back up the solution to the initial position in R_0 with just i' invocations of reverse, set union, set intersection, and set difference. Empirically, the main gain there is from dropping from $2i'$ to i' invocations of reverse, since each invocation of reverse contains many similiarly sized invocations of the set operations. For games with bounded numbers of moves, this also appears favorable compared to just retrograde analysis, since only one invocation of reverse is needed per ply vs

2-4 invocations for retrograde analysis depending on symmetries. However, this is not necessarily always the case since retrograde analysis may need fewer ply to solve all positions that we care about, and intersections with reachable sets of positions may increase the complexity of the sets involved.

Most of the results that we present later will be computed with this meet in the middle approach using various numbers of ply for the pure retrograde analysis. If we start our computations from an i, j choice where $RU_{i,j}$ is empty, then we will solve all positions reachable within i ply. In that case, $RW_{i,j} = R_i \cap W_\infty$ and $RL_{i,j} = R_i \cap L_\infty$ and we denote them as $RW_{i,\infty}$ and $RL_{i,\infty}$ respectively. This may not be a complete solution since positions that are at least $i + 1$ ply from the beginning and needing at least $j + 1$ additional ply to solve will be missed. However, we expect that most of the missed positions will be easily solved in practice using search and the already computed W_j and L_j.

4   Compressed Game Solving

We have argued so far that a set-oriented perspective on game solving gives a simple view of the game solving process, but these arguments are moot if we cannot make use of a more efficient set representation. We seek compressed set representations decreasing space usage by a fractional polynomial (e.g. $O(n^{0.5})$ space to store n positions), time linear in that representation size for move generation, and very fast membership testing. To be clear, we do not expect sublinear space usage for arbitrary sets of positions which would be impossible, but we hope for fractional polynomial space usage on interesting sets of positions such as "first player to move and win within 20 ply". Using deterministic finite automata (DFAs) to represent positions, we empirically achieve sublinear space usage, heuristically linear move generation, and constant time membership testing. The most similar previous application of compression used ordered binary decision diagrams to compress small chess endgame databases [14], but yielded much lower compression rates, and crucially, only after solving all the positions.

We compare the empirical tradeoffs that we seek versus previous approaches considering the space used by the representation, the time used for reverse move generaton, and the time used for membership tests to check if a position is in a set. Our baseline, retrograde analysis, uses linear space in the number of the positions, linear time for move generation, and constant time for membership tests. Previous compression work only compressed the output of retrograde analysis yielding constant factor improvements to space while preserving constant time membership tests [8,14]. An alternative symbolic approach using quantified boolean formulas describes sets of positions with formulas taking time and space linear in the number of plys to construct those formulas, but taking exponential time in the number of ply to test membership. Or more extreme, the minimax algorithm would take space logarithmic in the number of ply (to record that number), and time exponential in the number of ply for membership testing.

4.1 Representing Positions as Strings

We represent game positions simply with a one-to-one mapping to the natural game state. The games that we consider are played on a rectangular board with pieces played on a grid of squares. We represent positions from those games using a row-wise traversal with one character specifying the contents of each square. This order is sufficient to demonstrate the compression benefits of our approach and we show approximate scaling for Amazons, Breakthrough and Chess in Fig. 1c based on the largest R_i that we computed in our experiments. However, we are aware that there are potential optimizations in changing the traversal order [14] and expect those to be essential for harder games.

For the DFA alphabet, we use the first character for an empty board square for convenience sharing counting DFA code, and then enumerate the other possible contents of a board square as the remaining characters. For the game Amazons, the alphabet is `empty`, `player 1 queen`, `player 2 queen`, and `arrow`. For the game Breakthrough, the alphabet is `empty`, `player 1 piece`, `player 2 piece`. For the game Chess, the alphabet is `empty`, black and white versions of each piece type, plus extra versions of pawns and rooks to represent en-passant and castling status. This suffices for any game where all information of the position is visible looking at the board. Other approaches are possible - extra characters could have been added at either end of the position string to denote the status for these special moves, but we felt this was the simplest mapping that would add the fewest complications to move generation.

4.2 Generating Moves from Sets of Positions

Generating moves from a set of positions mostly consists of set operations, but we will need to add an operation to apply particular moves to sets of positions. First, let us define forward move generation.

$$\text{forward}(S) = \{p \in P \mid \exists p_S \in S \text{ s.t. there is a move from } p_S \text{ to } p\}$$

This definition is essentially the same as the reverse function used for retrograde analysis, but with the opposite direction in the move condition. For any particular game, we will decompose forward into further operations to implement distinct moves. As part of the definition of a game, we will require a list of moves M_i where

$$M_i = \langle \text{Pre}_i, \text{Changes}_i, \text{Post}_i \rangle$$
$$\text{Changes}_i = [\text{Change}_{i,j}]$$
$$\text{Change}_{i,j} = \langle \text{Index}_{i,j}, \text{Before}_{i,j}, \text{After}_{i,j} \rangle$$

In essence, each move has a pre-condition, a list of changes to the board, and a post-condition. Both the pre- and post-conditions can be represented as sets of positions. Each move's list of changes specifies each index in the string (position on the board) to change, its value before the move, and its value after the move. To avoid ambiguity, the before and after values should be included in the pre- and post-conditions respectively. With this specification, we can define a function change_i which applies the changes of move M_i assuming the preconditions Pre_i hold.

$$\text{change}_i(S) = \{p \in P \mid \exists p_S \in S \text{ s.t. move } M_i \text{ can be made from } p_S \text{ to } p\}$$

We can then implement $\text{forward}(S)$ as follows -

$$\text{forward}(S) = \bigcup_i \left(\text{change}_i(S \cap \text{Pre}_i) \cap \text{Post}_i\right)$$

Reverse move generation can be implemented similarly by swapping the pre- and post-conditions, and using change_i^{-1} to denote the same change operation swapping before and after values.

$$\text{reverse}(S) = \bigcup_i \left(\text{change}_i^{-1}(S \cap \text{Post}_i) \cap \text{Pre}_i\right)$$

These implementations of forward and reverse simplify the requirements for our set representations to basic set operations – set union ($\cup$), set intersection ($\cap$), and set difference ($\backslash$) – and the new change functions. Whatever set representation that we choose, we will want it to be compact and fast for these operations.

In practice, we found that this formulation of moves was theoretically suffi-cient, but stifling for games of only moderate complexity. For example, if each side has more than one kind of piece, capture moves such as in Checkers or Chess need to be replicated for each type of piece captured, since the $\text{Before}_{i,j}$ values differ. Similarly, shared state changes such as clearing en-passant status in Chess would multiply all moves to handle each possible position of an en-passant pawn and the case where there was none. To reduce these blowups in the numbers of moves, we implemented a more general move graph. We omit the details for space, but illustrate the simple and general graph formulations in Figs. 1a and 1b, and show the sizes of move graphs that we have implemented in Fig. 1c.

4.3 Compressing Sets of Positions Using Deterministic Finite Automata

We use deterministic finite automata (DFAs) to represent sets of positions. DFAs are a classic data structure used both in complexity theory and for parsing. A DFA has a fixed number of states, and a transition table mapping pairs of current state and input character to the next state. Using the transition table, a DFA can process a string in time linear in the number of characters. Set operations with DFAs usually take quadratic time – computing the set union, intersection, or difference of an m state DFA and an n state DFA can be done in $\Theta(mn)$ time. This quadratic performance is well above our linear target, but we empirically

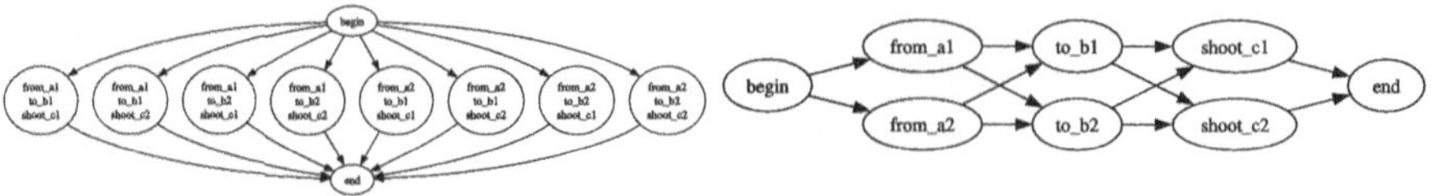

(a) Simple Parallel Move Generation   (b) General Move Graphs

Game	Move Graph Size	Reachable Position Scaling
Amazons (6x6)	110	states $\approx n^{0.82}$
Breakthrough (6x6)	111	states $\approx n^{0.45}$
Chess (8x8)	3822	states $\approx n^{0.78}$

(c) Move Graph Sizes and DFA Scaling

Fig. 1. Move Generation using Sets of Strings

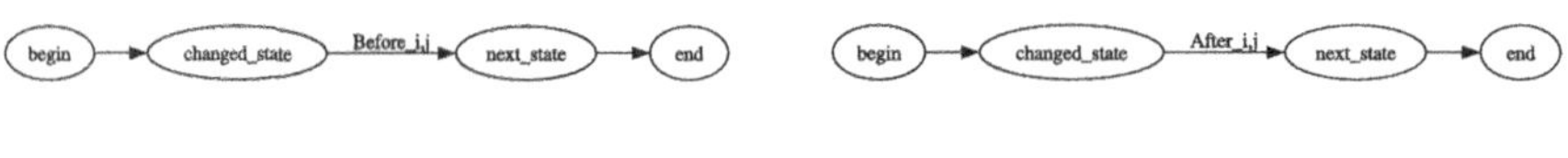

(a) A DFA before the change.   (b) A DFA after the change.

Fig. 2. An example of the change operation on DFAs.

find that the performance is closer to linear for the sets that arise solving games. The last kind of operation that we need from our compressed set representation is the change operations.

We can implement the change operation in time linear in the number of DFA states by rewriting the transition table in one pass. Since we are using DFAs to encode fixed length strings with one character per board position, we can easily map individual states in the transition table to string indexes using depth-first search. For any string index where the values will be changed, we already required the DFA to require the before value. That means that for any DFA state for that string index, there will be at most one non-rejecting transition, and it must be for the before character. To implement the change operation, that non-rejecting transitioned is simply swapped from the before character to the after character. This can be done for all string indexes in one pass, so the change operations take time linear in the number of DFA states. Additionally, change operations do not change the number of DFA states. Figure 2 shows an example DFA change.

How long do the forward and reverse functions take? Each function starts by intersecting the input set with the pre or post condition. Those conditions are fixed for a given move, so those take linear time and increase the number of DFA states by at most a constant factor. Then a change operation is applied which also takes linear time and does not change the number of states. And then the post- or pre-condition is applied which again takes linear time and increases the number of DFA states by at most a constant factor. So generating the results of a specific move takes linear time. What about the final union combining all of the moves?

We have not proven bounds on the final union of forward and reverse move generation. Empirically, the cost appears linear from our game solving usage, but we speculate that if it is linear for a given game, the constant factor is exponential in either the number of moves or the number of changes across moves. This linear cost and constant factor blowup does allow the total work to grow exponentially with the number of ply analyzed. This is not surprising, and we can still gain an advantage as long as the constant factor blowup tends to be lower than the branching factor of the game for relevant sets of positions. However, it does mean that games where those factors are close will show minimal gains from our techniques.

5 Results

We implemented compressed game solving using deterministic finite automata, and implemented the rules of a number of different games. We briefly check the solutions for Nim to confirm that they match the known analytical results. We then present our headline results for Breakthrough [9] where we solved several new board sizes on just a laptop. All results presented here were achieved on a 2016 MacBook Pro with a 2.9GHz Quad-Core Intel Core i7, 16GB RAM and 1TB storage.

5.1 Nim

Nim is an ancient game with the distinction of having had a complete mathematical solution since 1901 [4]. The game starts with a few heaps of sticks, and each player in turn removes at least one stick from a non-empty heap. We consider the normal play version of Nim, so a position is losing if and only if the binary XOR of all heap sizes is zero. With such a trivial analytical solution, Nim is rarely a target of search or brute-force methods. We applied our methods briefly to Nim and confirmed that they match the analytical solution. Nim is likely the most extreme case of leverage for our methods – for an initial position of m heaps of n sticks each, the number of possible states is $(n + 1)^m$, but the number of DFA states is only $\Theta(mn)$.

5.2 Breakthrough

Breakthrough is a relatively new game which won the first 8x8 Game Design Competition in 2001 [9]. Breakthrough has just one piece type for each player, trivial setup (two rows of pawns starting on their respective sides), and simple movement rules. Pawns may move straight forward or diagonally forward, and may capture if moving diagonally. A player wins if they move one of their pawns to the farthest row from their start or capture their opponent's last piece. Those rules are sufficient to play Breakthrough, but play exhibits non-trivial complexity, as an enemy's piece may only stopped from advancing by capturing it; simply blocking it is impossible. Previous work weakly solved Breakthrough for sizes up to 3x7, 4x6, and 6x5 using a mixture using novel search strategies, proof number search and identifying patterns [5,18,23]. We are not even the first to apply retrograde analysis to Breakthrough [13,26], but anecdotally, piece-limited endgame databases do not help much, as Breakthrough games tend to end with many pieces on the board.

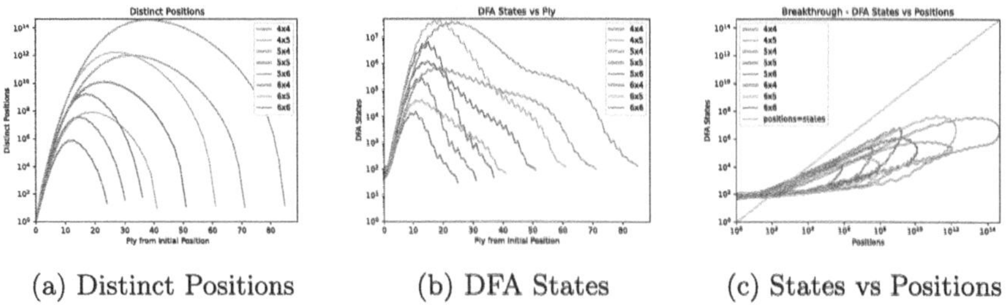

(a) Distinct Positions   (b) DFA States   (c) States vs Positions

Fig. 3. Reachable Breakthrough Positions

We initially tested our Breakthrough implementation generating all the reachable positions by ply for several different board sizes. Breakthrough games have bounded length that can be easily computed from the board size, so we were able to completely enumerate all reachable Breakthrough positions for those board sizes. Figure 3 shows those statistics. Figure 3c plots the states vs positions at different ply, and shows loops due to declining position counts in the end game. For the 6×6 board size, the highest number of reachable positions is at 39 ply. The number of positions was $|R_{39}| \approx 4.28 \times 10^{14}$ and the number of states was $3.78 \times 10^6 \approx |R_{39}|^{0.49}$. The reachable exponent of 0.49 gave us confidence that we had an effective compressed representation for Breakthrough. We then applied the set-based meet-in-the-middle strategy previously described using W_0 and L_0 for our initial retrograde solutions. We strongly solved all the sizes of Breakthrough that were previously solved weakly, and additionally solved a few new bigger sizes, including the 5x6 size that thwarted previous efforts. Table 2 shows all known Breakthrough solving results to date.

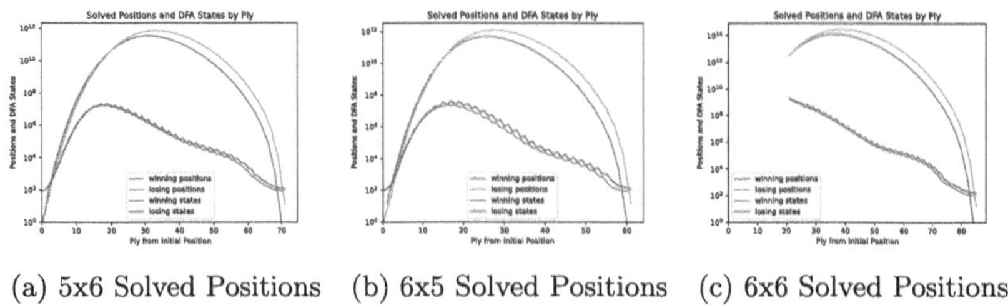

(a) 5x6 Solved Positions   (b) 6x5 Solved Positions   (c) 6x6 Solved Positions

Fig. 4. Breakthrough Largest Solutions

Table 2. Breakthrough Solved Board Sizes

width x height	4	5	6	7	8
2	P2	P2	P1	P2	P1 (new)
3	P2	P2	P1	P2 [10]	P1 (new)
4	P2	P2 [18]	P1 [26]	P1 (new)	
5	P2	P2 [11]	P1 (new)		
6	P2	P2 [18]			
7	P2 (new)				
8	P2 (new)				

P1 denotes a first player win. P2 denotes a second player win.

Figure 4 shows statistics for the 5x6, 6x5, and 6x6 board sizes. The 6x5 board size was previously the largest solved size, while 5x6 previously resisted efforts. We solved both of those easily, and saw substantial compression gains solving both – see Figs. 4a and 4b to compare the numbers of positions solved and the states to represent them, and note those charts are in log scale.

Our solution to the 6x6 board size is still running after about two months of computation. We have already solved R_{21} through the end of the game, and have already passed the ply with peak positions. Separately, we have computed W_{16} and L_{16} for this board size and determined that there are only 1.3×10^{11} positions remaining, so solving the remaining positions is easily within the range of brute force. This partial solution already includes more than 7×10^{15} reachable positions, making this the largest solution known to us. This 6x6 solution has averaged 3.05×10^4 positions per byte with our simple DFA encoding using 12 bytes per state. The peak compression rate has been 1.2×10^7 positions per byte to store the 9.5×10^{13} positions of $RL_{50,\infty}$ in 6.4×10^5 states. For comparison, the ten piece endgame database for Checkers averaged 154 positions per byte [21].

6 Conclusions and Future Work

In this work, we argued for the used of compressed sets for game solving. We demonstrated the efficacy of this approach with the game of Breakthrough, and look forward to solving more games using this approach. We have already started testing these ideas with Amazons and Chess, and while we saw less leverage, they also appear to have sublinear compressed set representations. We also intend to investigate the integration of knowledge into this approach to take advantage of symmetries and combinatorial game theory.

References

1. Allis, L.V., van den Herik, H.J., Huntjens, M.P.H.: Go-moku solved by new search techniques. In: Proceedings of AAAI Fall Symposium on Games: Planning and Learning, pp. 1–9 (1993)

2. Allis, L.V.: Searching for solutions in games and artificial intelligence (1994)
3. Allis, V.: A knowledge-based approach of connect-four. Master's thesis, Department of Mathematics and Computer Science, Vrije Universiteit (1988)
4. Bouton, C.L.: Nim, a game with a complete mathematical theory. Ann. Math. **3**(1/4), 35–39 (1901)
5. Finnsson, H., Björnsson, Y.: Game-tree properties and MCTS performance. In: Proceedings of the ICJAI Workshop on General Intelligence in Game-Playing Agents (GIGA 2011), pp. 23–30 (2011)
6. Fraenkel, A.S., Lichtenstein, D.: Computing a perfect strategy for n × n chess requires time exponential in n. J. Comb. Theory, Ser. A **31**(2), 199–214 (1981). https://doi.org/10.1016/0097-3165(81)90016-9
7. Gasser, R.: Solving nine men's morris. Computational Intelligence **12** (1996)
8. Gomboc, D., Shelton, C.R.: Chess endgame compression via logic minimization. In: Browne, C., Kishimoto, A., Schaeffer, J. (eds.) Advances in Computer Games, pp. 153–162. Springer International Publishing, Cham (2021). https://doi.org/10.1007/978-3-031-11488-5_14
9. Handsomb, K.: 8x8 game design competition: the winning game: breakthrough... and two other favorites. Abstract Games (2001)
10. Haugland, J.K.: Breakth37. https://www.neutreeko.net/Breakth37.java
11. Haugland, J.K.: Breakth55. https://www.neutreeko.net/Breakth55.java
12. Irving, G.: Pentago is a first player win: Strongly solving a game using parallel in-core retrograde analysis. CoRR abs/1404.0743 (2014). http://arxiv.org/abs/1404.0743
13. Isaac, A.W.: Generating an end game tablebase for the game of breakthrough using quasi-retrograde analysis. Master's thesis (2016)
14. Kristensen, J.T.: Generation and compression of endgame tables in chess with fast random access using OBDDs. Master's thesis, University of Aarhus (2005)
15. von Neumann, J., Morgenstern, O.: Theory of games and economic behavior (1945)
16. Patashnik, O.: Qubic: 4 × 4 × 4 tic-tac-toe. Math. Mag. **53**(4), 202–216 (1980)
17. Romein, J.W., Bal, H.E.: Awari is solved. J. Int. Comput. Games Assoc. **25**, 162–165 (2002)
18. Saffidine, A., Jouandeau, N., Cazenave, T.: Solving breakthrough with race patterns and job-level proof number search. In: Advances in Computer Games (2011)
19. Best play in fanorona leads to draw: Schadd, M.P.D., Winands, M.H.M., Uiterwijk, J., H., van den Herik, J., Bergsma, M.H.J. New Math. Nat. Comput. **04**, 369–387 (2008)
20. Schaeffer, J., Björnsson, Y., Burch, N., Lake, R., Lu, P., Sutphen, S.: Building the checkers 10-piece endgame databases. In: Advances in Computer Games (2003)
21. Schaeffer, J., et al.: Checkers is solved. Science **317**(5844), 1518–1522 (2007). https://doi.org/10.1126/science.1144079
22. Schwalbe, U., Walker, P.: Zermelo and the early history of game theory. Games Econom. Behav. **34**(1), 123–137 (2001). https://doi.org/10.1006/game.2000.0794
23. Skowronski, P., Björnsson, Y., Winands, M.H.M.: Automated discovery of search-extension features. In: Advances in Computer Games (2009)
24. Takizawa, H.: Othello is solved. ArXiv abs/2310.19387 (2023)
25. Turing, A.M.: Proposed electronic calculator. National Report (1946)
26. de Vink, E.: Solving breakthrough using binary decision diagrams and retrograde analysis. Bachelor's Thesis (2022)

Anytime Sequential Halving
in Monte-Carlo Tree Search

Dominic Sagers, Mark H. M. Winands, and Dennis J. N. J. Soemers[✉]

Department of Advanced Computing Sciences, Maastricht University, Paul-Henri
Spaaklaan 1, 6229 EN Maastricht, The Netherlands
{m.winands,dennis.soemers}@maastrichtuniversity.nl

Abstract. Monte-Carlo Tree Search (MCTS) typically uses multi-armed bandit (MAB) strategies designed to minimize cumulative regret, such as UCB1, as its selection strategy. However, in the root node of the search tree, it is more sensible to minimize simple regret. Previous work has proposed using Sequential Halving as selection strategy in the root node, as, in theory, it performs better with respect to simple regret. However, Sequential Halving requires a budget of iterations to be pre-determined, which is often impractical. This paper proposes an *anytime* version of the algorithm, which can be halted at any arbitrary time and still return a satisfactory result, while being designed such that it approximates the behavior of Sequential Halving. Empirical results in synthetic MAB problems and ten different board games demonstrate that the algorithm's performance is competitive with Sequential Halving and UCB1 (and their analogues in MCTS).

Keywords: Sequential Halving · Anytime · Monte-Carlo Tree Search

1 Introduction

Monte-Carlo Tree Search (MCTS) [7,13] is a search algorithm used for different sequential decision-making problems. It has been thoroughly studied within the context of game playing agents, but also seen use in other planning, optimization, and control problems [4]. The algorithm consists of four strategic steps, each of which can be implemented using a variety of different strategies [4,19]. Strategies for the *selection* step tend to use Multi-Armed Bandit (MAB) algorithms, which balance exploration (sampling actions that are less explored) with exploitation (more deeply searching actions that appear more promising).

The most commonly used selection strategy is UCB1 [2], which focuses on minimizing *cumulative regret*. Sequential Halving (SH) [12], which focuses on *simple regret*, may be argued to be a more suitable choice in MCTS [6,16]. Integrations of SH into MCTS have been described in research on partially observable games [15], variants of MCTS that take additional guidance from scores learned through online or offline learning [9], and the state-of-the-art Gumbel AlphaZero and MuZero [8], which also integrate deep neural networks.

M. Hartisch et al. (Eds.): CG 2024, LNCS 15550, pp. 91–102, 2025.
https://doi.org/10.1007/978-3-031-86585-5_8

Running through the four strategic steps of MCTS once is referred to as an iteration, and MCTS typically runs multiple iterations, after which it returns a final decision (e.g., move to play or action to take). It is common to use either a time budget, where MCTS keeps running iterations until it runs out of time, or an iteration budget, where it runs a predetermined number of iterations. SH requires the number of iterations that can be executed to be known in advance, which means that MCTS using SH as selection strategy does not have the *anytime* property. The algorithm cannot be terminated at any arbitrary point in time and be expected to have the quality of its final decision smoothly increasing as processing time increases (barring pathological cases [14]). When dealing with known games (for which the average number of iterations per unit of time could be measured) and a fixed per-move time budgets, a reasonable approximation of a fixed iteration budget may be calculated and used. However, when dealing with particularly large and varied sets of games [18], automatically generated games that must be played quickly in the context of an evolutionary search [20], or agents that automatically manage their time in an intelligent manner [3,11], the lack of anytime property can be more problematic.

This paper proposes *anytime SH*: a MAB algorithm with the anytime property, which can be used as selection strategy in (the root node of) MCTS. Its design was heavily inspired by the original SH, with anytime SH essentially being the original SH turned inside out. While we leave formal analyses of bounds on regret for future work, empirical results in synthetic MAB problems as well as a diverse set of ten board games demonstrate that anytime SH performs competitively with UCB1 (or UCT in games) as well as SH (only used in root node in games) in practice, whilst—in contrast to SH—retaining the anytime property.

2   Background

The Multi-armed Bandit (MAB) problem assumes an environment in which an agent repeatedly chooses one from a set of K arms to pull at time steps $t = 1, 2, \ldots$. Each of the arms is associated with a stationary, unknown probability distribution, and whenever the agent pulls an arm with index i_t at time t, it receives a reward sampled from the corresponding distribution with (unknown) mean μ_{i_t}. The most common measure of performance in MAB problems is the *cumulative regret* $R(T) = \sum_{t=1}^{T} (\mu^* - \mu_{i_t})$, which accumulates the regret of not having always picked the optimal arm (with the highest mean μ^*) over a sequence of T time steps. The *simple regret* $r(T) = \mu^* - \mu_{i_{T+1}}$, which solely measures the regret of a single choice made after a period of T exploration steps, is an alternative measure of performance [1,5,10]. Simple regret is a more appropriate measure of performance when it is only an ultimate single decision that matters, with all prior decisions simply serving as a learning or training phase.

UCB1 [2] is a common MAB algorithm, used as the selection strategy in the canonical UCT [13] variant of MCTS. It is designed primarily to minimize cumulative regret. At any give time step t, UCB1 selects an arm j_t to pull using

---

Algorithm 1. Sequential Halving

Input total budget T, K arms

 1: $S_1 \leftarrow \{1, ..., K\}, B \leftarrow \lceil \log_2 K \rceil$
 2: **for** $k = 1 \ldots B$ **do**
 3:     Sample each arm $i \in S_k$, $n_k = \frac{T}{|S_k| \times B}$ times
 4:     Update the average reward for each arm relative to the found rewards
 5:     $S_{k+1} \leftarrow$ the $\lceil |S_k| / 2 \rceil$ best arms from S_k
 6: **end for**
 7: **return** the sole remaining arm of S_{B+1}

$$j_t = \underset{1 \leq j \leq K}{\operatorname{argmax}} X_j + C \sqrt{\frac{\ln\left(\sum_{k=1}^{K} n_k\right)}{n_j}},$$ where X_j is the average reward collected from previous pulls of arm j so far, C is a tunable hyperparameter, which affects the balance between exploration and exploitation, and n_i is the number of times an arm i has been pulled so far.

Sequential Halving (SH) [12] is a different MAB algorithm, designed to optimize for simple regret rather than cumulative regret. It assumes prior knowledge of the budget of arm pulls (or time steps) T, as well as the fixed number of arms K. It calculates how many times the number of arms can be halved before narrowing down to a single arm as $B = \lceil \log_2 K \rceil$, and operates in B separate phases. The total budget T gets spread out evenly over these B phases. Within every phase, the algorithm distributes the number of arm pulls uniformly over all remaining arms (in the first phase, this is the full set of all K arms). After every phase, the worst-performing half of all arms get discarded. Algorithm 1 provides pseudocode for SH, and Fig. 1 gives a visual depiction of the algorithm.

Outside of affecting rewards that are collected and information that is gathered by an agent, decisions made in earlier time steps have no effect on later time steps in MAB problems. In contrast, games are examples of *sequential* decision-making problems, where actions taken (moves played) in early states affect which states the agent transitions into. Monte-Carlo Tree Search (MCTS) [7,13] can handle this sequential nature by gradually building up and traversing through a search tree, with nodes representing different states, connected by the actions that lead to transitions between the states. When traversing the tree, MCTS views the problem of selecting a branch from each node it reaches as a MAB problem. After running many iterations, it will use the information it has collected from simulations to make a final decision as to which move to play. Because only this final move selection truly matters—any choices made for tree traversal during the search itself only result in fictitious rewards—it can be argued that algorithms that optimize for simple regret (such as SH) are more suitable than ones that optimize for cumulative regret (such as UCB1) in the root node [6,10,16]. Outside of the root node, the argument in favor of simple regret minimization still holds due to the minimax structure of zero-sum games. However, simultaneously there is an argument to be made in favor of cumulative regret minimization, as this leads to a more focused best-first search that wastes

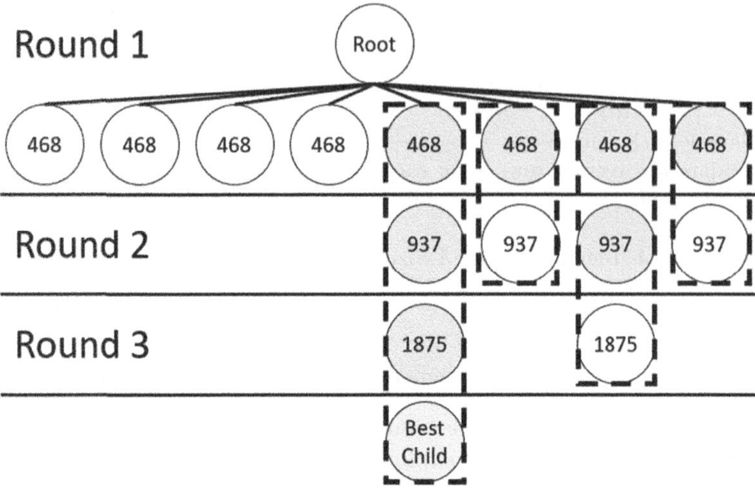

Fig. 1. Example of one complete run of Sequential Halving with 15,000 iterations. Only the root node and its immediate children are depicted. Circles in the same vertical bar depict the same node, in different rounds of the algorithm. The best half of nodes in each round are colored. Numbers inside the nodes denote the total number of iterations allocated to that node up to and including the corresponding round.

less time on seemingly uninteresting parts of the search space—in particular for small search budgets. Hybrid MCTS (H-MCTS) [16] therefore introduces a parameter that dynamically adjusts from using SH in and close to the root, to using UCB1 further down the tree, depending on the available budget. As a simplified version of this, we use H-MCTS with SH only in the root node, and UCB1 in all other nodes, as a baseline in our experiments.

3   Time-Based and Anytime Sequential Halving

As an initial step towards an anytime variant of SH, we consider *Time-based SH*. Standard SH requires a budget of iterations to be known in advance, because it spreads this number of iterations evenly over all of its phases. If every iteration takes approximately the same amount of time, a simple but effective algorithm with a time budget could simply divide the time budget over the phases instead of the iteration budget. This is a trivial variant of SH, but not one that we have seen in prior literature. It does not have the anytime property, as it still expects the time budget to be predetermined.

We propose *Anytime SH* as an anytime variant of the algorithm, which works as follows. It starts operating like the standard SH, albeit with an assumed budget of iterations that is only the bare minimum required for a valid, "complete" run of SH. In the first phase it allocates exactly one iteration to each arm. Then it halves the arms, allocating two additional iterations to each remaining arm, and

---

Algorithm 2. Anytime Sequential Halving

Input K arms
1: $S \leftarrow \{1, ..., K\}$
2: $T \leftarrow S$
3: $N \leftarrow 1$
4: **repeat**
5:      Every arm in T is sampled N times.
6:      Update the average reward for each arm.
7:      $T \leftarrow$ the $\lceil |T|/2 \rceil$ best arms from T
8:      $N \leftarrow N \times 2$
9:      **if** $|T| = 1$ **then**
10:          $T \leftarrow S$
11:          $N \leftarrow 1$
12:      **end if**
13: **until** stopping condition
14: **return** The highest-reward arm from S

---

so on, until only a single arm remains. We refer to this as one pass of the algorithm. After the first pass, if there is still time remaining, the algorithm resets back to considering the full set of arms again, and repeats the same process. If the ordering of arms' empirically observed mean rewards never changes (for example, if every arm i deterministically gives the same reward μ_i on each pull, with no randomness), this algorithm distributes its pulls over the arms in the same way as SH would have done in hindsight (if the iteration budget had been known in advance). If the ordering of arms based on their empirically observed mean rewards can vary over a run of the algorithm, it is possible to end up with different allocations of iterations than in the original SH. Algorithm 2 provides pseudocode for the algorithm, and Fig. 2 visualises two passes of the algorithm.

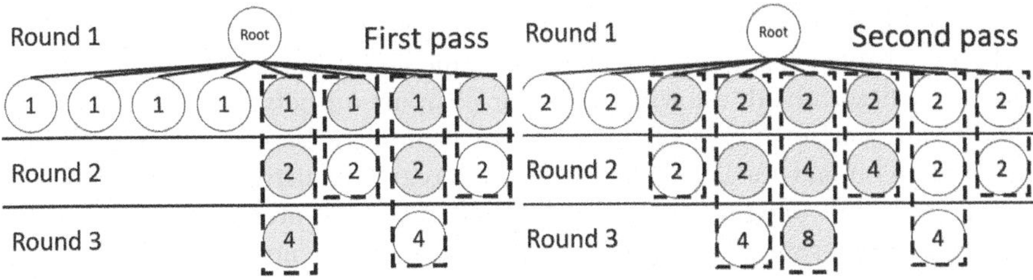

Fig. 2. Visualization of two passes made by Anytime Sequential Halving. Only the root node and its immediate children are depicted. Circles in the same vertical bar depict the same node, in different rounds of the algorithm. The best half of nodes in each round of each pass are colored. Numbers inside the nodes denote the total number of iterations allocated to that node up to and including the corresponding pass and round.

Table 1. Mappings between time and iteration budgets for 10-armed MAB problems.

Milliseconds	500	1000	1500	2000	2500	3000	3500	4000	4500	5000
Iterations		18500	37000	55500	73000	93000	112500	131000	150500	167500	186500

4   Experiments

This section describes the experiments used to evaluate the novel *Anytime SH* algorithm.[1] The algorithm is compared to appropriate baselines in synthetic MAB problems (Subsect. 4.1), and in a set of ten different board games (Subsect. 4.2). In the board games, the algorithm is not used standalone, but as selection strategy in the root node for MCTS.

4.1   Synthetic Multi-armed Bandit Problems

For an evaluation of the raw MAB algorithms, without the added complexity of sequential decision making and combining with tree search in games, we construct a set of 100 synthetic MAB problems as follows. For every MAB problem, we sample ten different means $\mu_1, \ldots, \mu_{10}$ for $K = 10$ arms from a normal distribution with mean 0 and unit variance. Within each problem, when an arm i is pulled, a reward is drawn from another normal distribution with mean μ_i and unit variance. The following algorithms are compared on this suite of problems:

- **UCB1**: UCB1 [2] using an exploration constant $C = \sqrt{2}^{-1}$, as described in Sect. 2.
- **Base SH**: standard Sequential Halving [12], as described in Sect. 2.
- **Time SH**: the trivial Time-based variant of SH, as described in Sect. 3.
- **Anytime SH**: the novel algorithm as described in Sect. 3.

Every algorithm was run on each MAB problem for up to 5000 milliseconds (or 186,500 iterations in the case of Base SH) using Python 3, on an i7-10700k Intel CPU. Table 1 lists mappings between time and iteration budgets that were empirically determined, allowing for a fair comparison between algorithms that support only certain types of budgets. For each time budget listed in Table 1 (or iteration budget for Base SH), the simple regret incurred by each algorithm running with that budget is recorded for each of the 100 problems, and averaged over those 100 problems. Figure 3 depicts 95% confidence intervals for these averaged simple regret measures.

4.2   Board Games

The second experiment evaluates the performance of Anytime SH, when used as selection strategy in the root node of MCTS, in a set of ten different board games (listed in Table 2). Three different agents are considered in this experiment:

---

[1] Source code: https://github.com/dominic-sagers/Anytime-Sequential-Halving.

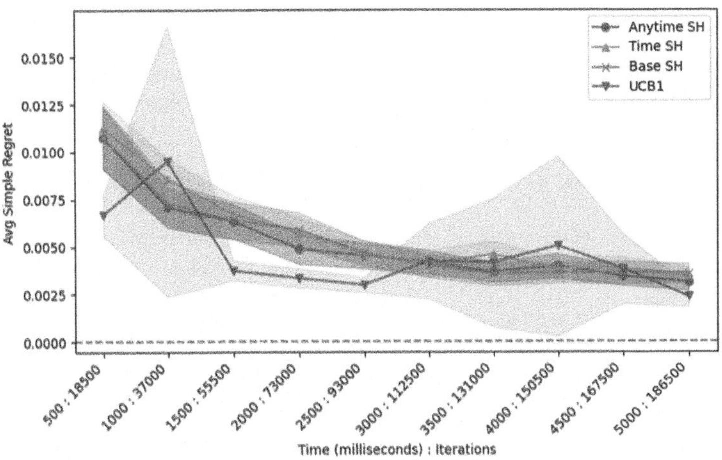

Fig. 3. Simple regret, averaged over 100 MAB problems, for four MAB algorithms.

- **UCT**: a standard implementation of MCTS, using UCB1 with $C = \sqrt{2}$ as selection strategy, adding one new node to the tree per iteration, and running uniformly random play-outs.
- **H-MCTS**: a simplified version of Hybrid MCTS [16], using SH as selection strategy in the root node, but otherwise running as described above for UCT.
- **Anytime SH**: uses anytime SH as selection strategy for the root node, but otherwise runs as described above for UCT.

Each of these agents played 150 times (75 as first and 75 as second player) against each of the other two agents, across ten different board games. For each matchup, seven different MCTS iteration budgets per move were used, ranging from 1000 to 50,000. We used iteration budgets rather than time budgets, because H-MCTS can only function with the former, whereas the other two algorithms can handle either type of budget. Table 2 lists 95% Agresti-Coull confidence intervals for win percentages, with any draws being counted as half-wins. All listed games were run using their default settings in the Ludii general game playing system [17], except for Atari Go and Clobber being played on boards of size 9×9 and 7×7, respectively. In addition to the table with results per game, Fig. 4 depicts the win percentages when averaging over all ten games.

5   Discussion

The results for the MAB problems in Fig. 3 show that Anytime SH performs on par with the naive time-based SH and the standard SH in terms of simple regret. In this setting, adjusting the algorithm to introduce the anytime property does not harm performance. UCB1 appears to have better performance for some budgets, which is somewhat surprising as this algorithm is not necessarily designed

Table 2. 95% Agresti-Coull confidence intervals for win percentages of row agents against UCT (top half) or H-MCTS (bottom half) in ten different board games.

MCTS iterations per move:	1000	5000	10,000	20,000	30,000	40,000	50,000
Win percentages against UCT (95% Agresti-Coull confidence intervals)							
Amazons							
H-MCTS	46.10 ± 7.88	56.50 ± 7.83	55.85 ± 7.85	51.95 ± 7.90	51.30 ± 7.90	46.75 ± 7.88	55.85 ± 7.85
Anytime SH	51.95 ± 7.90	52.60 ± 7.89	50.00 ± 7.90	47.40 ± 7.89	46.10 ± 7.88	48.70 ± 7.90	48.05 ± 7.90
Atari Go (9×9)							
H-MCTS	64.30 ± 7.57	56.50 ± 7.83	61.70 ± 7.68	64.30 ± 7.57	65.60 ± 7.51	59.10 ± 7.77	52.60 ± 7.89
Anytime SH	44.80 ± 7.86	46.75 ± 7.88	61.05 ± 7.71	53.25 ± 7.88	51.30 ± 7.90	49.35 ± 7.90	45.45 ± 7.87
Breakthrough							
H-MCTS	47.40 ± 7.89	51.30 ± 7.90	51.30 ± 7.90	52.60 ± 7.89	58.45 ± 7.79	48.70 ± 7.90	55.20 ± 7.86
Anytime SH	51.95 ± 7.90	53.90 ± 7.88	57.80 ± 7.80	61.05 ± 7.71	55.20 ± 7.86	52.60 ± 7.89	52.60 ± 7.89
Clobber (7×7)							
H-MCTS	54.55 ± 7.87	52.60 ± 7.89	46.10 ± 7.88	56.50 ± 7.83	51.95 ± 7.90	49.35 ± 7.90	48.70 ± 7.90
Anytime SH	44.15 ± 7.85	51.95 ± 7.90	49.35 ± 7.90	51.95 ± 7.90	47.40 ± 7.89	51.30 ± 7.90	45.45 ± 7.87
Gomoku							
H-MCTS	75.35 ± 6.81	78.60 ± 6.48	80.55 ± 6.25	76.65 ± 6.69	79.25 ± 6.41	72.75 ± 7.04	74.05 ± 6.93
Anytime SH	55.20 ± 7.86	55.20 ± 7.86	50.00 ± 7.90	45.45 ± 7.87	45.45 ± 7.87	47.40 ± 7.89	59.10 ± 7.77
Hex							
H-MCTS	79.25 ± 6.41	63.00 ± 7.63	57.80 ± 7.80	53.25 ± 7.88	48.70 ± 7.90	59.10 ± 7.77	54.55 ± 7.87
Anytime SH	32.45 ± 7.40	40.90 ± 7.77	52.60 ± 7.89	46.10 ± 7.88	53.90 ± 7.88	54.55 ± 7.87	48.05 ± 7.90
Pentalath							
H-MCTS	62.35 ± 7.66	59.75 ± 7.75	56.50 ± 7.83	50.00 ± 7.90	48.70 ± 7.90	53.90 ± 7.88	52.60 ± 7.89
Anytime SH	52.60 ± 7.89	44.80 ± 7.86	51.30 ± 7.90	51.30 ± 7.90	53.25 ± 7.88	57.80 ± 7.80	47.40 ± 7.89
Reversi							
H-MCTS	50.98 ± 7.90	51.95 ± 7.90	51.30 ± 7.90	53.25 ± 7.88	46.10 ± 7.88	45.77 ± 7.87	49.35 ± 7.90
Anytime SH	45.45 ± 7.87	53.25 ± 7.88	52.28 ± 7.89	55.85 ± 7.85	51.63 ± 7.90	51.95 ± 7.90	49.35 ± 7.90
Tablut							
H-MCTS	57.15 ± 7.82	50.65 ± 7.90	50.00 ± 7.90	50.00 ± 7.90	49.35 ± 7.90	50.00 ± 7.90	50.65 ± 7.90
Anytime SH	48.05 ± 7.90	50.00 ± 7.90	50.65 ± 7.90	50.00 ± 7.90	51.95 ± 7.90	50.00 ± 7.90	49.35 ± 7.90
Yavalath							
H-MCTS	57.15 ± 7.82	46.10 ± 7.88	37.00 ± 7.63	40.25 ± 7.75	45.45 ± 7.87	49.67 ± 7.90	48.37 ± 7.90
Anytime SH	57.15 ± 7.82	44.15 ± 7.85	43.82 ± 7.84	48.05 ± 7.90	43.17 ± 7.83	53.25 ± 7.88	48.70 ± 7.90
Win percentages against H-MCTS (95% Agresti-Coull confidence intervals)							
Amazons							
UCT	53.90 ± 7.88	43.50 ± 7.83	44.15 ± 7.85	48.05 ± 7.90	48.70 ± 7.90	53.25 ± 7.88	44.15 ± 7.85
Anytime SH	38.95 ± 7.71	37.00 ± 7.63	41.55 ± 7.79	51.95 ± 7.90	40.90 ± 7.77	44.15 ± 7.85	40.25 ± 7.75
Atari Go (9×9)							
UCT	35.70 ± 7.57	43.50 ± 7.83	38.30 ± 7.68	35.70 ± 7.57	34.40 ± 7.51	40.90 ± 7.77	47.40 ± 7.89
Anytime SH	33.75 ± 7.47	42.20 ± 7.80	33.75 ± 7.47	45.45 ± 7.87	41.55 ± 7.79	40.25 ± 7.75	50.00 ± 7.90
Breakthrough							
UCT	52.60 ± 7.89	48.70 ± 7.90	48.70 ± 7.90	47.40 ± 7.89	41.55 ± 7.79	51.30 ± 7.90	44.80 ± 7.86
Anytime SH	50.65 ± 7.90	52.60 ± 7.89	53.90 ± 7.88	46.75 ± 7.88	50.65 ± 7.90	56.50 ± 7.83	50.65 ± 7.90
Clobber (7×7)							
UCT	45.45 ± 7.87	47.40 ± 7.89	53.90 ± 7.88	43.50 ± 7.83	48.05 ± 7.90	50.65 ± 7.90	51.30 ± 7.90
Anytime SH	54.55 ± 7.87	46.75 ± 7.88	47.40 ± 7.89	51.95 ± 7.90	50.65 ± 7.90	53.25 ± 7.88	49.35 ± 7.90
Gomoku							

(continued)

Table 2. (*continued*)

MCTS iterations per move:	1000	5000	10,000	20,000	30,000	40,000	50,000
	Win percentages **against UCT** (95% Agresti-Coull confidence intervals)						
UCT	24.65 ± 6.81	21.40 ± 6.48	19.45 ± 6.25	23.35 ± 6.69	20.75 ± 6.41	27.25 ± 7.04	25.95 ± 6.93
Anytime SH	32.45 ± 7.40	31.80 ± 7.36	18.15 ± 6.09	10.35 ± 4.81	25.30 ± 6.87	18.15 ± 6.09	26.60 ± 6.98
Hex							
UCT	20.75 ± 6.41	37.00 ± 7.63	42.20 ± 7.80	46.75 ± 7.88	51.30 ± 7.90	40.90 ± 7.77	45.45 ± 7.87
Anytime SH	12.30 ± 5.19	22.70 ± 6.62	38.30 ± 7.68	45.45 ± 7.87	51.95 ± 7.90	50.00 ± 7.90	48.70 ± 7.90
Pentalath							
UCT	37.65 ± 7.66	40.25 ± 7.75	43.50 ± 7.83	50.00 ± 7.90	51.30 ± 7.90	46.10 ± 7.88	47.40 ± 7.89
Anytime SH	24.65 ± 6.81	35.70 ± 7.57	44.80 ± 7.86	50.00 ± 7.90	43.50 ± 7.83	54.55 ± 7.87	55.20 ± 7.86
Reversi							
UCT	49.02 ± 7.90	48.05 ± 7.90	48.70 ± 7.90	46.75 ± 7.88	53.90 ± 7.88	54.23 ± 7.87	50.65 ± 7.90
Anytime SH	50.98 ± 7.90	51.95 ± 7.90	54.23 ± 7.87	48.05 ± 7.90	64.95 ± 7.54	54.23 ± 7.87	59.43 ± 7.76
Tablut							
UCT	42.85 ± 7.82	49.35 ± 7.90	50.00 ± 7.90	50.00 ± 7.90	50.65 ± 7.90	50.00 ± 7.90	49.35 ± 7.90
Anytime SH	43.50 ± 7.83	47.40 ± 7.89	48.70 ± 7.90	49.35 ± 7.90	48.05 ± 7.90	48.05 ± 7.90	47.40 ± 7.89
Yavalath							
UCT	42.85 ± 7.82	53.90 ± 7.88	63.00 ± 7.63	59.75 ± 7.75	54.55 ± 7.87	50.33 ± 7.90	51.63 ± 7.90
Anytime SH	47.40 ± 7.89	57.15 ± 7.82	58.45 ± 7.79	57.48 ± 7.81	52.60 ± 7.89	51.30 ± 7.90	53.90 ± 7.88

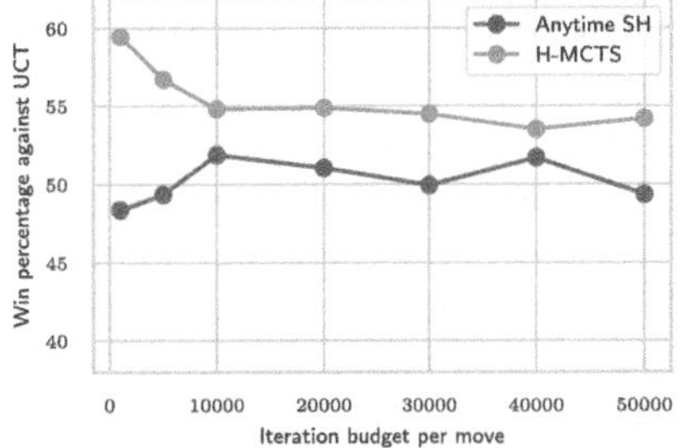
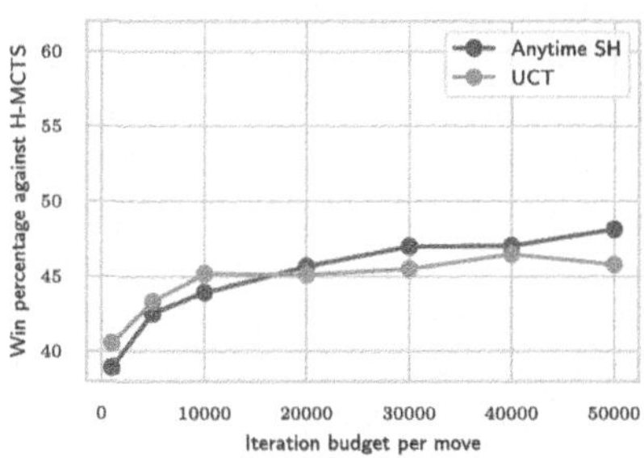

Fig. 4. Win percentages averaged over all ten games against UCT (left) and H-MCTS (right). 95% confidence intervals are too small to be visible.

to optimize simple regret. However, for many budgets, UCB1 has substantially greater variance in its performance level than the three SH-based algorithms do.

When averaging results over all ten board games (Fig. 4), we find that (i) H-MCTS (which is not an anytime algorithm) tends to perform better than the other two algorithms, in particular for low iteration budgets, and (ii) anytime SH appears to be possibly weaker than UCT by a slight margin for low iteration budgets, but evenly-matched or slightly stronger for medium and large iteration budgets. At the level of individual games, these trends can differ (see Table 2). The results in the game of Gomoku stand out in particular, with H-MCTS having particularly high win percentages of around 75% against UCT for all budgets, and ranging between approximately 70% and 90% against Anytime SH. While a sample size of ten games (with 150 plays per game, per pair of agents) is no less than is customary in the literature, it is still small enough for a single game with relatively extreme results such as Gomoku to have an outsized effect on a plot that averages over the games like Fig. 4. Especially in the direct matchup against H-MCTS (the left subfigure), Anytime SH would be substantially closer to H-MCTS if the results for Gomoku were excluded (and, plausibly also if the experiment were extended with more other games, if Gomoku is an outlier).

6   Conclusion and Future Work

This paper proposed Anytime Sequential Halving: an algorithm designed in an effort to approximate the behavior of the standard Sequential Halving (SH) algorithm, whilst having the *anytime* property. Experiments in a set of synthetic Multi-Armed Bandit problems show that Anytime SH performs on par in terms of simple regret with the standard SH, as well as a trivial time-based variant of SH, which can handle time-based budgets (but is not truly anytime). While the performance in terms of simple regret remains unchanged, Anytime SH does bring the benefit of having the anytime property. When used as selection strategy for the root node in Monte-Carlo Tree Search (MCTS) for game playing, Anytime SH appears to perform slightly below the Hybrid MCTS baseline (which has the downside of not being an anytime algorithm). Its performance level is competitive with UCT, appearing to be possibly slightly worse for low search budgets, but slightly better for higher budgets.

We see potential for ample future work to further improve Anytime SH. The Anytime SH algorithm as proposed in this paper was kept simple and straightforward. We expect that there is likely room to improve the algorithm, in particular by more carefully investigating how it should behave in situations where its ordering of arms changes between different passes of the algorithm (a situation that cannot occur in the standard SH). When Anytime SH "changes its mind" about ordering of any pair of arms, one of them will have had fewer iterations so far than it should have had in hindsight (fewer iterations than the standard SH would have allocated if the current total number of iterations were the full budget). In our implementation, we ignore this, but it is worth investigating if correcting for this would be worthwhile. This could potentially make the algorithm more adaptive to the level of complexity of a problem than the standard SH is, which always halves sets of arms at specific intervals regardless of how many arms are close or far from each other in terms of expected rewards. Furthermore, it would be interesting to investigate how the algorithm interacts with different values of hyperparameters, such as the exploration constant still used for UCB1 in nodes below the root node in MCTS.

Disclosure of Interests. The authors have no competing interests to declare that are relevant to the content of this article.

References

1. Audibert, J.Y., Bubeck, S.: Best arm identification in multi-armed bandits. In: Kalai, A.T., Mohri, M. (eds.) COLT 2010 - The 23rd Conference on Learning Theory, pp. 41–53 (2010)
2. Auer, P., Cesa-Bianchi, N., Fischer, P.: Finite-time analysis of the multiarmed bandit problem. Mach. Learn. **47**(2–3), 235–256 (2002)
3. Baier, H., Winands, M.H.M.: Time management for Monte Carlo tree search. IEEE Trans. Comput. Intell. AI Games **8**(3), 301–314 (2015)
4. Browne, C., et al.: A survey of monte carlo tree search methods. IEEE Trans. Comput. Intell. AI Games **4**(1), 1–49 (2012)
5. Bubeck, S., Munos, R., Stoltz, G.: Pure exploration in finitely-armed and continuous-armed bandits. Theor. Comput. Sci. **412**(19), 1832–1852 (2011)
6. Cazenave, T.: Sequential halving applied to trees. IEEE Trans. Comput. Intell. AI Games **7**(1), 102–105 (2015)
7. Coulom, R.: Efficient selectivity and backup operators in Monte-Carlo tree search. In: van den Herik, H.J., Ciancarini, P., Donkers, H.H.L.M.J. (eds.) CG 2006. LNCS, vol. 4630, pp. 72–83. Springer, Heidelberg (2007). https://doi.org/10.1007/978-3-540-75538-8_7
8. Danihelka, I., Guez, A., Schrittwieser, J., Silver, D.: Policy improvement by planning with Gumbel. In: International Conference on Learning Representations (ICLR 2022) (2022)
9. Fabiano, N., Cazenave, T.: Sequential halving using scores. In: Browne, C., Kishimoto, A., Schaeffer, J. (eds.) Advances in Computer Games. ACG 2021. LNCS, vol. 13262, pp. 41–52. Springer, Cham (2022). https://doi.org/10.1007/978-3-031-11488-5_4
10. Feldman, Z., Domshlak, C.: Simple regret optimization in online planning for Markov decision processes. J. Artif. Intell. Res. **51**, 165–205 (2014)
11. Huang, S.C., Coulom, R., Lin, S.S.: Time management for Monte-Carlo tree search applied to the game of Go. In: Proceedings of the 2010 International Conference on Technologies and Applications of Artificial Intelligence, pp. 462–466 (2010)
12. Karnin, Z., Koren, T., Somekh, O.: Almost optimal exploration in multi-armed bandits. In: Proceedings of the 30th International Conference on Machine Learning PMLR, vol. 28, pp. 1238–1246 (2013)
13. Kocsis, L., Szepesvári, C.: Bandit based monte-carlo planning. In: Fürnkranz, J., Scheffer, T., Spiliopoulou, M. (eds.) ECML 2006. LNCS (LNAI), vol. 4212, pp. 282–293. Springer, Heidelberg (2006). https://doi.org/10.1007/11871842_29
14. Nguyen, K.P.N., Ramanujan, R.: Lookahead pathology in Monte-Carlo tree search. In: Proceedings of the International Conference Automated Planning and Scheduling, vol. 34, pp. 414–422 (2024)
15. Pepels, T., Cazenave, T., Winands, M.H.M.: Sequential halving for partially observable games. In: Cazenave, T., Winands, M.H.M., Edelkamp, S., Schiffel, S., Thielscher, M., Togelius, J. (eds.) CGW/GIGA -2015. CCIS, vol. 614, pp. 16–29. Springer, Cham (2016). https://doi.org/10.1007/978-3-319-39402-2_2
16. Pepels, T., Cazenave, T., Winands, M.H.M., Lanctot, M.: Minimizing simple and cumulative regret in Monte-Carlo tree search. In: Cazenave, T., Winands, M.H.M., Björnsson, Y. (eds.) CGW 2014. CCIS, vol. 504, pp. 1–15. Springer, Cham (2014). https://doi.org/10.1007/978-3-319-14923-3_1

17. Piette, É., Soemers, D.J.N.J., Stephenson, M., Sironi, C.F., Winands, M.H.M., Browne, C.: Ludii – the ludemic general game system. In: Giacomo, G.D., Catala, A., Dilkina, B., Milano, M., Barro, S., Bugarín, A., Lang, J. (eds.) Proc. 24th European Conference Artificial Intelligence. Frontiers in Artificial Intelligence and Applications, vol. 325, pp. 411–418. IOS Press (2020)
18. Soemers, D.J.N.J., et al.: Towards a characterisation of Monte-Carlo tree search performance in different games. In: Proceedings of the IEEE Conference Games, pp. 1–4 (2024)
19. Świechowski, M., Godlewski, K., Sawicki, B., Mańdziuk, J.: Monte Carlo tree search: a review of recent modifications and applications. Artif. Intell. Rev. **56**, 2497–2562 (2022)
20. Todd, G., Padula, A., Stephenson, M., Piette, É., Soemers, D.J.N.J., Togelius, J.: GAVEL: Generating games via evolution and language models (2024). https:// arxiv.org/abs/2407.09388

Monte Carlo Search Algorithms Discovering Monte Carlo Tree Search Exploration Terms

Tristan Cazenave[✉]

LAMSADE, Université Paris Dauphine - PSL, CNRS, Paris, France
Tristan.Cazenave@dauphine.fr

Abstract. Monte Carlo Tree Search and Monte Carlo Search have good results for many combinatorial problems. In this paper we propose to use Monte Carlo Search to design mathematical expressions that are used as exploration terms for Monte Carlo Tree Search algorithms. The Monte Carlo Tree Search algorithm we aim to optimize is SHUSS (Sequential Halving Using Scores). We automatically design the SHUSS root exploration term. For small search budgets of 32 evaluations the discovered root exploration term makes SHUSS competitive with usual PUCT (Predictor Upper Confidence bounds for Trees).

1 Introduction

Monte Carlo Tree Search [13,23] is a well known family of algorithms that were designed for the game of Go and then applied to many different combinatorial problems [2,42].

Our goal in this paper is to use Monte Carlo Search to improve Monte Carlo Tree Search. This is part of a longstanding goal of using Artificial Intelligence to improve Artificial Intelligence [33].

The usual way to design an exploration term is to make a theoretical analysis [1]. We take another empirical approach. We randomly generate many exploration terms and keep the ones that work well in practice. This is a simpler approach, yet it can find exploration terms that work well in practice and that surpass the ones found with a theoretical analysis.

Another approach to the automatic improvement of Monte Carlo Tree Search exploration terms is to use Genetic Programming. It could evolve Monte Carlo Tree Search algorithms, improving on UCT and RAVE for the game of Go [5]. However this approach relies on making the exploration terms play against each other which is time consuming. It is also more complicated than the method we propose in this paper.

Monte Carlo Tree Search combined with Deep Reinforcement Learning has been used to improve algorithms. AlphaTensor discovered new fast matrix multiplications algorithms playing the tensor game [16]. AlphaTensor as well as other Monte Carlo Tree Search algorithms have also been used for quantum circuit

M. Hartisch et al. (Eds.): CG 2024, LNCS 15550, pp. 103–115, 2025.
https://doi.org/10.1007/978-3-031-86585-5_9

optimization [20,34,35,43]. New fast sorting algorithms were discovered thanks to Monte Carlo Tree Search with the AlphaDev system [27].

Monte Carlo Search has been used for discovering mathematical expressions that maximize a given score function [6,7]. This was applied to different domains including physics [41], finance [10], and the automated design of functions [21].

Refinements of the Monte Carlo Search approach to mathematical expressions discovery include incorporating actor-critic in Monte Carlo Tree Search for symbolic regression [25], using a grammar of Monte Carlo Search algorithms [26], controlling the size [29], and using GPT as a prior [24].

The automated discovery of optimization algorithms with symbolic program search recently enabled to discover a simple and effective optimization algorithm, Lion (evoLved sIgn mOmeNtum). Lion is more memory-efficient than Adam as it only keeps track of the momentum [12].

Our work is in line with these uses of Artificial Intelligence to discover new Artificial Intelligence algorithms. Our goal is to use Monte Carlo Search to discover a new root exploration term for the SHUSS algorithm [15].

Our contributions are:

- An efficient method to empirically design exploration terms.
- The AMAF prior for non uniform playouts in Monte Carlo Search applied to the discovery of mathematical expressions.
- The design of a curriculum learning dataset for discovering exploration terms.
- A better way of selecting moves for SHUSS according to their priors given by the policy network.

The second section presents various Monte Carlo Tree Search algorithms. The third section explains how we generate mathematical expressions for the exploration terms. The fourth section details experimental results.

2   Monte Carlo Tree Search

In this section we present various Monte Carlo Tree Search algorithms, starting with PUCT the most popular one which is used in Alpha Zero and that is standard in computer games. We then define the AMAF prior that can be used to play non uniform playouts biased toward the actions that give better playouts scores. It uses statistics on the playouts that contain an action to calculate its probability of being played as explained in the following subsection on sampling. We then present the Sequential Halving algorithm as well as the related Sequential Halving Using Scores (SHUSS) algorithm. We end this section explaining how generated exploration terms can be used for SHUSS.

2.1   PUCT

Monte Carlo Tree Search was designed for computer Go and made a revolution in computer Go [13,23] and then in computer game playing [17,28]. The current

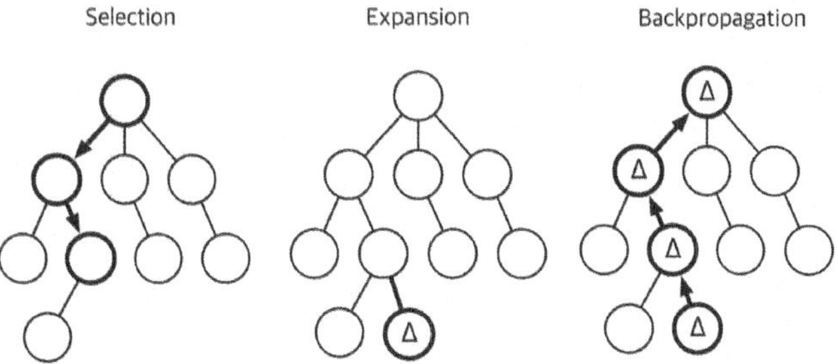

Fig. 1. The three steps of MCTS. The first step is the tree descent using the exploration term to choose among the children. The second step is adding a new leaf associated to an evaluation of the state by the value network. The third step is updating the statistics in the tree with the evaluation.

standard algorithm for Monte Carlo Tree Search is PUCT. This is the search algorithm used in AlphaGo [38], AlphaGo Zero [39], AlphaZero [40] and MuZero [37].

Figure 1 gives the three steps of MCTS. The principle of the algorithm is to memorize the already explored states as well as the associated statistics for the possible actions in these states. When the algorithm encounters a state he has already explored, it uses an exploration term to choose the next action to play. The average of the previous evaluations associated to an action a in state s is $Q(s, a)$. The number of descents that have passed by state s is $N(s)$ and the number of descent in s that have played action a is $N(s, a)$.

A neural network is used at the leaves of the tree to evaluate the leaf and calculate probabilities for the possible actions. The probability, as estimated by the neural network, that action a is the best in state s is $P(s, a)$.

The exploration term which is added to $Q(s, a)$ in PUCT is:

$$c_p \times P(s, a) \times \frac{\sqrt{N(s)}}{1 + N(s, a)}$$

The constant c_p is an hyper parameter that has to be tuned for each problem.

In the following we use pr for $P(s, a)$ the probability for action a in state s given by the neural network policy head.

2.2   The AMAF Prior

The All Moves As First (AMAF) heuristic comes from computer Go [4]. It calculates statistics on moves independently of when the moves were played in a playout. It is used in General Game Playing [32] in the MAST algorithm [18]. It was also used in computer Go in the RAVE [19] algorithm. The principle of RAVE is to bias the tree policy with the AMAF statistics of the node. RAVE is much better than UCT for the game of Go. RAVE was later generalized to GRAVE [8] by using AMAF statistics of an ancestor node of the tree instead of the AMAF statistics of the node. GRAVE has much better results than RAVE for many games. It has good results in General Game Playing. It is the standard Monte Carlo Tree Search algorithm used in the Ludii system [3].

We now define a more elaborate version of AMAF. If $\mathcal{P}$ is the set of the playouts and $s(p)$ is the score of playout $p \in \mathcal{P}$, we define:

$$\mu = \frac{\sum_{p \in \mathcal{P}} s(p)}{|\mathcal{P}|}$$

$$\mathcal{P}_a = \{p \in \mathcal{P} \mid a \in p\}$$

$$\mu_a = \frac{\sum_{p \in \mathcal{P}_a} s(p)}{|\mathcal{P}_a|} - \mu$$

$$maxi = \max_a(|\mu_a|)$$

$$z = \sum_a e^{\frac{\mu_a}{maxi}}$$

$$AMAF(a) = \frac{e^{\frac{\mu_a}{maxi}}}{z}$$

2.3 Sampling

The basic algorithm in Monte Carlo Search is sampling. It performs playouts by randomly choosing actions until it reaches a terminal state.

It usually improves the results of the playout to adopt a non uniform strategy for sampling. A policy can attribute different probabilities to the possible actions in a state. The sampling algorithm can then choose the next action to play according to these probabilities.

It is also possible to use a temperature τ to make the policy more or less exploratory. In the case of AMAF, if $\mathcal{A}$ is the set of the possible actions in state s, sampling with a temperature τ consists in choosing the next action a with probability p_a:

$$p_a = \frac{e^{\frac{log(AMAF(a))}{\tau}}}{z}$$

$$z = \sum_{a \in \mathcal{A}} e^{\frac{log(AMAF(a))}{\tau}}$$

2.4   Sequential Halving

Sequential Halving [22] is an algorithm that minimizes the simple regret. It has successfully been used as an alternative to UCB in Monte Carlo Tree Search, in particular as a replacement in the root node with UCB used in the rest of the tree [31], or even in the whole tree with SHOT [9]. It was applied to games as well as to partially observable games [30]. Sequential Halving was also used as a root policy with Gumbel MuZero [14]. The outputs of the Sequential Halving at the root were used for reinforcement learning in the MuZero algorithm. Gumbel MuZero was successfully applied to Go, Chess and Atari games.

Algorithm 1 gives the Sequential Halving algorithm used in SHUSS [15]. This is the one we use in this paper with $\lambda = \frac{1}{2}$. The principle of the algorithm is to allocate the same number of playouts to all the actions in the set of actions S_r. It then selects half of the actions in S_r that have the best empirical average. This best half constitutes S_{r+1}. The algorithm continues to allocate playouts to remaining actions and to select the best half until there is only one action remaining in S_R.

Algorithm 1. Sequential Halving

> **Parameter:** cutting ratio λ
> **Input:** total budget T, set of arms S
> $S_0 \leftarrow S,\ T_0 \leftarrow T$
> $R \leftarrow$ number of rounds before $|S_R| = 1$
> **for** $r = 0$ **to** $R - 1$ **do**
> $\quad t_r \leftarrow \lfloor \frac{T_r}{|S_r| \cdot (R-r)} \rfloor$
> $\quad T_{r+1} \leftarrow T_r - t_r |S_r|$
> $\quad$ sample t_r times each arm in S_r
> $\quad S_{r+1} \leftarrow S_r$ deprived of the fraction $1 - \lambda$ of the worst arms
> **end for**
> **Output:** arm in S_R

2.5   Sequential Halving Using Scores

SHUSS [15] is an improvement of Sequential Halving that uses a prior to improve the move selection at the root. The prior can be used either to eliminate moves or to bias the selection of the actions.

When the prior is standard AMAF it selects the moves to keep using:

$$\tilde{Q}_a = Q_a + C \times \frac{StandardAMAF(a)}{N(root, a)}$$

$$StandardAMAF(a) = \frac{\sum_{p \in \mathcal{P}_a} s(p)}{|\mathcal{P}_a|}$$

In case of a prior given by a neural network, it uses the classic Sequential Halving algorithm restricted to a fixed number of moves that have the best priors.

2.6 Using an Exploration Term for the Selection of Moves in SHUSS

In the same spirit as SHUSS it is possible to use various exploration terms for choosing the moves to keep at the end of a round of Sequential Halving. Algorithm 2 gives the move selection process with an exploration term. The principle is to take the best half of the moves that maximize the expression. If the expression is the usual empirical average then the algorithm is the usual Sequential Halving algorithm.

Algorithm 2. Selection of the moves to keep for the next round

---

    Parameter: cutting ratio λ
    Input: set of moves S_r
    $S_{r+1} \leftarrow \emptyset$
    for $i = 0$ **to** $\lambda \times |S_r|$ **do**
      $bestScore \leftarrow -\infty$
      for $j = 0$ **to** $|S_r|$ **do**
        if $S_r[j] \notin S_{r+1}$ **then**
          if $expression(S_r[j]) > bestScore$ **then**
            $bestMove \leftarrow S_r[j]$
            $bestScore \leftarrow expression(S_r[j])$
          end if
        end if
      end for
      $S_{r+1} \leftarrow S_{r+1} \cup \{bestMove\}$
    end for
    return S_{r+1}

---

3 Generating Mathematical Expressions

In this section we detail the algorithms we use to discover mathematical expressions. We first define the expression discovery game, and then explain how to sample expressions for this game.

3.1 The Expression Discovery Game

The expression discovery game is used to generate and evaluate expressions that are used as the SHUSS exploration term. Expression trees are represented as stacks in reverse polish notation. For example the generated expression [+, pr, *, *, 2, sc, sc] corresponds to the exploration term $pr + 2 \times sc \times sc$ where sc is the sum of the scores of the playouts starting with the move to evaluate and pr the prior for that move. The evaluation of an expression in reverse polish notation is algorithmically simple as it uses a straightforward depth first search.

In order to limit the size of the generated expressions, we maintain the number of open leaves of an incomplete expression. This is the total number of children of the atoms of the expression that are not yet associated to an atom. In the root node the number of open leaves of the empty expression is 1. If for example a '+' atom is assigned to the root, then there is one open leaf less due to the assignment and two open leaves more due to the '+' having two children not yet assigned. In order to generate expressions that are smaller than the maximum length, the legal moves function does not return atoms that make the number of already assigned atoms plus the number of open leaves plus the number of children of the atom greater than the maximum length.

The atoms we used to generate expressions are:

- 1, 2, 3 and 100 numbers.
- sc: the sum of the scores of the playouts starting with the move.
- pr: the prior for the move given by the policy head.
- nbp: the number of playouts starting with the move.
- nb: the total number of playouts.
- +, -, *, /, log, exp, =, max and min operators.

3.2 Sampling

The default sampling procedure is uniform sampling. It is possible to replace it with non uniform sampling using the AMAF prior.

In our code for sampling mathematical expressions, the possible atoms are defined in a list and the number of children of each atom is defined in the corresponding children list. A state is a possibly incomplete mathematical expression in reverse polish notation. It is associated to a number of open leaves which is the minimum number of atoms that have to be added to the expression in order to have a complete expression.

The usual functions to define a problem for Monte Carlo Search are defined as follows for the mathematical expression discovery game:

- The legal moves function takes as parameters an incomplete expression and the number of associated open leaves. It returns the list of atoms that can be added to the incomplete expression. It verifies that adding an atom does not exceed the maximal number of atoms for the final complete expression.
- The play function just adds the selected atom to the expression and also returns the updated number of open leaves.
- The terminal function returns True when the expression is complete.
- The playout function is the usual uniformly random playout function that randomly adds authorized atoms to the expression until the expression is complete.

4   Experimental Results

In this section we experiment the discovery of Monte Carlo Tree Search root exploration terms in the game of Go. We present the computer Go dataset that was used to train a transformer network for the game of Go. The transformer network is used to generate the SHUSS dataset that is in turn used to evaluate generated root exploration terms. We compare uniform sampling to AMAF sampling for the discovery of root exploration terms. We apply the framework to the discovery of root exploration terms for SHUSS. We then test the discovered exploration terms in a Go program, making the new algorithm play against standard PUCT.

4.1   The Computer Go Dataset

The computer Go dataset is composed of games played by Katago [44] against itself in 2022. There are 1,000,000 different games in total in the training set. The input data is composed of 31 19x19 planes (color to play, ladders, current state on two planes, two previous states on four planes). The output targets are the policy (a vector of size 361 with 1.0 for the move played, 0.0 for the other moves), and the value (close to 1.0 if White wins, close to 0.0 if Black wins). The test set is composed of 50,000 states taken randomly from 50,000 games that are not used in the training set.

4.2   The Neural Network

We trained a computer Go vision transformer network [36] using 2,000 epochs with 100,000 states per epoch. The loss for the policy head is a categorical cross entropy and the loss for the value head is a binary cross entropy. The optimizer is Adam and the learning rate decreases according to a cosine annealing [11]. The network reached an accuracy of 57.75% on Katago moves, a Mean Squared Error (MSE) of 0.0334 and a Mean Absolute Error (MAE) of 0.117.

4.3   The SHUSS Dataset

The time required to precisely evaluate a generated expression in a real Go playing program can be huge. For example making a Sequential Halving algorithm with a generated expression play against a standard PUCT for 500 games with 1024 playouts per move takes days.

In order to have a fast evaluation of a given exploration term we built a dataset of states associated to their cached search. The policy learned by the neural network is of high quality. Out of the 2,000 states taken from the test set only 77 of them have a prior less than 0.01. In the remaining of the experiments, we only use moves that have a prior greater or equal to 0.01 for Sequential Halving. For each of the moves that have a prior greater or equal to 0.01, we call PUCT starting with the move a fixed number of times (e.g. 32) and store the sequence of evaluations returned by the successive calls to PUCT after the fixed first move. Therefore for all moves we have an associated sequence of 32 evaluations that can be used to simulate the calls made by Sequential Halving while not using the inference by the neural network. This enables a very fast evaluation of a given Sequential Halving exploration term as the neural network is not used anymore to calculate the accuracy of the exploration term. The label of a state is the move found by Sequential Halving with 128 evaluations. The accuracy of an exploration term is defined as the percentage of labeled moves found by the Sequential Halving algorithm with 32 evaluations on the 2,000 cached states.

In order to speed up the evaluation of the exploration terms we stop evaluating the accuracy of an exploration term if it scores less than a threshold of 80 after 200 states. We also use memorization of the scores of the exploration terms in a dictionary as well as the memorization of the sums of scores for a given number of playouts and a given first move.

In the experiments we run 100 processes generating exploration terms in parallel for 512 s. It results in 354,400 exploration terms being evaluated.

4.4 AMAF Sampling

The evolution of the best accuracy on the Sequential Halving moves with 128 evaluations is given in Fig. 2 both for uniform sampling and for AMAF sampling. AMAF sampling is much better.

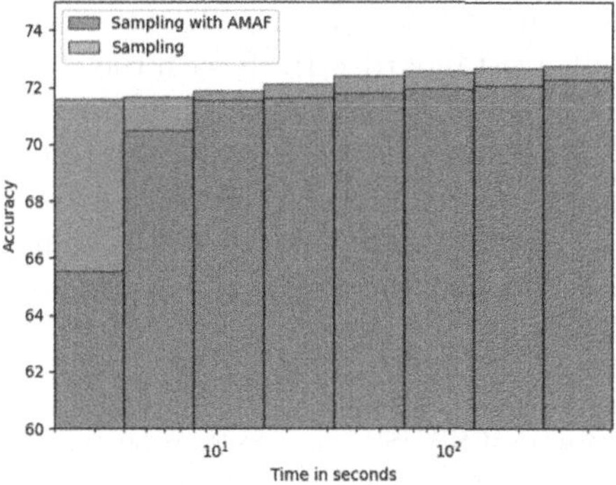

Fig. 2. Evolution of the best expression accuracy with the logarithm of the sampling search time with doubling search times. Each measure is the average of 100 runs of the sampling algorithms. Using the AMAF prior improves the results. It finds the same accuracy more than 8 times faster than the uniform sampling algorithm. The temperature of the AMAF sampling is set to $\frac{1}{5}$. The dataset used is the Sequential Halving moves with 128 evaluations dataset and the exploration terms are scored using 32 evaluations on each state out of the 2,000 states.

4.5   Discovering a SHUSS Exploration Term

Table 1 gives the accuracy of different exploration terms for the Sequential Halving moves. The prior pr is much worse than the standard Sequential Halving algorithm sc on this dataset. The sampling algorithm finds the $sc \times (pr + sc \times sc)$ exploration term that is better than both.

Table 1. Accuracy of SHUSS with 32 evaluations on the SHUSS dataset. The SHUSS label moves are found using Sequential Halving with 128 evaluations. The accuracy is calculated on the moves found by SHUSS with 32 evaluations and the depicted exploration term for halving. The sc exploration term corresponds to standard SHUSS. The $pr + 2 \times sc \times sc$ has a slightly better accuracy on the SHUSS dataset.

Exploration Term	Accuracy on the SHUSS dataset
pr	44.85%
sc	71.45%
$pr + 2 \times sc \times sc$	72.85%

4.6   Testing the SHUSS Exploration Term in a Go Program

We evaluate the different exploration terms by using them in a computer Go program. The SHUSS algorithm using an exploration term plays 400 games against PUCT. Both algorithms use 32 evaluations for choosing their move. PUCT chooses the most simulated move and SHUSS chooses the only remaining move in S_R. The results for standard SHUSS with the usual exploration term sc are given in Table 2. We can observe that the standard SHUSS is weaker than PUCT. The exploration term $pr + 2 \times sc \times sc$ is also tested against PUCT. For all the PUCT constants we tested, SHUSS with the discovered exploration term is better than PUCT. The best result for PUCT is that SHUSS wins 51.00% of its games. So we can say that the discovered exploration term made SHUSS competitive with PUCT.

Table 2. Winrates of standard SHUSS (the exploration term is sc) and SHUSS with the $pr + 2 \times sc \times sc$ exploration term against PUCT. The two SHUSS algorithms use 32 evaluations and the 5 best prior moves. PUCT also uses 32 evaluations. We see that the discovered exploration term is an improvement on standard SHUSS. The 400 starting states are taken from the Katago dataset test set games by playing 20 moves by Katago from the beginning of the games. The resulting states are balanced according to Katago.

Exploration Term	Winrate against PUCT
sc	42.50%
$pr + 2 \times sc \times sc$	51.00%

If we analyze the discovered exploration term $pr + 2 \times sc \times sc$, we see that when there are only a few playouts it takes into account the prior so as not to eliminate moves that have a great prior. When the number of playouts is greater, the $2 \times sc \times sc$ value becomes much greater than the prior and the moves are sorted according to the square of the sum of their scores and not much according to their prior anymore.

5 Conclusion

We presented a simple yet efficient method to find new exploration terms for Monte Carlo Tree Search. It uses sampling of mathematical expressions and a fast evaluation of the generated expressions. The generated exploration terms are simple. For search with a small number of evaluations, the method discovered an exploration term that works better than the usual exploration term for Sequential Halving. The discovered exploration term also beats the canonical PUCT algorithm for small equivalent search times. We also proposed the AMAF prior for sampling mathematical expressions. It reaches a score approximately 8 times faster than uniform sampling.

Our method to discover new exploration terms is simple, fast, general and empirically adapts the generated mathematical expressions to the problem at hand.

Future work involves accelerating the discovery of the expressions and applying the algorithm to other problems. It would also be interesting investigating the generation of more general expressions by evaluating them on more varied data, for example with different numbers of playouts or even for different games or problems.

From a more general point of view, Artificial Intelligence is becoming powerful enough to help discover new Artificial Intelligence algorithms. There are many further developments along the line of using Artificial Intelligence to improve Artificial Intelligence.

References

1. Auer, P., Cesa-Bianchi, N., Fischer, P.: Finite-time analysis of the multiarmed bandit problem. Mach. Learn. **47**(2–3), 235–256 (2002)
2. Browne, C., et al.: A survey of monte carlo tree search methods. IEEE TCIAIG **4**(1), 1–43 (2012)
3. Browne, C., Stephenson, M., Piette, É., Soemers, D.J.: A practical introduction to the Ludii general game system. In: ACG 2019, pp. 167–179. Springer (2020). https://doi.org/10.1007/978-3-030-65883-0_14
4. Brügmann, B.: Monte Carlo Go. Tech. rep., Max-Planke-Inst. Phys., Munich (1993)
5. Cazenave, T.: Evolving monte carlo tree search algorithms. Dept. Inf., Univ. Paris **8** (2007)
6. Cazenave, T.: Nested monte-carlo expression discovery. In: ECAI 2010, pp. 1057–1058. IOS Press (2010)

7. Cazenave, T.: Monte-carlo expression discovery. Int. J. Artif. Intell. Tools **22**(01), 1250035 (2013)
8. Cazenave, T.: Generalized rapid action value estimation. In: Yang, Q., Wooldridge, M.J. (eds.) IJCAI 2015, pp. 754–760. AAAI Press (2015)
9. Cazenave, T.: Sequential halving applied to trees. IEEE Trans. Comput. Intell. AI Games **7**(1), 102–105 (2015)
10. Cazenave, T., Hamida, S.B.: Forecasting financial volatility using nested monte carlo expression discovery. In: IEEE SSCI, pp. 726–733 (2015)
11. Cazenave, T., Sentuc, J., Videau, M.: Cosine annealing, mixnet and swish activation for computer Go. In: Advances in Computer Games. Springer (2021). https://doi.org/10.1007/978-3-031-11488-5_5
12. Chen, X., et al.: Symbolic discovery of optimization algorithms. In: Advances in Neural Information Processing Systems, vol. 36 (2024)
13. Coulom, R.: Efficient selectivity and backup operators in monte-carlo tree search. In: van den Herik, H.J., Ciancarini, P., Donkers, H.H.L.M.J. (eds.) CG 2006. LNCS, vol. 4630, pp. 72–83. Springer, Heidelberg (2007). https://doi.org/10.1007/978-3-540-75538-8_7
14. Danihelka, I., Guez, A., Schrittwieser, J., Silver, D.: Policy improvement by planning with gumbel. In: International Conference on Learning Representations (2021)
15. Fabiano, N., Cazenave, T.: Sequential halving using scores. In: Advances in Computer Games, pp. 41–52. Springer (2021). https://doi.org/10.1007/978-3-031-11488-5_4.pdf
16. Fawzi, A., et al.: Discovering faster matrix multiplication algorithms with reinforcement learning. Nature **610**(7930), 47–53 (2022)
17. Finnsson, H., Björnsson, Y.: Simulation-based approach to general game playing. In: AAAI, pp. 259–264 (2008)
18. Finnsson, H., Björnsson, Y.: Learning simulation control in general game-playing agents. In: AAAI (2010)
19. Gelly, S., Silver, D.: Monte-Carlo tree search and rapid action value estimation in computer Go. Artif. Intell. **175**(11), 1856–1875 (2011)
20. Hummel, A., Cazenave, T.: Monte carlo qubit routing. In: Quantum Machine Learning at ECML PKDD (2022)
21. Illetskova, M., Elnabarawy, I., Da Silva, L.E.B., Tauritz, D.R., Wunsch, D.C.: Nested monte carlo search expression discovery for the automated design of fuzzy ART category choice functions. In: GECCO, pp. 171–172 (2019)
22. Karnin, Z.S., Koren, T., Somekh, O.: Almost optimal exploration in multi-armed bandits. In: ICML, pp. 1238–1246 (2013)
23. Kocsis, L., Szepesvári, C.: Bandit based monte-carlo planning. In: Fürnkranz, J., Scheffer, T., Spiliopoulou, M. (eds.) ECML 2006. LNCS (LNAI), vol. 4212, pp. 282–293. Springer, Heidelberg (2006). https://doi.org/10.1007/11871842_29
24. Li, Y., et al.: Discovering mathematical formulas from data via GPT-guided monte carlo tree search. arXiv preprint arXiv:2401.14424 (2024)
25. Lu, Q., Tao, F., Zhou, S., Wang, Z.: Incorporating actor-critic in monte carlo tree search for symbolic regression. Neural Comput. Appl. **33**, 8495–8511 (2021)
26. Maes, F., St-Pierre, D.L., Ernst, D.: Monte carlo search algorithm discovery for single-player games. IEEE Trans. Comput. Intell. AI Games **5**(3), 201–213 (2013)
27. Mankowitz, D.J., et al.: Faster sorting algorithms discovered using deep reinforcement learning. Nature **618**(7964), 257–263 (2023)
28. Méhat, J., Cazenave, T.: Monte-Carlo tree search for general game playing. Univ. Paris **8** (2008)
29. Moudřík, J., Křen, T., Neruda, R.: Algorithm discovery with monte-carlo search: controlling the size. In: ICTAI, pp. 390–395. IEEE (2017)

30. Pepels, T., Cazenave, T., Winands, M.H.M.: Sequential halving for partially observable games. In: Cazenave, T., Winands, M.H.M., Edelkamp, S., Schiffel, S., Thielscher, M., Togelius, J. (eds.) CGW/GIGA -2015. CCIS, vol. 614, pp. 16–29. Springer, Cham (2016). https://doi.org/10.1007/978-3-319-39402-2_2
31. Pepels, T., Cazenave, T., Winands, M.H.M., Lanctot, M.: Minimizing simple and cumulative regret in monte-carlo tree search. In: Cazenave, T., Winands, M.H.M., Björnsson, Y. (eds.) CGW 2014. Communications in Computer and Information Science, vol. 504, pp. 1–15. Springer (2014). https://doi.org/10.1007/978-3-319-14923-3_1
32. Pitrat, J.: Realization of a general game-playing program. In: IFIP Congress, vol. 2, pp. 1570–1574 (1968)
33. Pitrat, J.: A step toward an artificial artificial intelligence scientist (2008). LIP6 Research Report
34. Rosenhahn, B., Osborne, T.J.: Monte carlo graph search for quantum circuit optimization. Phys. Rev. A **108**(6), 062615 (2023)
35. Ruiz, F.J., et al.: Quantum circuit optimization with alphatensor. arXiv preprint arXiv:2402.14396 (2024)
36. Sagri, A., Arjonilla, J., Saffidine, A., Cazenave, T.: Vision transformers for computer Go. In: EvoApps. Springer (2024). https://doi.org/10.1007/978-3-031-56855-8_23
37. Schrittwieser, J., et al.: Mastering Atari, go, chess and shogi by planning with a learned model. Nature **588**(7839), 604–609 (2020)
38. Silver, D., et al.: Mastering the game of go with deep neural networks and tree search. Nature **529**, 484–489 (2016)
39. Silver, D., et al.: Mastering chess and shogi by self-play with a general reinforcement learning algorithm. CoRR abs/1712.01815 (2017). http://arxiv.org/abs/1712.01815
40. Silver, D., et al.: A general reinforcement learning algorithm that masters chess, shogi, and go through self-play. Science **362**(6419), 1140–1144 (2018)
41. Sun, F., Liu, Y., Wang, J.X., Sun, H.: Symbolic physics learner: discovering governing equations via monte carlo tree search. arXiv preprint arXiv:2205.13134 (2022)
42. Świechowski, M., Godlewski, K., Sawicki, B., Mańdziuk, J.: Monte carlo tree search: a review of recent modifications and applications. Artif. Intell. Rev. **56**(3), 2497–2562 (2023)
43. Wang, P., Usman, M., Parampalli, U., Hollenberg, L.C., Myers, C.R.: Automated quantum circuit design with nested monte carlo tree search. IEEE Trans. Quant. Eng. **4**, 1–20 (2023)
44. Wu, D.J.: Accelerating self-play learning in go. arXiv preprint arXiv:1902.10565 (2019)

Nonograms

Generating Difficult and Fun Nonograms

Milo Roucairol$^{(\boxtimes)}$ ⓘ and Tristan Cazenave ⓘ

LAMSADE, Université Paris Dauphine - PSL Place du Maréchal de Lattre de Tassigny, 75016 Paris, France
`milo.roucairol@dauphine.eu`

Abstract. Nonograms are Japanese logic puzzles where the player must find a 2D black-and-white image using information on the columns and rows. Here we present a new method to generate nonograms of varying difficulties and enjoyability using a human-like solver to estimate the difficulty of a puzzle, and Monte Carlo Tree Search algorithms to optimize the estimation of the difficulty.

Keywords: Nonogram · Monte Carlo · puzzle

1 Introduction

Logic puzzles are a staple of the gaming landscape. Widespread as early as 1913 thanks to newspapers, or even in 1783 with Euler's Latin square. Every living person has encountered one (be it crossword or sudoku), and likely solved one in their life. They are especially popular among retired people and computer scientists, as they are very similar to many computer science logic problems. Solving or programming a solver for these problems is common in CS studies and research.

Sudoku and Sokoban are two of the most notable logic puzzles of the 20th century. Another notable Japanese logic puzzle from the 80's was the Nonogram. It was quickly taken over by Nintendo with the Picross series for the Game Boy and the SNES with Mario's Picross in 1995 and entries using the sprites from Nintendo's most popular franchises. Spinning off multiple variants, like color nonograms, mosaic nonograms, nonograms with unknowns, mega-picross, etc. We are interested in the original version of the nonograms.

A nonogram is a grid-based logic puzzle. The player has to fill a grid with either black or white squares until there are no more unknown cells and the picture is fully formed. The player is given instructions on the rows and columns in the form of numbers on top and left of the grid. Each number n indicates that there are exactly n adjacent black squares. The order in which the numbers appear is important too, the groups of adjacent black squares must appear in the same order as on the clue.

Here we set out to generate Nonogram puzzles of varying difficulties, this has been the subject of some research. First in 2009, K. Joost Batenburg et al. [1] introduced a method to evaluate the difficulty and generate simple nonograms.

M. Hartisch et al. (Eds.): CG 2024, LNCS 15550, pp. 119–129, 2025.
https://doi.org/10.1007/978-3-031-86585-5_10

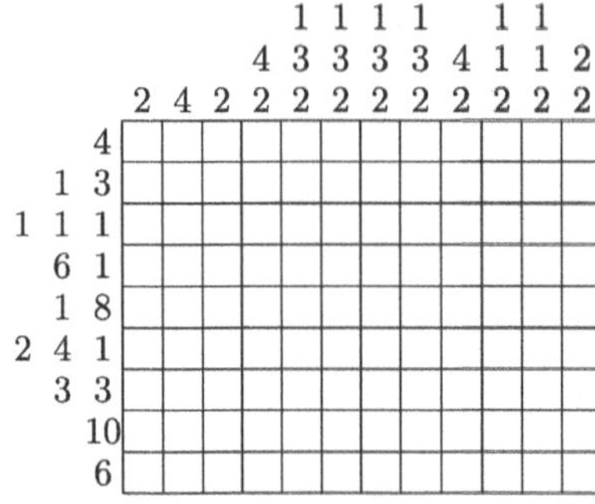 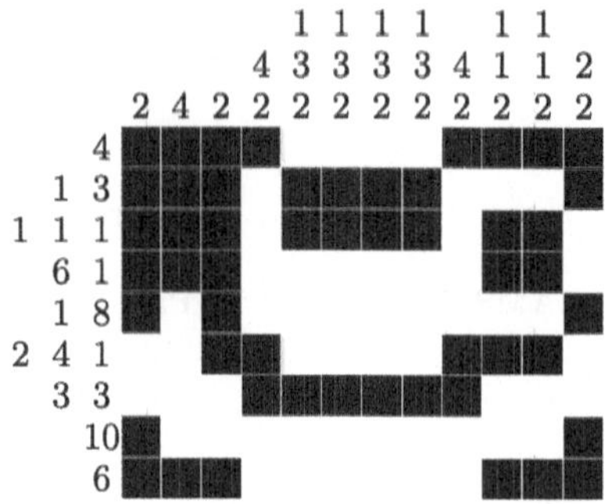

Fig. 1. Example of a medium sized nonogram, it depicts a cup of coffee on a saucer

Followed in 2012 by another assessment of the difficulty of nonograms [2]. However, both research papers do not focus on player-related difficulty but only on a solver/mathematical-related difficulty, here we intend to explore the nonogram design with human players in mind. Solvers for nonograms are also another point of interest, with genetic approaches like in Wiggers' work [12].

In this paper we will use a human-like deterministic solver to evaluate the difficulty and enjoyability (fun) of the generated nonograms, and state of the art Monte Carlo Search algorithms for the generation process. Our goal is to make a fast nonogram generator with targetable difficulty to allow for new ways of playing nonograms: time attack, survival, or endless modes, with a set or increasing difficulties (Tetris-like gameplay).

2 "Human" Solver

An optimization process requires a way to evaluate the quality of a state. A state of our search tree is a small black-and-white image. We imagine two ways to evaluate the difficulty and enjoyability of that image:

1. A neural network trained on a set of images and their evaluation by humans
2. A solver that emulates human logic and stores data about the resolution

We decided to use a solver because designing a human-like solver is an interesting and intuitive task, and the neural network training datasets are not publicly available yet.

One technique that is commonly used when solving nonograms is to check the possible extreme positions of a group of adjacent filled tiles and see if they overlap. If they do, the part where they overlap is necessarily black. This is the main technique used by humans, as such it is also the main one used by the solver. Conversely, spaces where no constraint-satisfying configuration had a black square on add a white square

In Fig. 2, first the 8 white cells are deduced given all positions of the 10 consecutive white cells overlap on these 8 cells. Then, all possible positions of

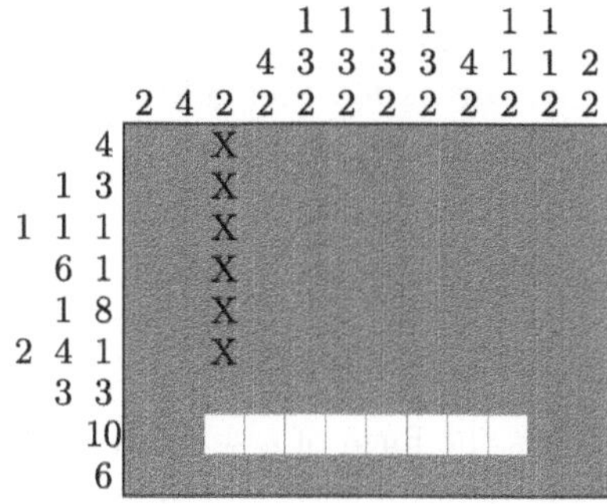

Fig. 2. Example of column and row swipes

the 2 in the third column exclude the 6 first cells from top to bottom (denoted with black "X"). These 6 cells must be black. This in turn helps us fill the 1st, 4th, 5th, and 6th lines from the top.

Our method takes a line or columns, its clue, and the already-filled cells, and computes all possible fillings that meet the requirements of the clue. Then if for a cell in this line, all possible filling leaves it black or white, the cell is filled in the grid. This method is called over the rows and columns according to the last cells modified, this mimics human solving as the attention and memory of a human player are focused on the last cells modified too.

This simple method is enough to solve most nonograms, but the hardest ones may require more advanced techniques, like the one called "edge solving". Edge solving is a type of deterministic guessing, it is done by guessing a white square, usually on the edges of the grid, and unrolling the usual resolution until a contradiction is found. Once a contradiction is found, the cell that was guessed as white is colored black. That technique is unknown by most players, and should be avoided unless the difficulty target is high and it only happens 1 to 3 times in the puzzle.

The algorithm has a stack of rows and lines to check (starting with all rows and columns), it checks them all until if finds a line/row move, it then applies that move to the row or columns and adds the rows and columns of all modified cells to the stack. If the algorithm does not find a line/row move, it tries to find a deterministic guessing move that gives a contradiction. If no move is found it returns the grid in its state, completed or not. We decided to not allow the solver to make another deterministic guess while one is active, thus used as a score function it does not produce nonograms unsuitable for humans. If a nonogram is solvable but necessitates the use of nested deterministic guessing it is deemed unsolvable by the solver, and discarded during the generation process (see next section). This is not a problem since deterministic guessing is almost never used in most nonogram games, and never in a nested fashion to the best of our knowledge.

The solving time of the algorithm is a metric sufficient to design hard nonograms by maximizing it. But for more precise difficulty targets, the solver returns other metrics such as the number of time it used edge solving, the number of step, the length of each backtracking, and others. These metrics are used to estimate the fun and the difficulty of a puzzle.

3   Generation

3.1   Search Space

The generation process takes the form of a search tree search as we use Monte-Carlo Tree Search and other deterministic search algorithms. All the algorithms share the same search tree (or search space). The root of the search tree is the initial nonogram that is submitted to the algorithm: an empty grid with black cells only. From that state, the available moves are swapping the value (white or black) of any rectangle inside the grid.

This simple single move allows the search algorithms to reach diverse grids in fewer moves than setting the value of each cell. It also allows for drastic changes in difficulty and grid layout in very few moves, while also setting the value of each cell individually if needed.

It is possible to start from an already existing nonogram, or from an image, and input a list of cells that cannot have their value swapped to preserve the depiction: nonograms usually depict objects.

3.2   Algorithms

Monte Carlo search algorithms are a family of search algorithms that use sampling (playouts) to learn about a search space to guide the search. They are a key element of recent breakthroughs in game playing such as Deepmind's AlphaGo [11], but are also widely used in other machine learning applications like multi-step retrosynthesis [5] or graph theory [9]. We selected the following algorithms.

1. UCT: Upper Confidence bound applied to Trees, the most commonly used MCTS algorithm. [6]
2. RAVE: Rapid Action Value Estimation, a variant of UCT using All Moves As First (AMAF), a machine learning technique appropriate to our search model because the order of the moves does not matter. [4]
3. NMCS: Nested Monte Carlo Search, a method that recursively calls lower level version of themselves on child states to find the route leading to the best score. A level 0 NMCS is a playout. [3]
4. LNMCS; Lazy Nested Monte Carlo Search, a variant of NMCS that introduces the exploitation/exploration dilemma and prunes lower level LNMCS using playout based evaluation. [10]
5. NRPA: Nested Rollout Policy adaptation, an algorithm inspired by NMCS that learns online a policy to guide the playouts. [8]

For combinatorial optimization, two families of MCS exist. The main and most commonly used one is called MCTS and uses an iterative approach, it includes UCT and RAVE. The other family is recursive, it includes NMCS, LNMCS, and NRPA.

Deterministic search algorithms are simpler search algorithms that do not involve sampling or machine learning. Intuitively we could expect them to provide inferior results compared to methods using machine learning. Recent approaches show that this is not always the case, they can outperform even the most complex state-of-the-art machine learning on certain problems, as shown in [7,9]. We selected two widely known deterministic search algorithms:

1. BFS: Best First Search uses a list to keep track of the best candidates, it opens the best one, evaluates its child, inserts them in the list according to their evaluation, and repeats. This algorithm is complete, it will explore the entire search space given enough time.
2. BEAM: Beam Search keeps width w states open at all depth. From a depth n it opens all the children of the w states and keeps the w best ones for depth $n + 1$.

4   Results

4.1   Experimental Setup

The experiments were made using a 2.60 GHz i5-13600K Intel single core.
We define three goals of optimization:

1. Difficulty for the solver program: time spent solving it by the solver.
2. Difficulty for players: estimation by the solver.
3. Fun: estimation by the solver.

Nonograms also come in many different sizes, we decided to compare our program on sizes 5x10, 10x10, and 15x15 as these are the most common nonogram sizes used in games. Larger nonograms exist too, but the focus is usually on the picture depicted and not on the difficulty or the puzzling aspect.

Monte Carlo Search experiments require multiple runs. We observed an important standard deviation among preliminary runs, so we decided to run each algorithm 10 times over each combination of size and goal.

Finally, this method is intended to be used in real-time by games for player versus player, or survival (like Tetris for example) game modes for example. In these game modes small new nonograms must be generated as fast as the player solves them so we decided to set the optimization time to 60 s on an Intel Core i5-13600K using a single core. This method is also fit for generating regular low-quality nonogram games, or daily challenges.

For Hyperparameters, BEAM uses a width of 10, UCT a learning ratio of 1, RAVE a threshold of 5, NMCS a level of 2, NRPA a level of 2, and LNMCS a level of 3, pruning ratio of 0.8 and 3 playouts per estimation.

4.2 Optimizing the Solver Difficulty

The solver was made to behave like a human, thus the time taken to solve a nonogram is indicative of its difficulty, but it is also an interesting task by itself as a benchmark for estimating MCS algorithms performances. The solving times of graphs optimized to be more complex to the solver by all algorithms are presented in Table 1.

Table 1. Mean solving times of 10 nonograms each generated in 60 s in seconds, greater values indicate success from the Monte Carlo optimization algorithm

	BFS	BEAM	UCT	RAVE	NMCS	LNMCS	NRPA
5x5	0.000417	0.000181	0.00150	0.00121	0.00179	0.00180	0.000131
5x10	0.0200	0.00219	0.226	0.145	0.103	0.0963	0.00272
10x10	0.0221	0.00305	0.591	0.568	0.308	0.563	0.0286
15x15	0.00995	0.00254	9.578	10.466	3.066	13.07	1.741

4.3 Optimizing the Estimated Player Difficulty

To estimate the difficulty for a human player, we focus on three metrics:

1. The number of steps required to solve the puzzle
2. The number of times edge guessing is required
3. The number of times backtracking is required (the next available move is not in vicinity)

Only focusing on the number of steps like in [1] would not result in an actually difficult puzzle, but in tedious ones (like the one shown in Fig. 4 of their paper). While the difficulty and tediousness often overlap in nonograms, and a minimum number of steps is required to make a hard enough puzzle, the number of steps is not sufficient to build difficult nonograms, and is here the least important part of the evaluation. The other two members of the difficulty estimation are the number of times the player must backtrack to find a new available move (the move is N cells away from any modified cells last), this is the most important part of the equation and where we think resides the true difficulty. The last part of the equation is the number of advanced deterministic guessing techniques the player must use (edge guessing), puzzles must refrain from using too many of these in order to remain enjoyable, as such only the reward follows a square root function.

$$difficulty(N) = n(N) + \sqrt{g(N)} * 50 + d(N) * 10$$

where N is the solution to the nonogram, $n(N)$ the number of steps in that solution, $g(N)$ the number of deterministic guessing, and $d(N)$ the number of times no move is found in the 7 lines and rows checked after making a move. The factors (50 and 10) were set to these values because a long backtracking is approximately 10 times more complex and time-consuming for a human than executing moves found directly. A deterministic guessing can be simple or very hard, for the sake of the method's simplicity it is set 50, but could be computed more accurately depending on what happens during the guessing, or set to higher values like 100 by default.

The estimated difficulty scores of graph optimized by all algorithms are presented in Table 2.

Table 2. Mean estimated difficulty scores of 10 nonograms each generated in 60 s

	BFS	BEAM	UCT	RAVE	NMCS	LNMCS	NRPA
5x5	103.710	103.710	158.670	148.930	168.956	166.241	96.536
5x10	112	112	197.533	184.609	211.582	212.475	116.202
10x10	181.602	217	277.778	280.949	271.944	272.314	198.370
15x15	299	401	308.975	313.443	320.596	296.749	282.483

4.4 Optimizing the Fun

Estimating the human player's fun is a harder task as it is even more subjective. According to players, the fun is "like dominos or finishing a jigsaw puzzle, seeing something meticulously set up and solved line by line finally stepping back to look at the result, it's satisfying because of completion itself", or "solving any nonogram gives me a dopamine hit, but the bigger ones definitely hit harder.". Other players find satisfaction in hard puzzles (but we are not going to use this definition of fun in this section), otherwise the puzzles are generally fun by default, unless they are unfun.

An unfun puzzle can be defined as unnecessarily tedious and frustrating. As such, the number of total steps, edge guessing, and backtracking must be limited with some tolerance to avoid making the puzzles so simple they become tedious again.

To avoid puzzles so easy they become unfun, one of the terms in the parenthesis favors balance between the number of black and white cells. The other is the kurtosis value of the lengths of the moves of the solution. Both are multiplied by the number of unique lengths of the moves of the solution because players enjoy the most variety.

$$fun(N) = \left(\frac{4 * b(N)w(N)}{s(N)^2} - k(N) \right) * u(N) + 5 - max(d(N), 5) - g(N)^2$$

where N is the solution to the nonogram, $s(N)$ the size of the grid (number of cells), $k(N)$ the kurtosis of the lengths of the moves used, $u(N)$ the number of moves of different lengths used, $b(N)$ the number of black cells, $w(n)$ the number of white cells, $n(N)$ the number of steps in that solution, $g(N)$ the number of deterministic guessing, and $d(N)$ the number of times no move is found in the 7 lines and rows checked after making a move. Like with the difficulty, this function is an attempt to model the fun. It is to be improved, ideally supported by puzzles rated by players, which we do not have.

The estimated fun scores of graph optimized by all algorithms are presented in Table 3.

Table 3. Mean estimated fun scores of 10 nonograms each generated in 60 s

	BFS	BEAM	UCT	RAVE	NMCS	LNMCS	NRPA
5x5	12.765	12.765	12.765	12.696	12.765	12.765	11.099
5x10	14.008	0	16.523	15.642	16.959	17.072	14.326
10x10	18.596	0	19.807	18.540	20.213	19.888	16.417
15x15	18.976	0	13.577	12.113	11.663	13.235	16.225

4.5   Overview of the Solver's Estimations

To assess our estimation function and solver, we ran it on 150 nonograms, in Fig. 3 we show 15 of them and their fun scores, difficulty scores, and solving times.

5   Discussion

With the optimization of the solver's time on Table 1: finding nonograms complex enough to maximize the time spent by the solver solving it, the size 15x15 is too large for most algorithms and does not allow to collect reliable data as the solver is rapidly countered by UCT, RAVE, LNMCS, and even NMCS despite showing inferior solving times. The standard deviation is high enough that LNMCS performance can be attributed to luck (UCT 5.019, RAVE 3.550, LNMCS 8.323, NMCS 2.544, NRPA 0.869). But this does not indicate that the solver is underperforming as seen in Fig. 3 where it solves most nonograms rapidly. On lower grid sizes, LNMCS, UCT and RAVE are similar, with standard deviations of approximately 0.3 on 10x10. NMCS and NRPA are outperformed by the other MCS algorithms. BFS and BEAM results are even lower, this may be due to the use of playouts which produce complex puzzles without the need to evaluate at each step (MCS algorithms only evaluate at the end), leading the deterministic algorithms to be left behind with larger grids. However, deterministic algorithms seem to perform better on small grids.

The optimization of the estimation of difficulty with a handmade function on Table 2 shows most MCS algorithms providing similar scores. The standard deviation is approximately 30 with all the MCS algorithms for size 15x15. Differences

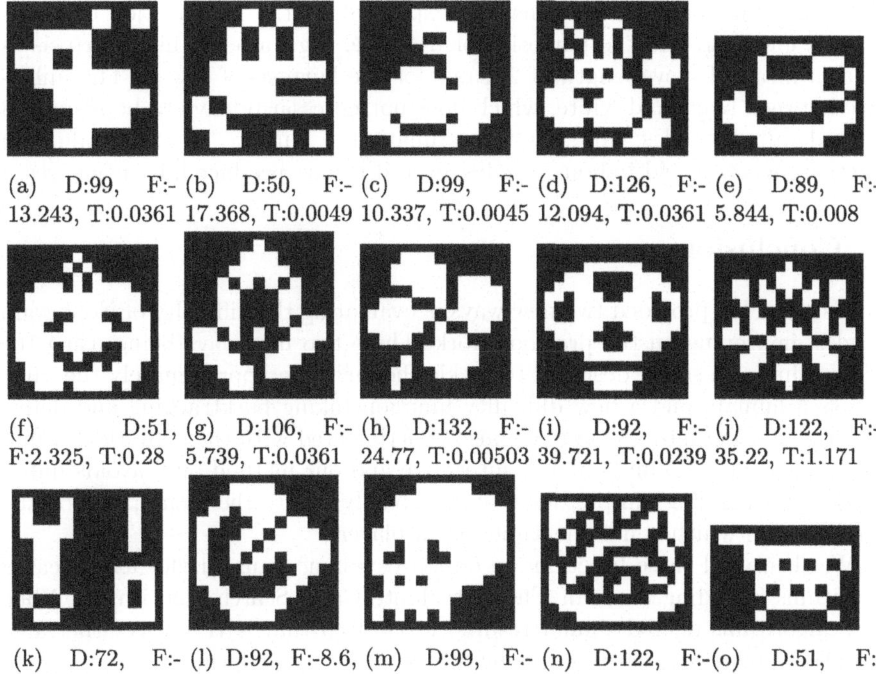

(a) D:99, F:- (b) D:50, F:- (c) D:99, F:- (d) D:126, F:- (e) D:89, F:-
13.243, T:0.0361 17.368, T:0.0049 10.337, T:0.0045 12.094, T:0.0361 5.844, T:0.008

(f)   D:51, (g) D:106, F:- (h) D:132, F:- (i) D:92, F:- (j) D:122, F:-
F:2.325, T:0.28 5.739, T:0.0361 24.77, T:0.00503 39.721, T:0.0239 35.22, T:1.171

(k) D:72, F:- (l) D:92, F:-8.6, (m) D:99, F:- (n) D:122, F:-(o) D:51, F:
1.833, T:0.0207 T:0.0289   13.243, T:0.0361 81.372, T:9.812 2.325, T: 0.235

Fig. 3. Solver and its estimations applied to 15 nonograms, D: difficulty score, F: fun
score, T: solving time by the solver in seconds

between UCT, RAVE, NMCS, and LNMCS are minimal and can be attributed
to their random nature. However, NRPA, the only algorithm learning a policy,
underperforms, while the BEAM search outperforms all MCS algorithms. The
proximity of the 10x10 and 15x15 difficulty scores for the MCS algorithms seem
to indicate that the solving times become too important and block the algorithms at the beginning of the search trees. BEAM evaluates the children of 10
states and goes down the search tree, thus allowing it to reach a harder puzzle.

The optimization of the estimation of fun with a handmade function on
Table 3 shows that BEAM locks itself in a local maximum. Again the MCS
algorithms share similar results, with a slight advantage for LNMCS, they all
have a standard deviation of approximately 1 for sizes 10x10 and 15x15 and
less than 0.5 for sizes 5x5 and 10x5. The 15x15 size is where our optimization
process starts to struggle to optimize the fun further, it seems adequate since the
tediousness of a puzzle increases faster than its fun with the size in our opinion.

The application of the evaluations to select 15 nonograms in Fig. 3 shows
that the difficulty score, while far from being perfect, is quite correlated to the
difficulty of the puzzles and is sometimes better at evaluating the difficulty than
the solver time. However, our attempt at a fun function is able to produce fun
puzzles when used as a goal function for optimization but fails to recognize the

fun in these nonograms. This may be explained by the penalization of deterministic guessing, and the kurtosis, for example, Fig. 3n has a high kurtosis as it has a mean of move length of 2, same for the kurtosis of Fig. 3j. The imbalance between black and white, which does not necessarily have to be respected in handcrafted puzzles, can skew the estimation of fun too. The fun evaluation function aims to avoid tedious puzzles, even if it may produce false negatives.

6   Conclusion

In this paper we provided two new ways of evaluating the difficulty of Nonogram puzzles, improving on the previous work. These two new ways being using the solving time of a solver designed to tackle the puzzle in approximately the same way as a human, and a new difficulty function taking backtracking and deterministic guessing into account. We also experimented with the definition of fun, with mixed success, fun is highly subjective and our method only avoids unfun puzzles, but can flag fun puzzles as unfun, partly due to the assumption on the fun definition which is not the same for all players.

We then used these functions to design new nonogram puzzles using search algorithms including State of The Art Monte Carlo Search algorithms. While MCS algorithms offered similar results, we noticed that NRPA was either able to learn a policy and outperform the others, or be outperformed.

Our method is apt for this task and can generate many nonograms of target difficulty rapidly. You can find the code here:

https://github.com/RoucairolMilo/nonoGen

References

1. Batenburg, K.J., Henstra, S., Kosters, W.A., Palenstijn, W.J.: Constructing simple nonograms of varying difficulty. Pure Math. Appl. (Pu. MA) **20**, 1–15 (2009)
2. Batenburg, K.J., Kosters, W.A.: On the difficulty of nonograms. ICGA J. **35**(4), 195–205 (2012)
3. Cazenave, T.: Nested Monte-Carlo Search. In: Boutilier, C. (ed.) IJCAI, pp. 456–461 (2009)
4. Gelly, S., Silver, D.: Monte-carlo tree search and rapid action value estimation in computer go. Artif. Intell. **175**(11), 1856–1875 (2011)
5. Genheden, S., et al.: AiZynthFinder: a fast, robust and flexible open-source software for retrosynthetic planning. J. Cheminf. **12**(1), 70 (2020)
6. Kocsis, L., Szepesvári, C.: Bandit based monte-carlo planning. In: Fürnkranz, J., Scheffer, T., Spiliopoulou, M. (eds.) ECML 2006. LNCS (LNAI), vol. 4212, pp. 282–293. Springer, Heidelberg (2006). https://doi.org/10.1007/11871842_29
7. Mehrabian, A., et al.: Finding increasingly large extremal graphs with alphazero and tabu search. arXiv preprint arXiv:2311.03583 (2023)
8. Rosin, C.D.: Nested rollout policy adaptation for monte carlo tree search. In: In IJCAI, pp. 649–654 (2011)
9. Roucairol, M., Cazenave, T.: Refutation of spectral graph theory conjectures with monte carlo search. In: International Computing and Combinatorics Conference, pp. 162–176. Springer (2022). https://doi.org/10.1007/978-3-031-22105-7_15

10. Roucairol, M., Cazenave, T.: Solving the hydrophobic-polar model with nested monte carlo search. In: International Conference on Computational Collective Intelligence, pp. 619–631. Springer (2023). https://doi.org/10.1007/978-3-031-41774-0_49
11. Silver, D., et al.: Mastering the game of Go with deep neural networks and tree search. Nature **529**, 484–489 (2016)
12. Wiggers, W., van Bergen, W.: A comparison of a genetic algorithm and a depth first search algorithm applied to Japanese nonograms. In: Twente student conference on IT. Citeseer (2004)

Solving Nonograms: A Constraint Satisfaction Approach

Abik Aramian[(⊠)] and Varduhi Yeghiazaryan[iD]

American University of Armenia, Yerevan, Armenia
{aaramian,vyeghiazaryan}@aua.am
https://cse.aua.am/

Abstract. This paper explores automated Nonogram solving using a constraint satisfaction problem (CSP) formulation. Nonograms require players to use numerical clues to color cells in a grid and reveal a hidden image. Our approach decomposes the puzzle into separate CSPs for each row and column, where the starting positions of clues are treated as variables, with constraints ensuring non-overlapping and sufficient spacing. Once these individual CSPs are solved, the entire puzzle board is modeled as a single CSP, with rows and columns as variables and constraints enforcing cell color consistency at intersections. To efficiently solve the puzzle, we employ inference and backtracking techniques, enhanced by Nonogram-specific logical analysis. We conduct comparative analyses with established solving methods to evaluate the effectiveness of our proposed approach. Experimental results demonstrate the efficiency of our CSP formulation and automated solving algorithm.

Keywords: CSP · Nonogram · Inference · Backtracking · Bitmasking · Artificial intelligence · Constraint programming · Puzzle solving

1 Introduction

Nonograms [3,4], also known as Picross, Griddlers, or 'picture logic puzzles,' are engaging logic puzzles from Japan that challenge players to reveal hidden images on a grid using numerical clues. These puzzles come in both black-and-white and color variants, with the clues indicating the lengths of consecutive filled cells in each row and column. Our focus is on black-and-white Nonograms, where players systematically fill or leave cells blank. A sample black-and-white Nonogram puzzle is shown in Fig. 1a; Fig. 1b shows the solution of the same puzzle.

The focus on Nonograms arises from their complexity and problem-solving potential. They are well-suited for constraint satisfaction problems [9] (CSPs) because they involve managing multiple interacting constraints. Using CSPs, one can devise an optimal Nonogram solving process, demonstrating practical uses of advanced computational methods. Existing CSP-based methods [3,10] often model the entire puzzle as a single CSP, which makes solving the puzzle

M. Hartisch et al. (Eds.): CG 2024, LNCS 15550, pp. 130–141, 2025.
https://doi.org/10.1007/978-3-031-86585-5_11

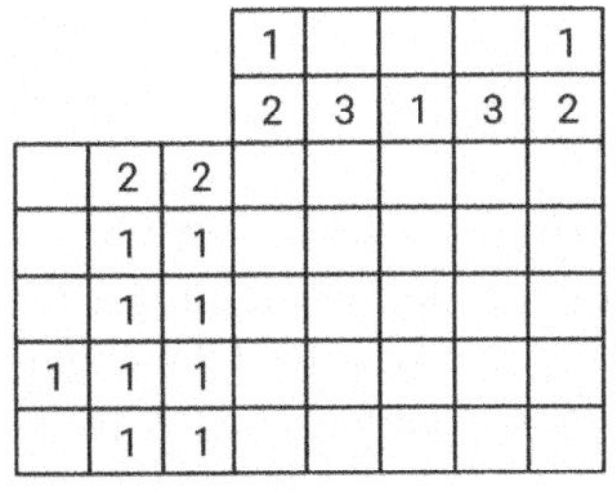

(a) 5 × 5 Nonogram

(b) solved Nonogram

Fig. 1. (a) An empty Nonogram puzzle and (b) its solution. The first row clue sequence, 2 and 2, denotes two adjacent filled cells, then another two adjacent filled cells, separated by at least one blank cell.

inherently sequential and computationally intensive. By contrast, our approach decomposes the Nonogram problem into smaller, independent row and column CSPs. This decomposition simplifies the initial solving stages. It enables efficient parallelization, allowing each row/column CSP to be processed concurrently through multiprocessing. This increases the scalability of the solution, particularly for large puzzles. Once the row and column CSPs are solved, the main Nonogram CSP is formulated as the task of correctly combining the solutions of individual rows and columns into a Nonogram solution. To the best of our knowledge, no prior CSP formulations and solvers of Nonograms have decomposed the puzzle into multiple CSPs or utilized parallelization for row/column solving.

We formulate Nonogram puzzles as CSPs and solve them using inference and backtracking techniques [9], complemented by Nonogram-specific logical analysis methods, to enhance solution efficiency. A CSP consists of variables, each with a domain of possible values, and constraints that limit the combinations of these values. For Nonograms, we break down the puzzle into distinct CSPs for each row and column, treating the starting positions of clues as variables constrained to ensure proper spacing and non-overlap. The entire puzzle board is then modeled as a single CSP where the rows and columns become the variables with domains derived from the solutions of the row and column CSPs. Constraints are applied to maintain color consistency at cell intersections. By narrowing down the solution space through deductive reasoning and by adopting a bitmasking [6] approach, we minimize computational complexity while maintaining accuracy, thus enhancing the scalability of our solution. The bitmasking approach stores each cell in a single bit, significantly reducing memory usage compared to the boolean approach and enabling efficient processing of large, complex puzzles.

We evaluate the efficiency of our CSP approach through comparisons with alternative Nonogram solving techniques, demonstrating our approach's capability to efficiently solve various puzzles.

2   Literature Review

2.1   Nonogram Solving Approaches

Various innovative approaches have been developed to automatically solve Nonograms, enhancing both efficiency and accuracy. Khan [7] proposes an integer linear programming (ILP) formulation with binary decision variables to navigate the solution space, employing techniques such as *branch and bound* to prune infeasible branches and improve computational performance. Tran [10], with a CSP formulation, assigns a variable to each cell with a Boolean filled/blank domain, utilizing regular and ternary constraints. The solving process is streamlined through consistency algorithms and heuristics.

Więckowski and Shekhovtsov [11] comparatively analyze a modified depth-first search (DFS) and a soft computing algorithms, that tackle the problem through recursive exploration and heuristic-driven grid filling, respectively. While efficiency in solving the puzzles is important, their results reveal that for larger Nonograms, these algorithms' performance degrades in case of complex puzzles. The comparative analysis in the thesis by Zavistanavičius [15] highlights that while depth-first search is effective for smaller puzzles, constraint programming outperforms it for larger grids (over 20×20) and is suitable for mobile devices.

In [14], logical rules are first utilized to fill in cells that can be solved deterministically, and then chronological backtracking is employed to address the remaining cells, offering a balanced approach of logic-based solving followed by exploration. A similar strategy is observed in [13], where fast dynamic programming (DP) is used for line solving, and fully probing (FP) methods are proposed to solve more cells, further enhancing efficiency in complex grids, before resorting to backtracking.

The WebPBN survey [12] showcases notable solvers like those by Wolter, Wu, Syromolotov, Olšák, Lagerkvist, Kjellerstrand, Wilk, and from Ben-Gurion University (BGU). These solvers employ diverse strategies, including backtracking, logical inference, heuristic-driven search, constraint satisfaction, SAT solvers, and constraint logic programming (CLP), greatly contributing to the understanding and efficiency of Nonogram solving.

Recently, in a wave of massive innovation, neural networks (NNs) [8] have been explored to enhance traditional algorithms such as DFS and genetic algorithms (GAs). By leveraging pattern recognition and heuristic generation, fully connected NN architectures transform puzzle clues into board states, significantly advancing the capabilities of Nonogram solvers. However, direct comparisons with any additional approaches are not covered in [8].

2.2   Benchmarking Platforms and Datasets

In the realm of Nonogram-solving research, the availability and selection of benchmarking datasets play a crucial role in the evaluation of algorithmic effectiveness. Several datasets have emerged as standard benchmarks, enabling researchers to compare the performance of their methods across a variety of puzzle complexities and sizes.

Survey of Paint-by-Number Puzzle Solvers: A notable dataset in this field is the collection of 2491 black and white Nonogram puzzles from the 'Survey of Paint-by-Number Puzzle Solvers' [12]. This dataset is widely used for its diverse range of puzzle complexities and structures and has served as a benchmark for evaluating various algorithms. Although the original developers—Syromolotov (C++), Wu (C), BGU (MiniZinc), Olšák (C++), Lagerkvist (C++), Wilk (C), and Kjellerstrand (C++, MiniZinc)—did not directly use this dataset for development, Wolter collected and compared their algorithms in the survey, benchmarking the major Nonogram-solving techniques of the time.

Hanjie Dataset: A comprehensive collection of 8151 black and white puzzles is available in the online Hanjie dataset [2]. This dataset contains puzzles of varying difficulty levels and sizes, providing a robust platform for testing algorithm scalability and performance. The diversity within this dataset makes it an excellent benchmark for thoroughly evaluating Nonogram solvers.

3   Nonogram CSP: Formulations and Solving Techniques

Nonograms are grid-based logic puzzles that can be effectively formulated as a CSP. We formulate the puzzle as a set of row and column CSPs, where each row and column is treated independently, and a single Nonogram CSP that relies on the solutions of the individual row/column CSPs.

Our approach is different for several reasons. First, we introduce two types of CSPs: row/column CSPs and Nonogram CSP. In our formulation, the row/column CSPs are solved independently first, where the variables are linked to the number of clues in each row or column. Once these CSPs are solved, the Nonogram CSP becomes significantly smaller, reducing the complexity of the problem. Specifically, while traditional approaches might handle a large number of variables at once, our method reduces the Nonogram CSP to just $n + m$ variables (where n is number of rows and m is number of columns) leading to fewer variables than other CSP approaches. Additionally, solving the row/column CSPs first reduces the domain sizes for the variables in the Nonogram CSP, which streamlines the final solving process and improves overall efficiency.

3.1   Row and Column CSPs

In this approach, each row and column of the Nonogram is represented as a separate CSP $(r_1, r_2, \ldots, r_n, c_1, c_2, \ldots, c_m)$, resulting in a total of $n + m$ CSPs, where n is the number of rows and m is the number of columns.

The variables $\mathcal{X}$ for these CSPs are the starting positions of the sequences of filled cells, and the number of variables, $|\mathcal{X}|$, in each CSP is the total number of clues in that specific row/column. In Fig. 1, the variables of r_1, r_2, c_1, c_2, for example, are $\mathcal{X}^{r_1} = \{X_1^{r_1}, X_2^{r_1}\}$, $\mathcal{X}^{r_2} = \{X_1^{r_2}, X_2^{r_2}\}$, $\mathcal{X}^{c_1} = \{X_1^{c_1}, X_2^{c_1}\}$, $\mathcal{X}^{c_2} = \{X_1^{c_2}\}$, respectively.

The domain D for each variable (i.e. clue) in $\mathcal{X}$ constitutes all potential starting positions within its respective row/column for the sequence it specifies. The size of the domain of each variable is $l + 1 - v$, where $l \in \{m, n\}$ is the length of the corresponding row/column and v is the value of the clue. The domains of all variables in the first row CSP, r_1, are

$$\mathcal{D}^{r_1} = \left\{ D_1^{r_1} = \{1, 2, 3, 4\}, D_2^{r_1} = \{1, 2, 3, 4\} \right\}. \tag{1}$$

The domain of the only variable in the second column CSP, c_2, is

$$\mathcal{D}^{c_2} = \left\{ D_1^{c_2} = \{1, 2, 3\} \right\}. \tag{2}$$

The constraints in Nonogram puzzles require each row and column to adhere to the sequence lengths given by the clues, with sequences separated by at least one blank cell. These must fit within the grid without overlapping. There is a constraint between each pair of adjacent clues. Hence, each row/column CSP has one less constraint than the number of its variables. A CSP with only one variable has no constraints.

For the Nonogram in Fig. 1, r_1 has two variables, $X_1^{r_1}, X_2^{r_1}$. Hence, it has only one constraint $C_1^{r_1}$:

$$C_1^{r_1} : X_1^{r_1} + 2 < X_2^{r_1}. \tag{3}$$

This constraint enforces that the block of 2 filled cells (as per variable $X_1^{r_1}$ for the left clue) strictly precedes the block of 2 filled cells (as per variable $X_2^{r_1}$ for the right clue) with at least one blank cell between them.

The number of solutions for each row/column CSP varies due to differing clues. The minimum is 1 when the sum of clues and gaps equals the row/column length. The maximum occurs with only clues of value 1, calculated as $\binom{l-j+1}{j}$, where j is the number of clues on that specific row/column.

3.2   Nonogram CSP

While the row and column CSPs help decompose the Nonogram puzzle into manageable units, the Nonogram CSP integrates these elements into a complete problem representation.

In the Nonogram CSP, variables are the rows and columns, encoded as binary sequences based on clues. There are $n + m$ variables. For the Nonogram in Fig. 1, with 5 rows and 5 columns, there are 10 variables: $R_1, \ldots, R_5$ for rows and $C_1, \ldots, C_5$ for columns.

The domain of each variable includes all valid configurations based on the row/column clues. The domains are denoted as $D_{R_1}, \ldots, D_{R_n}, D_{C_1}, \ldots, D_{C_m}$. Each solution of the row CSP r_i ($i \in 1..n$) or column CSP c_j ($j \in 1..m$) corresponds to a value in the domain D_{R_i} or D_{C_j}, respectively. Thus, the domain size $|D_{R_i}|$ equals the number of solutions for r_i, and $|D_{C_j}|$ equals the number of solutions for c_j.

For the Nonogram in Fig. 1, the variable domains in the Nonogram CSP are $D_{R_1}, \ldots, D_{R_5}, D_{C_1}, \ldots, D_{C_5}$. The domain D_{R_2} of the second row, e.g., is

$$D_{R_2} = \{10100, 10010, 10001, 01010, 01001, 00101\}. \tag{4}$$

The domain D_{C_2} of the second column is

$$D_{C_2} = \{11100, 01110, 00111\}. \tag{5}$$

The constraint in the Nonogram CSP is consistency at each cell where row and column variables intersect. If a row variable indicates a cell should be filled, the corresponding column variable must agree, and vice versa. The number of constraints equals the grid size, $n \times m$. For example, the first row variable R_1 participates in m constraints, one for each column variable. For the Nonogram in Fig. 1, there are $5 \times 5 = 25$ constraints.

For any row variable $R_i, i \in 1..n$, and any column variable $C_j, j \in 1..m$, there is a constraint Ct_{ij} that enforces the color of the jth cell of the row variable R_i to match the color of the ith cell of the column variable C_j:

$$Ct_{ij} : R_i[j] = C_j[i]. \tag{6}$$

For example, constraints with R_1 are $Ct_{11}, Ct_{12}, \ldots, Ct_{1m}$, and constraints with C_2 are $Ct_{12}, Ct_{22}, \ldots, Ct_{n2}$. As we can see R_1 and C_2 share the same constraint Ct_{12} because cell $(1, 2)$ is their intersection, and to satisfy the constraint their intersecting cell should have the same color in both variables:

$$Ct_{12} : R_1[2] = C_2[1]. \tag{7}$$

3.3   Solving Row/Column CSPs

In the row/column CSP representation, we perform backtracking search on each row CSP and each column CSP individually. We begin the search by generating the first solution with black cells on the left/top side of the row/column. We then initiate a shifting process by moving the last group of black cells towards the end of the row/column. When we successfully reach the end, we backtrack to the initial solution and proceed to shift the last two groups of black cells. The shifting process is repeated on the last group until reaching the end again. This cycle continues: when the last two groups reach the end, we backtrack to the initial solution and shift the last three groups, repeating the entire process. We progressively shift more groups until we generate the final solution where all black cells are placed on the far right/down side with a white space between each pair of consecutive groups. This shifting approach ensures the exploration and construction of all possible solutions within the given row/column CSP, automatically ensuring the satisfaction of all constraints.

The visualization in Fig. 2 shows the enumeration (left part of the figure) of all possible states for a row with 3 clues. The steps (right part of the figure) of our algorithm are provided to indicate how each solution is generated.

3.4 Solving Nonogram CSP

To solve the Nonogram CSP, we employ both constraint propagation and back-tracking search methods.

Constraint Propagation: This technique reduces the problem space by enforcing constraints early in the solving process. We propagate constraints by utilizing disjunction (OR) and conjunction (AND) operations on the domain of a selected row/column variable. This process yields two distinct tuples.

- The result of disjunction (OR) operations indicates guaranteed white cells.
- The result of conjunction (AND) operations indicates guaranteed black cells.

These two tuples are used to filter the domains of intersecting row/column variables for values that do not align with them. This iterative process significantly narrows down the domains of the variables and continues until no further reductions can be made. If the Nonogram has a unique solution and can be fully solved without guessing, constraint propagation alone solves the puzzle without the need for further search methods.

Figure 3a illustrates the generation of the AND-tuple by applying conjunction on D_{C_2}. Figure 4 demonstrates the filtering of D_{R_3} using C_2 AND-tuple. The filtering process is applied only to R_3 due to the presence of a single black guarantee in the third term in the AND-tuple. Figure 3b illustrates the follow-up generation of the OR-tuple by applying disjunction on D_{R_3}. There are two

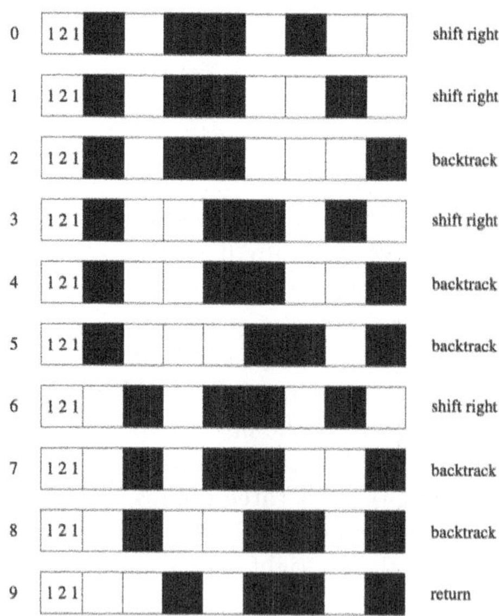

Fig. 2. Visualization of the backtracking process for solving a row CSP through shifts. The numbers on the left represent the order in which solutions are constructed. 'Shift right' moves the last group of black cells one cell to the right; 'backtrack' resets the tuple; 'return' stops the process.

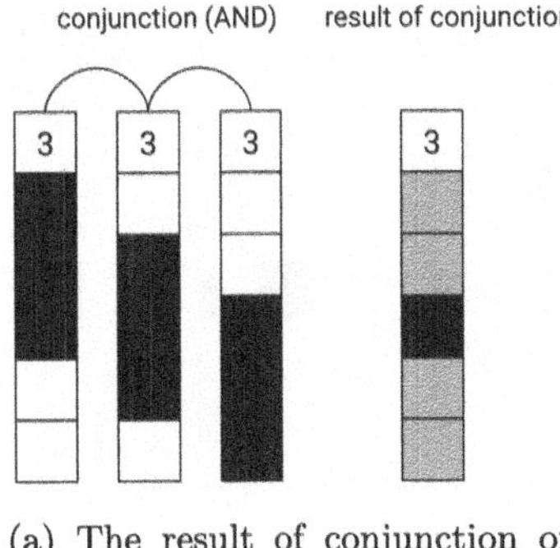

(a) The result of conjunction on the domain of C_2.

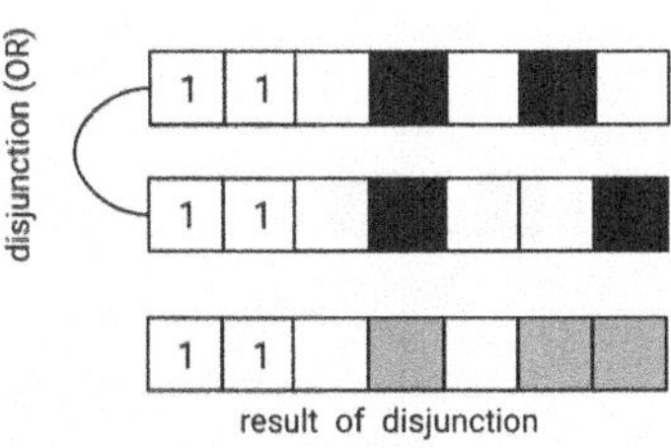

(b) The result of disjunction on the domain of R_3.

Fig. 3. Examples of conjunction and disjunction on row/column variable domains. The gray cells represent undecided values. The black cell in (a) is guaranteed to be black. The white cells in (b) are guaranteed to be white. (Color figure online)

white guarantees in the first and third terms, implying future filtering of D_{C_1} and D_{C_3}.

Backtracking Search: Some Nonograms have multiple solutions, requiring more than just constraint propagation. We use backtracking, but its efficiency, in general, depends on implementation. Our approach relies on a fixed ordering of variables: $R_1, C_1, R_2, C_2, \ldots$ To ensure value consistency between the next unassigned variable and all already assigned variables, we maintain values in domains in a sorted order (consistent with Eqs. 4 and 5) and utilize *binary search* to identify the sub-domain of consistent values.

3.5 Implementation Details

We use Java with an 8GB heap size. We employ bitmasking [6], where each cell is represented by a single bit. There are three types of bitmasks: values in domains of variables, AND-tuples, and OR-tuples. For values in domains, a 1-bit represents a filled cell, while a 0-bit is a blank. In an AND-tuple, a 1-bit corresponds to a guarantee filled cell (black in Fig. 3a), while a 0-bit denotes an undecided cell (gray in Fig. 3a). Finally, for OR-tuples, a 1-bit is an undecided cell (gray in Fig. 3b) and a 0-bit is a blank guarantee (white in Fig. 3b).

With bitmasking, 8 cells may require as little as 1 byte (8 bits) of storage instead of 8 bytes (64 bits) if using `booleans`. We store each value in an array of 32-bit integers. The size of the array becomes $\lceil \frac{l}{32} \rceil$, where $l \in \{m, n\}$. In the worst case, 31 bits may be wasted (e.g., if $l = 65$, we allocate an array of three `ints`, thus using 96 bits, out of which 31 are discarded). In Fig. 5, the visualization shows the difference between our bitmasking approach and the `boolean` approach in terms of memory consumption in bytes per number of cells. Since the `boolean` approach consumes 1 byte per cell, the memory increases linearly with the number of cells. The memory consumption of the bitmasking

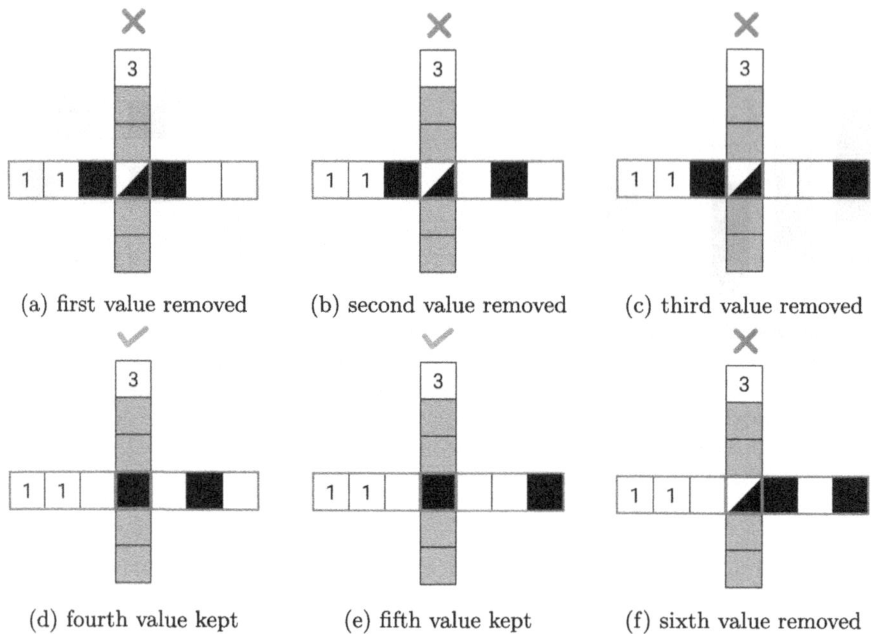

(a) first value removed   (b) second value removed   (c) third value removed

(d) fourth value kept   (e) fifth value kept   (f) sixth value removed

Fig. 4. Filtering D_{R_3} by utilizing C_2 AND-tuple. Gray cells represent undecided values, blank cells are white, filled cells are black, and half-black and half-white cells are a mismatch between the AND-tuple and the current value in D_{R_3}. (Color figure online)

approach is a step function. The `boolean` approach consumes less memory than the bitmasking approach when $l < 4$ and more memory when $l > 4$. Their difference becomes more significant with the increase of l.

To improve performance, parallelism is applied when solving row/column CSPs independently. The $n+m$ tasks are distributed dynamically across multiple execution processes using an `ArrayBlockingQueue` [1,5].

4   Experimental Evaluation

In this section, we present a benchmarking analysis of our algorithm against existing state-of-the-art (SOTA) methods. The experiments were performed on a MacBook Pro M1 with 16GB of RAM. Each solver was executed three times, and the average of the three execution times is reported to ensure consistent performance measurement. We used the earlier-discussed datasets [2,12] with 2491 and 8151 black-and-white Nonogram puzzles, respectively. All puzzles from these datasets have unique solutions and can be solved by humans, which allows our solver to use inference only, without the need for backtracking.

The SOTA algorithms tested include the seven top-performers from the Wolter survey [12] and the two algorithms from [11] (we denote them MDFS and SC). The implementations for the latter two were kindly provided by the authors,

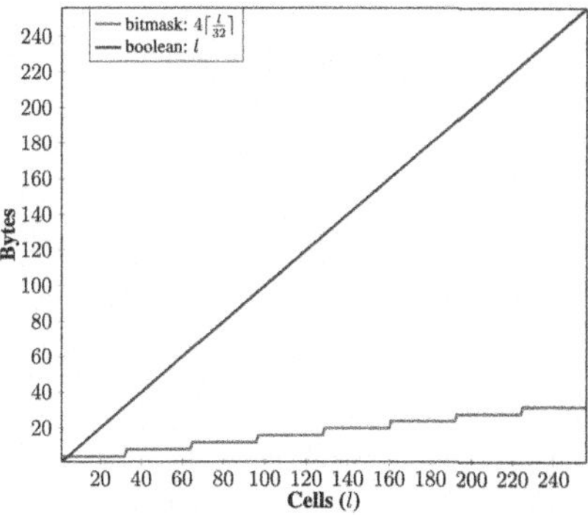

Fig. 5. Comparison between our bitmasking approach and `boolean` approach in terms of memory consumption.

per our request. We were unable to get implementations of any other SOTA algorithms. Unfortunately, this includes CSP-based solvers like [10]. It is important to note that the different algorithms expect different formats for the Nonogram input and are implemented using different programming languages and libraries. This makes a direct comparison of execution times somewhat biased, but it still allows us to draw general conclusions.

Table 1 summarizes the numbers of puzzles solved by each algorithm within specific time ranges, in seconds (s), on the 2491 puzzles. 100 puzzles were too large for the default setting of the Wu solver, hence we report results for 2391 puzzles. We report two implementations of our algorithm: $Our_{parallel}$ denotes the main version of our algorithm that utilizes parallel processing for row/column CSP solution; $Our_{sequential}$ makes this phase completely sequential. This separation allows for a fair comparison against traditionally sequential solvers.

Solvers by Wolter, Syromolotov, and our solver are highly efficient, solving more than 99% of all puzzles in under 0.1 s. Wolter's and Syromolotov's solvers overcome the hardest puzzle in under 0.5 s; ours achieves it in less than 10 s. All other solvers take at least 60 s for the hardest puzzles. Among these, MDFS and SC struggle with speed, taking significantly longer times for most puzzles. Lagerkvist's and Kjellerstrand's solvers display more balanced performance, overcoming 98–99% of the puzzles in under 60 s. Overall, the results highlight substantial differences in speed and effectiveness among the solvers; our solver performs comparably to the fastest two (both C++ in contrast to our Java).

Table 2 presents the percentage of puzzles solved by each algorithm within two minutes for the larger, more challenging dataset of 8,151 Nonogram puzzles [2]. These results provide insight into the solvers' efficiency across a diverse set of puzzles. The algorithm ranking is largely consistent with the results of the previous comparison.

The two implementations of our algorithm differ in the use of multiprocessing when solving row/column CSPs. For the dataset of 2491 puzzles, on average, this

Table 1. The performance of different solvers on the 2491 puzzles, categorized by the time taken to solve each puzzle (in seconds). Time ranges are divided into intervals from 0 to infinity, indicating the efficiency of each solver.

Solver	Number of puzzles solved per time range (s)								
	0.00 0.09	0.10 0.19	0.20 0.49	0.50 0.99	1.00 3.99	4.00 9.99	10.00 29.99	30.00 59.99	60 ∞
Wolter	2486	4	1	0	0	0	0	0	0
Olšák	2434	7	6	9	7	5	5	6	12
Wu	2380	5	4	2	0	0	0	0	0
Syromolotov	2484	4	3	0	0	0	0	0	0
Lagerkvist	2426	6	5	8	7	11	10	8	10
Kjellerstrand	2411	3	5	7	6	9	12	16	22
Wilk	2187	24	43	48	63	33	21	20	52
MDFS	49	112	98	86	51	62	611	512	910
SC	352	82	72	49	55	332	203	312	1034
$\text{Our}_{\text{sequential}}$	2450	31	3	5	1	1	0	0	0
$\text{Our}_{\text{parallel}}$	2472	9	3	5	1	1	0	0	0

Table 2. For each solver, percentage of the 8151 puzzles solved in < 2 mins.

Solver Name	Wolter	Syromolotov	$\text{Our}_{\text{parallel}}$	$\text{Our}_{\text{sequential}}$	Olšák	Lagerkvist	Kjellerstrand	Wilk	Wu	SC	MDFS
Solved (%)	87.1	86.9	**86.4**	**86.1**	85.4	85.1	84.8	82.0	69.6	30.3	18.5

phase in $\text{Our}_{\text{sequential}}$ is around 3.3 times slower in comparison with $\text{Our}_{\text{parallel}}$. As a result, the total time for solving a Nonogram puzzle is, on average, 2.7 times that of $\text{Our}_{\text{parallel}}$. This parallelization shows clear performance gains. Further speed-ups could be achieved with higher-core-count processors or a shift to a more performance-optimized language, such as C++.

5   Conclusion and Future Work

This paper proposed a novel CSP formulation and a solving technique for Nonogram puzzles. We formulated rows and columns as individual CSPs and the entire board as a single, more complex CSP. Our solving algorithm utilized specialized constraint propagation for unique-solution, no-guess puzzles, and introduced follow-up backtracking, otherwise. The algorithm was implemented with time and space efficiency and, hence, scalability in mind, through the utilization of bitmasking, parallelization and other algorithmic enhancements. The extensive benchmarking against the SOTA showed the efficiency of our algorithm.

Future work will focus on refining the backtracking algorithm and enhancing the inference process for multi-solution puzzles. We also aim to tackle color Nonograms, which add complexity with multiple colors and constraints, by developing specialized CSP formulations and algorithms for those.

References

1. ArrayBlockingQueue: JDK 21 api specification. https://docs.oracle.com/en/java/javase/21/docs/api/java.base/java/util/concurrent/ArrayBlockingQueue.html. Accessed Sept 11 2024
2. Hanjie dataset. https://github.com/susarip/test/blob/master/hanjie_scraper/hanjie_scraper/hanjie.csv. Accessed 20 Apr 2024
3. Batenburg, K.J., Henstra, S., Kosters, W.A., Palenstijn, W.J.: Constructing simple nonograms of varying difficulty. Pure Math. Appl. (Pu. MA) **20**, 1–15 (2009)
4. Berend, D., Pomeranz, D., Rabani, R., Raziel, B.: Nonograms: combinatorial questions and algorithms. Discret. Appl. Math. **169**, 30–42 (2014)
5. Deitel, P., Deitel, H.: Java: How to Program. Pearson Education, tenth edn. (2015)
6. Halim, S., Halim, F.: Competitive programming 3: The New Lower Bound of Programming Contests. Lulu, third edn. (2013)
7. Khan, K.A.: Solving nonograms using integer programming without coloring. IEEE Trans. Games **14**(1), 56–63 (2020)
8. Buades Rubio, J.M., Jaume-i-Capó, A., López González, D., Moyà Alcover, G.: Solving nonograms using neural networks. Entertain. Comput. **50**, 100652 (2024). https://doi.org/10.1016/j.entcom.2024.100652
9. Russell, S., Norvig, P.: Artificial Intelligence: A Modern Approach. Pearson, fourth edn. (2020)
10. Tran, T.H.: Modeling and Solving the Nonogram Puzzle Using Constraint Programming. Undergraduate thesis, Department of Computer Science and Engineering, University of Nebraska-Lincoln (2019)
11. Więckowski, J., Shekhovtsov, A.: Algorithms effectiveness comparison in solving nonogram boards. Proc. Comput. Sci. **192**, 1885–1893 (2021)
12. Wolter, J.: Survey of paint-by-number puzzle solvers. https://webpbn.com/survey/. Accessed Aug 5 2024
13. Wu, I.C., et al.: An efficient approach to solving nonograms. IEEE Trans. Comput. Intell. AI Games **5**(3), 251–264 (2013)
14. Yu, C.H., Lee, H.L., Chen, L.H.: An efficient algorithm for solving nonograms. Appl. Intell. **35**, 18–31 (2011)
15. Zavistanavičius, R.: Nonogram solving algorithms analysis and implementation for augmented reality system. Master's thesis, Kaunas University of Technology (2013)

Social Aspects of Games

Sexual Harassment in Valorant and Overwatch Voice Chats

Daniel Görlich[1]([⊠]) [iD], Max Wagner[2], and Markus Breuer[3]

[1] Offenburg University, Badstr. 24, 77652 Offenburg, Germany
daniel.goerlich@hs-offenburg.de
[2] Gameforge 4D GmbH, Albert-Nestler-Str 8, 76131 Karlsruhe, Germany
[3] SRH University Heidelberg, Ludwig-Guttmann-Str. 6, 69123 Heidelberg, Germany

Abstract. Unfortunately, sexism and sexual harassment are common in both private online gaming and professional esports. It has been repeatedly questioned whether the operators of multiplayer games, platforms and esports leagues are taking sufficient measures to adequately protect users, players, children, young gamers, and esports athletes. When measures are taken, such as censoring sexist or offensive chat messages or banning users, they tend to be undifferentiated. This may be partly due to a lack of surveys, studies, and data. This paper therefore presents the results of two consecutive studies using the games Overwatch and Valorant, two of the world's most popular multiplayer first-person shooters which are also played professionally in esports leagues. Participant observations were conducted on 28 Overwatch and Valorant game sessions in a first study and 120 Valorant game sessions in a second one. These sessions' voice chats were transcribed, coded, and statistically evaluated. The results indicate that female gamers are harassed in every seventh Valorant game, ranging from questions about their gender to unsolicited affection to threats of or jokes about rape.

Keywords: Harassment · E-Sport · Video Games

1 Introduction

In the US, 45% of all gamers are female [1]. In Europe [2] and in Germany [3] the figure is as high as 48%. While gaming as a hobby is enjoyed equally by all genders, playing video games is still considered by society as an activity with a male connotation [4]. This is partly due to gender-specific characteristics of usage behavior [5, 6]. Depending on different player motivations and genre preferences, there are male-dominated areas within the gaming communities where women are marginalized and negatively stereotyped [7].

In esports, the proportion of women is generally lower: [8] reported a 22% female share of esports viewers, whereby a distinction must be made between the purely online market and the market for live events [9, p. 281]. However, there are currently few reliable figures on active female players. One literature review puts the proportion of female esports players at 35% overall, but only 5% of professional players, and concludes "that women players rarely compete at the topmost level of esports" [10]. While there are games in which women make up the majority—e.g., 69% in Match3 games and family/farming simulations [6]—they are least represented in tactical shooters at 4.3%, in first-person shooters at 7.2% and in sports games at just 2% [6]. The most popular esports genres are therefore predominantly male-dominated. According to [11], the proportion of women in esports tournaments is also only around 5%.

This may be partly due to the rough interaction between players in competitive online and esports games. Female players of all ages, from children and teenagers to professionals (e.g. [12, p. 221–230]) repeatedly reported various forms of general and sexual harassment. With the Video Game Harassment Behavior (VGHB) scale, there is an instrument for recording, classifying and statistically evaluating such harassment.

2 State of the Art

Harassment, cyberbullying and hatred are widespread on the internet, in gaming and esports. A recent scoping review of 33 studies concluded that cybersexism and its manifestations "are a harsh reality" for female gamers [37]. Almost 75% of users of online multiplayer games reported experiencing at least one form of online harassment [13, 14]. Empirical studies show that women are more often victims of sexual harassment than men [15, 16]. The esports industry is largely male-dominated, with women and girls making up a smaller proportion of participants, fans, and employees [17]. In a study of ten esports participants and content creators, a glass screen (rather than a glass ceiling) not only hindered women's advancement, but participants also experienced toxic masculinity, a hostile culture toward women, and harassment.

Given the fully commercialized nature of the esports industry, it is important to assess the potential negative impact of sexism and harassment on economic figures. [18] reports that sexism is considered as a low risk threat, based on a survey sample of 1,500 esports fans. However, toxic behavior as a general issue is considered a medium risk threat. Apparently, unsportsmanlike conduct against women does not have the economic impact that would be needed to get sponsors etc. to address this issue. However, it is not just esports fans and players who have negative experiences: While most studies focus on female gamers and their experiences, [19] worked with leaders of Scandinavian esports organizations. The results showed that the experiences of the participants were highly gendered. All women reported experiences of discrimination and exclusion, while none of the male informants described such incidents.

Despite clear differences between traditional sports and esports (see [39]), sports combine masculinity, athleticism, and competition in very similar ways. The areas in which women are said to fall short (skills, ambitions, desires, and abilities) are presented as physical or mental discrepancies between the sexes and are reinforced by discursive, material, and behavioral confirmations of inferior and secondary roles for women. Any involvement in sexual harassment can be understood as reinforcing the premise of hegemonic masculinity in competitive gaming environments [10].

In addition to text chat, voice chat is a synchronous and largely unmoderated communication tool. In a 2019 survey of 1,045 participants, the Anti Defamation League (ADL) identified voice chat as the most frequently used communication tool for harassment (42%) [14]. On average, women received three times as many negative comments as men [20]. Women's successes and exceptional skills in esports are often derided or deliberately ignored [21], and their skills and achievements are judged to be inferior to those of men, despite equal performance [22, 23]. A telling example is Kim "Geguri" Seyeon from South Korea: Before she was able to start her professional career in Overwatch, she became the victim of insults, threats and mockery. Her skills were widely discredited and she was accused of using illegal third-party software [24]. This is not an isolated incident. Insults, harassment and sexism against women often occur not only in esports, but also in everyday use of the internet for gaming.

Many surveys are based solely on polls, interviews or personal experience reports and may therefore be subjectively biased. In a 2014 Pew Research Center survey of 2,800 US-American gamers, men reported more forms of online harassment, such as insults and ridicule, while women more frequently experienced more severe forms of harassment, such as harassment over a longer period of time, stalking or sexism [13]. An online survey of 151 selected MMO players about cyberbullying found that women and LGBTQ participants were more likely to be victims of sexism [15].

Currently, most data on sexism and harassment in the gaming community is based on subjective experiences. Participant observation data is much rarer. Kasumovic and Kuznekoff (2015) observed the behavior of 1,660 male and female players towards female subjects of different ranking ranges in 245 matches [25]. The number of negative comments was significantly higher for lower-ranked than for higher-ranked subjects. The authors suggest that higher-ranked players have already achieved a certain status within the game and therefore no longer need to distinguish themselves from their female teammates, while lower-ranked players compensate and defend their status by using insults and sexist harassment [25].

In [36], Fox and Tang argue that the problem of harassment in online gaming may be partly caused by anonymity: As described in the SIDE theory, deindividualization takes place, whereby the connection to oneself is lost and one becomes part of the emerging social construct. As a faceless part of a group, the anonymized person feels able to engage in anti-social behavior. Despite this anonymity, however, there are occasional clues to social identity or gender, e.g. through the choice of username, profile picture or game character [16]. In games such as League of Legends or Overwatch, there are heroes who are increasingly being played by women and are consequently more frequently the target of sexism [24, 26]. Female game characters are sometimes portrayed in a hypersexualized and objectified way. Men who predominantly confront female characters also tend to hold sexist attitudes towards women in real life [27].

In [16], Fox and Tang further describe five coping strategies for how gamers deal with sexual harassment. These include denial (e.g. ignoring or forgetting the situation), avoidance (e.g. leaving the game), seeking help (e.g. reporting the perpetrator in-game or talking to others about the experience), hiding one's identity (e.g. not using female avatars) and self-blame. These negative experiences lead affected female gamers to withdraw from the game in question. According to a survey of 2,100 participants conducted by Unity, 68% of the respondents have already been victims of at least one form of harassment in online multiplayer games. As a result, women are more likely than men to stop playing the respective video game for good [28].

3 Methodology

In order to determine through participant observation whether and what forms of harassment female gamers and e-athletes experience during voice chat gaming sessions, two female players (anonymized: P1 and P2) were initially accompanied by the second author of this paper during 19 Overwatch matches (P1) and 9 Valorant matches (P2), i.e. 28 matches in total, between February 27th, 2022, and March 7th, 2022 (9 days), as part of an initial study. Since an Overwatch match lasted an average of 13.9 min, but a Valorant match lasted an average of 30 min, the subjects played Overwatch for 264.1 min and Valorant for 270 min—almost the same amount of time.

The subjects were required to self-identify as female, use avatars and gamer tags that allowed them to be perceived as female by other players, and have extensive experience in their chosen game. They were allowed to choose which games they wanted to play as long as the games met four conditions: They had to be team-based multiplayer capable, have integrated voice chat, offer a ranked mode and belong to a genre with a low proportion of women. According to [6], tactical and first-person shooters were the main candidates in the competitive esports setting, but also sports simulations, multiplayer online battle arenas (MOBA) and massively multiplayer online games (MMOG). Subject P1 chose Overwatch. Her active playing time previously amounted to just under 600 h (as determined using the statistics in her Blizzard account). Her ranked mode was in the platinum range, corresponding to the top 37% according to the 2019 statistical update [35]. Subject P2 chose Valorant. At the start of the study, she was not yet ranked in ranked mode. In the previous season, her ranking corresponded to "Silver 3" and thus to the top 33%.

In the longer-term second study, four subjects were followed for 30 matches each between April 10th and June 25th, 2023, for a total of 120 matches, with each subject completing 3 matches of Valorant in ranked mode within 2½ hours per session. This provided more comparable conditions for the purpose of statistical evaluation. Valorant was chosen based on the results of the first study, but also because its operators are trying to make it as attractive as possible to female players and marginalized groups—with apparent success: In an interview with the Head of Esports Partnership, Matthew Archambault, at the GamesBeat Summit 2021, he stated that between 30 and 40% of the player base was female [29]. While it is debatable whether Valorant meets the aforementioned requirement of having a "low" proportion of women, the game can definitely be considered male-dominated. The four subjects selected for this second study were all in the Ascendant 1–3 ranking range at the start of the study, which corresponds to the top 7% of Valorant's player base [30].

All subjects were informed of the aim and methodology of the study when they were asked to participate. Each session took place in the familiar environment of the subjects, namely at home, a largely protected space. Team members participating via the matchmaking system, on the other hand, were not informed about the study. As audio and video recordings are not permitted under German law, the voice chats were recorded live in written form. The subjects were only given the task of playing in ranked mode and participating in the voice chat. They were neither given any instructions on how or how intensively to use the voice chat, nor were they required to actively use the voice chat. The use of voice chat was meant to be habitual and intuitive. Due to the explosive nature of the topic of sexual harassment and its potential consequences, the subjects were free to end a game or session at any time, use the tools available in Valorant to mute other players, or leave the voice chat. Nevertheless, it cannot be completely ruled out that the subjects used the voice chat differently than usual during the observation, or that they reacted to harassment differently than usual.

The data were collected and processed by the observer using a transcription system according to [31], i.e. the transcription rules were defined in advance and the names of all participants were anonymized using abbreviations such as TM1 for "team member 1". It was transcribed verbatim rather than phonetically or summarized. Word loops were approximated to the spoken content rather than transcribed. Dialects were translated as accurately as possible, but colloquial particles and reception signals were omitted. Word and sentence breaks, pauses as well as unintelligible words and sentences were marked, as were speaker overlaps and emotional expressions. Each speaker's contribution was given its own paragraph and time mark.

According to [38], it is important to distinguish between different types of harassment, in particular between general and sexual harassment. The Video Game Harassment Behaviour (VGHB) scale developed by Fox and Tang [32] makes this distinction (see Fig. 1). It was used to classify behaviors and to identify general and sexual harassment. When instances of general or sexual harassment occurred during the participant observation, they were color-coded and identified by shorthands in the transcript (see Fig. 1). A statistical analysis according to Baur and Blasius [33] was only carried out after all sessions had been completed. The transcribed data were recorded in Microsoft Excel 365 (version 2306, build 16529.20154) and analyzed in JASP 0.17.2.1.

4 Results

In the first study, subject P1 played 19 matches of Overwatch with an average duration of 13.9 min and a total of 264.1 min. Because an Overwatch team consists of six players, P1 met 95 unknown, new players. Including her participation in the voice chat, the participation rate was 40%. This means that an average of 2–3 people per match participated in voice chat communication in the Overwatch matches observed. In the case of a victory, the average number of spoken contributions over the course of the entire match was 63. In the case of a defeat, there were only 13.6 contributions.

In Valorant, a team consists of only 5 people. During the 9 matches played, subject P2 met 36 unknown new players. Including P2's own participation in the voice chat, the participation rate was 62%. This means that an average of 3 people per match participated in the voice chat communication in the observed Valorant matches. In the case of a win, the average number of voice contributions over the course of the match was 48. In the case of a loss, the average stayed rather close, at 41.3 contributions.

A total of 45 cases of harassment were documented in the first study. Of these, 40 fall into the category of general harassment ($32\times$ swearing, $4\times$ insults, $3\times$ derogatory comments about players' abilities to play, $1\times$ calling that own actions were in good fun) and 5 into the category of sexual harassment ($4\times$ sexist comments and insults, $1\times$ asking for sexual favors) (see Fig. 2). Specifically, 27 of the 45 cases of harassment were related to Overwatch (P1). Here, 24 cases of swearing, 2 cases of insults and 1 comment about a player's abilities to play were recorded. While not a single case of sexual harassment occurred, most cases of swearing still involved sexual or vulgar terms such as "fuck" or "shit". In almost all cases, the swearing was not targeted or directed at a specific person, but instead involved strong expressions of emotion such as anger, frustration, or surprise. In a few cases, the swearing was targeted, but always directed at an opposing player and never at the own team. The documented forms of verbal abuse were also directed at the opposing team, who were not in the same voice chat and therefore did not notice this harassment. Only one comment about players' abilities to play was directed at the own team: In the match with the ID OW_05, one of the players said "Thanks for lose tanks, thanks". This player blamed the defeat in the game on the players in the tank role in the voice chat and denounced their abilities.

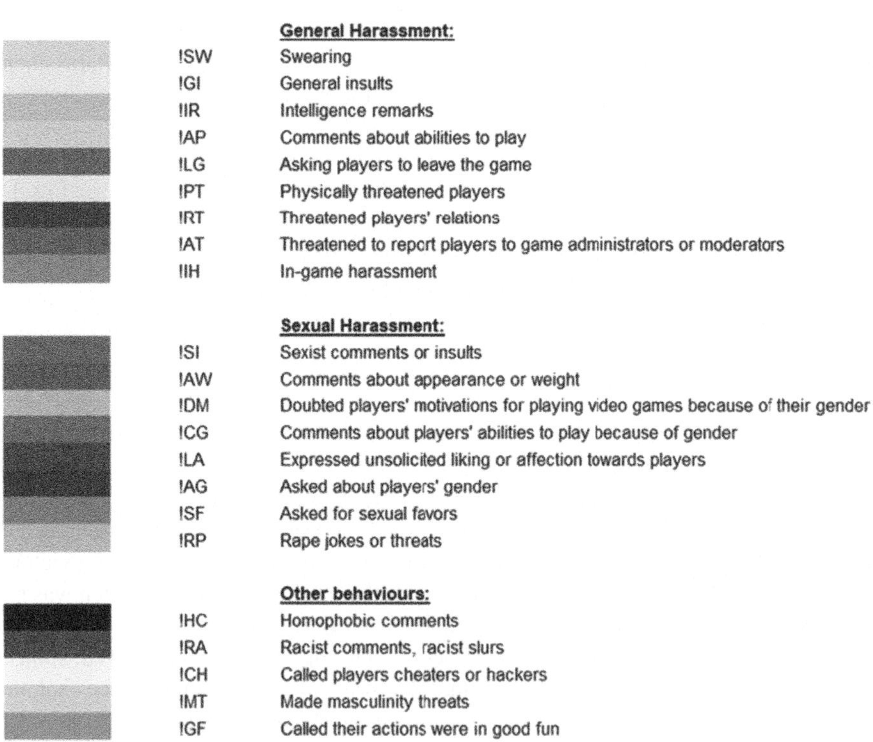

Fig. 1. Color-coding and shorthands/tokens for items of general and sexual harassment

In Valorant, 18 cases of harassment were documented, among them 8 cases of swearing, 2 cases of insults, 2 comments about players' abilities to play, 1 case of calling that a harassment was in good fun, 4 cases of sexist comments and insults and 1 case of asking for sexual favors (see Fig. 2). As in Overwatch, the documented cases of swearing contained sexual and vulgar terms as expressions of emotion and were not directed at specific people. However, apart from two cases of swearing, all forms of harassment in

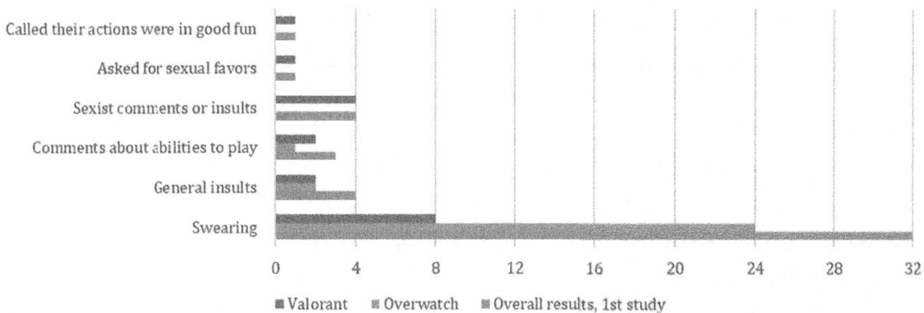

Fig. 2. Occurrences of general and sexual harassment in the first study

Valorant occurred within one match (match ID: VL_02, player TM2, see Table 1), which makes the value of its statistical analysis questionable.

The aggressive player TM3 repeatedly attracted negative attention during the VL_02 match with four instances of swearing, one disparagement of the playing skills of all team members, one attempt of calling that his own actions were in good fun, denial of previous harassment, as well as four instances of sexual harassment and one instance of asking for sexual favors. A single player thus created a negative experience for four teammates and turned the voice chat into an antisocial environment.

However, because all cases of sexual harassment were attributable to just a single player (TM2) in a single game (VL_02) in a single title (Valorant), the second study focused entirely on Valorant in order to obtain statistically more meaningful data. At the same time, the number of subjects was increased from 2 to 4 and the number of games was increased to 10 sessions of 2½ h playing time each. The total playing time in Valorant was thus increased by 455% from 270 to 1,500 min.

In the 120 matches of the second study, 742 cases of general harassment were recorded, an average of 6.18 per match. Swearing occurred 582 times (mean value 4.85 (SD 5.759) per match, minimum of 0, maximum of 31). Swearing occurred at least once in 80.8% of the matches. General verbal abuse occurred 67 times (mean 0.558(1.208), min 0, max 6). In 25.8% of the matches, at least one participant was insulted, but no one in the other 74.2%. Mocking or questioning skills of fellow players occurred 54 times, in 18.33% of the matches and not in 81.67% (mean 0.45(1.099), min 0, max 5).

Threats of violence only occurred in 1 of the 120 matches, but twice there (mean 0.017(0.183), min 0, max 2). However, this classification as a threat of violence is questionable. According to Fox and Tang's classification, requesting another person to commit suicide should be interpreted as a threat of violence. In the specific case (match Valo_16D) there was an exchange of words not with the subject P, but between the participants TM2 and TM4. (P had already muted TM4 due to previous sexist insults.) At time index 00:20:23, TM2 asked TM4 to "kill yourself" (see Table 2), albeit in reference to TM2's decision to lose the round without putting up a fight after he had previously been mocked by TM4 for not getting enough kills: "you want me to get some more deaths? i got you. no problem". TM2's asking TM4 to "kill yourself" could therefore also be interpreted as a request to leave the game according to the VGHB scale.

Table 1. Excerpts of the transcript of voice chat VL_02 in the first study.

20:43:00 P2: Why do you want to surrender already?

20:43:07 TM3: because.

20:43:57 TM3: this is why we surrender

20:44:02 P2: yeah but I'm bad so

20:44:07 TM3: nah we can move on then. Think about it we could already go next game. (unintelligible)

20:44:20 P2: oh you are perfect?

20:44:23 TM3: facts yeah

20:44:32 P2: What? say that again, I don't understand idiot !GI

20:44:34 TM3: Neither do I

20:44:40 P2: but you are one

20:44:42 TM3: You're a bitch !SI

20:45:10 P2: why are you so mean? // TM2: someone on (unintelligible)

20:45:11 TM3: who

20:45:14 P2: you

20:45:18 TM3: I don't know what I did

20:45:28 P2: so you are bottom fragging and insulting people? !AP

20:45:33 TM3: but I'm not, I just said that I wanna kill myself

20:45:38 P2: I thought you said that I should kill me

20:45:47 TM3: Nah I said that I should kill myself, not directed at you

20:45:55 P2: Ohh didn't you call me a bitch?

20:46:00 TM3: Nah I called myself a bitch because I'm trash !GF

20:46:04 P2: ok alright then

20:48:59 TM3: we got some rad players here !AP

20:59:27 TM3: I've been flashed (…)

20:59:30 TM3: flashed some titties (laugs) !SI

21:01:50 TM3: really really when I reload? (yells)

21:01:53 TM2: oh dude

21:02:02 P2: you are a bit impulsive

21:02:09 TM3: YOU ARE A PUSSY (shouts) !SI

21:02:16 TM2: I think I'm just gonna mute him

21:02:19 TM3: FUCK YOU PUSSY (loud) !SI

21:02:27 P2: can you try to be a little less sexist?

21:06:32 TM1: gg guys

21:06:33 TM3: gg

21:06:35 TM2: gg

21:06:36 P2: gg

21:06:41 TM3: SUCK MY DICK (yells) !SF

In the second study, there were again individual players such as TM2 who frequently attracted negative attention in a variety of ways. Although trolling did not occur in 90% of the games, it occurred all the more frequently in other games (56 times in total, min 0, max 26, mean 0.417(2.482)). Three out of four subjects (A, B and D) experienced trolling between 3 and 26 times; subject B was spared. However, a single player was again responsible for 52% of the trolling cases: 26 out of 50. Table 2 with a transcript of match Valo_16D makes it clear, though, that the various forms of harassment merge almost seamlessly into one another, can sometimes hardly be distinguished from trash talk and can sometimes only be specifically assigned from the context. In Valo_16D, for example, P wanted to say something at the start of the round but was interrupted and imitated by TM4. Due to this rude interruption, TM2 intervened and forbade TM4 to speak. TM2 was then sarcastically described by TM4 as a hero who wanted to save the woman, which can be seen as trolling towards TM2 and/or—due to the context of the imitation—as sexual harassment. After TM1 also got involved ("yeah you are right it doesn't matter"), this voice chat escalated between the parties P vs TM2 and TM1 vs TM4. The battle of words included swearing, general insults, intelligence remarks and threats of violence as well as sexual insults, sexual comments and comments about the subject's abilities based on her gender. The situation could only be defused by muting the aggressors. At the end (see the last three lines in Table 2), P thanks her teammate TM2 for his intervention: "thank you it's sometimes really hard".

Furthermore, 16 cases of discrimination occurred in the 120 matches of the second study (mean 0.133(0.593), min 0, max 5). For example, in match Valo_04A a player named Mark insults another: "Who the fuck do you think you are french fuck?" The offended player replies: "you are a big racist fuck mark".

For some players, discrimination, insults, harassment, swearing, and trash talk seem to be part of gaming. In such cases, previous comments are sometimes glossed over, for example by trying to call that they occurred "in good fun". According to the Video Game Harassment Behavior (VGHB) scale, such glossing over must be classified as harassment under "other behaviors" [32]. In the second study, such cases occurred five times, in three matches once and in one game twice (min 0, max 2, mean 0.042(0.239)). Thereby, two of the four subjects (C and D) experienced this form of harassment; only subject A was spared. It is worth mentioning that in the game Valo_18B it is the remaining subject B herself who, in an attempt to relativize a previous behavior of TM3, glosses over statements made by her teammate TM4 (see Table 3). Unfortunately, TM3's reaction remained acoustically unintelligible.

Cases of sexual harassment occurred alarmingly frequently in the second study: 82 cases were logged in 120 matches, including 32 cases of sexist comments and insults (min 0, max 8, mean 0.267(0.905)) in a total of 14.17% of the matches. All subjects were affected by this between 4 and 16 times.

With a total of 8 cases, comments about the appearance and weight of subjects or participants only occurred in 2.5% of the matches (mean 0.067(0.463), min 0, max 4) and affected three of the subjects (A, B and D) between 1 and 4 times. Comments about player abilities based on gender occurred even less frequently, a total of 6 times (min 0, max 2, mean 0.050(0.254)). They occurred in 4.17% of the matches, i.e. not in 95.83%,

Table 2. Excerpts of the transcript of voice chat VL_16D in the first study.

00:07:19 P: by the way guys uhm you see
00:07:29 TM4: // uhm uh by the way guys uh shut the fuck up !SI
00:07:32 TM2: shut the fuck omen !SW
00:07:33 TM1: haha
00:07:36 TM4: oh my god the hero is coming to save her !SI
00:07:38 P: I just wanted to say something but I guess it doesn't matter
00:07:48 TM1: yeah you are right it doesn't matter
00:18:51 TM1: Killjoy take the spike please
00:18:55 P: I'm going mid brother you can take it
00:18:59 TM1: bro stop lurking play with the team
00:19:10 P: no I just told you I'm going for a pick in mid //
00:19:14 TM4: // shut the fuck up !SW
00:19:17 TM1: just take the fucking bomb man !SW
00:19:19 P: No. You understand that word?
00:19:22 TM4: you're so bad you stupid girl !CG
00:19:29 P: I'm so bad but you lose a duel against !AP
00:19:37 TM4: are you premades idiot? !GI
00:19:41 P: no I'm solo-queue what are you talking about
00:19:43 TM4: then why does this jett?
00:19:49 P: because he is a decent human being you know
00:19:52 TM4: decent human being !IR
00:19:54 TM1: shut the fuck up I'm carrying this shit !AP
00:19:56 TM1: thank you guys for talking you bots lurking around like bots !AP
00:20:00 TM2: shut your bitch ass up !SI
00:20:03 TM2: you little faggot !GI
00:20:14 TM1: you didn't hit a single shot
00:20:18 TM4: you're so bad killjoy you little faggot // !GI
00:20:20 TM2: // you're a faggot // !GI
00:20:21 TM4: // and this killjoy is just sucking dicks in the back // !SI
00:20:23 TM2: // kill yourself // !PT
00:20:25 TM4: // and this jett is simping thinking he will get his virginity taken // !SI
TM1, TM4 muted
00:20:36 P: yo jett thank you I muted them but thanks buddy
00:20:38 TM2: huh what?
00:20:41 P: I said thank you it's sometimes really hard

but nevertheless affected all subjects between 1 and 3 times. In total, there were also 3 questions about gender (min 0, max 2, mean 0.025(0.203)).

Table 3. Excerpt of the transcript of voice chat Valo_18B in the second study.

00:34:30 P: dude we just joking bro !GF
00:34:34 P: you just need to calm bro
00:34:40 TM3: (unintelligible)
00:34:45 P: you need to calm down
00:34:52 P: you outplay yourself by dumb plays
00:34:59 TM4: we know you can do better just focus

Table 4. Excerpts of the transcript of voice chat Valo_29C in the second study.

00:19:06 TM4: okay
00:19:13 TM1: we will gangbang you TM3 bro !RP
00:19:21 TM3: my ass is deep !SF
00:19:27 TM4: we will gangbang you bro !RP
00:19:37 P: are you comparing or what?
00:19:47 TM1: I will fuck him now TM3 bro !RP
00:19:50 TM3: (unintelligible)
00:19:52 TM2: oh my god
00:20:01 TM1: you make me horny mid game bro !SF
00:33:44 TM1: fucking girl talks so much bullshit to me bro !SW
00:33:48 TM1: fucking girl so toxic to me !SW
00:33:50 TM3: bro they ultra
00:33:51 TM3: one ct
00:33:53 TM3: one elbow
00:33:55 TM4: one TP behind
00:33:58 TM1: see?
00:34:03 TM1: I show your pussy my big cock !RP
tm1 muted

Three of the four subjects (A, C and D) experienced cases of unsolicited affection between 5 and 9 times, one even 4 times in the same match (min 0, max 4, mean 0.175(0.669)). In addition, there were 12 requests for sexual favors. Although no such incidents occurred in 93.33% of the matches, persistent players made up to 3 such requests per match (min 0, max 3, mean 0.100(0.418)). Thus, sexual favors were requested in a total of 6.67% of the Valorant games in the second study.

One of the 120 games was particularly extreme. There, subject C experienced jokes about rape according to the VGHB scale four times (min 0, max 4, mean 0.033(0.365)), the last one (at 00:34:03 in Table 4) directly aimed at her.

5 Conclusions

The focus on Valorant in the second study resulted in a significantly higher number of cases and therefore a much more statistically analyzable and comprehensive database than in the first study. It can be assumed that if Overwatch had been chosen as the game for the second study, at least more and more diverse cases of harassment according to the VGHB scale would have come to light, too. Voice chats from Valorant, Overwatch and other esports titles should therefore be scientifically analyzed on a larger scale.

The data collected here shows that general harassment is so common that hardly any player is spared from it for long. Swearing and trash-talking seem to be the order of the day, and it is sometimes difficult to distinguish between the two. In the second study, swearing occurred in 80.8% of the 120 matches, with an average of 6.18 times per match. General verbal abuse was identified 67 times in 25.8% of the matches.

Sexual harassment occurred 82 times in a total of 14.17% of the matches—objectively, much less frequent than general harassment. However, it affected all four subjects in the second study on average in every seventh Valorant match, confronting them with a wide range of harassing behavior, ranging from questions about their gender and unsolicited affection to jokes about rape. Considering that the four female test subjects in this study only played for 270 min each, it is statistically likely that it is only a matter of hours, days or weeks before regular players also experience or are exposed to sexual harassment.

Due to the growing importance of esports (see [34, p. 166]), which tends to have a young, tech-savvy and, above all, male following ([9, p. 228]), the problem of sexism runs through all leagues. Female players report such cases not only from their amateur and youth years, but also from their years as professional players (see e.g. [12, pp. 221–230]). Despite the many testimonials, however, there are still far too few reliable statistics. A scoping review published in 2024, [37], revealed that one of its main limitations was the lack of a general assessment of the prevalence of cybersexism in online gaming communities. Participant observation with ratings based on the Video Game Harassment Behavior scale appears to be an adequate, albeit time-consuming, means of collecting such data.

Disclosure of Interests.   The authors have no competing interests.

References

1. Entertainment Software Association: 2021 Essential Facts About the Video Game Industry (2021). https://www.theesa.com/2021-essential-facts-about-the-video-game-industry/
2. ISFE: Key facts about the european video games sector (2021). https://www.videogameseu rope.eu/data-key-facts/key-facts-from-2021-europe-video-games-sector/
3. GAME: Jahresreport der deutschen Games-Branche 2022 (2021). https://www.game.de/pub likationen/jahresreport-2022/. Accessed 30 Sept 2022
4. Paaßen, B., Morgenroth, T., Stratemeyer, M.: What is a true gamer? the male gamer stereotype and the marginalization of women in video game culture. Sex Roles 76(7–8), 421–435 (2017)
5. Scharkow, M., Festl, R., Vogelgesang, J., Quandt, T.: Beyond the "core-gamer": genre preferences and gratifications in computer games. Comput. Hum. Behav. 44, 293–298 (2015)

6. Yee, N.: Beyond 50/50: Breaking Down The Percentage of Female Gamers By Genre (2017). https://quanticfoundry.com/2017/01/19/female-gamers-by-genre/. Accessed 19 Jan 2017

7. Shaw, A.: Do you identify as a gamer? gender, race, sexuality, and gamer identity. New Media Soc. **14**(1), 28–44 (2011)

8. Nielsen: Meet the Female Esports Fan (2019). https://www.nielsen.com/us/en/insights/article/2019/meet-the-female-esports-fan/

9. Breuer, M., Görlich, D.: Gaming und E-Sport – Markt und Inszenierung des digitalen Sports. In: Horky, Th., Stiehler, H.-J., Schierl, Th. (eds.): Die Digitalisierung des Sports in den Medien, vol. 13. Herbert von Halem Verlag, Sportkommunikation (2018)

10. Rogstad, E.T.: Gender in eSports research: a literature review. Eur. J. Sport Soc. **19**(3), 195–213 (2021)

11. Rößner, S.: eSport und Gender: Interview mit Natalie Denk und Yvonne Scheer (2019). https://webcare.plus/esport-gender/

12. Görlich, D.: Sexismus im E-Sport – ein Interview mit Marlies "Maestra" Brunnhofer. In: Breuer, M., Görlich, D. (eds.): E-Sport – Status quo und Entwicklungspotenziale, pp. 221–230 (2022)

13. Duggan, M.: Online Harassment (2014). https://www.pewresearch.org/internet/2014/10/22/online-harassment/. Accessed 22 Oct 2014

14. Anti-Defamation League: Free to Play? Hate, Harassment, and Positive Social Experiences in Online Games. Survey Report (2019). https://www.adl.org/free-to-play#survey-report

15. Ballard, M.E., Welch, K.M.: Virtual warfare. Games Cult. **12**(5), 466–491 (2017)

16. Fox, J., Tang, W.Y.: Women's experiences with general and sexual harassment in online video games: rumination, organizational responsiveness, withdrawal, and coping strategies. New Media Soc. **19**(8), 1290–1307 (2017)

17. Darvin, L., Wells, J.E., Baker, T., Holden, J.: Breaking the glass monitor: examining the underrepresentation of women in esports environments. Sport Manag. Rev. **24**(3), 475–499 (2021)

18. Abreu Freitas, B.D., Contreras-Espinosa, R.S., Pereira Correia, P.A.: A model of the threats that disreputable behavior present to esports sponsors. Contemp. Manag. Res. **17**(1), 27–64 (2021)

19. Piggott, L.V., Tjønndal, A.: "It becomes a fight against who I am, rather than what I say": gender, positionality, and inclusion in esports leadership. In: International Review for the Sociology of Sport (2023)

20. Kuznekoff, J.H., Rose, L.M.: Communication in multiplayer gaming: examining player responses to gender cues. New Media Soc. **15**(4), 541–556 (2013)

21. Taylor, N., Jenson, J., de Castell, S.: Cheerleaders/booth babes/ Halo hoes: progaming, gender and jobs for the boys. Digital Creat. **20**(4), 239–252 (2009)

22. Kelly, D., Giolla Easpaig, B.N., Castillo, P.: 'You Game Like a Girl': perceptions of gender and competence in gaming. Games Cult. **18**(1), 62–78 (2023)

23. Vermeulen, L., Núñez Castellar, E., Van Looy, J.: Challenging the other: exploring the role of opponent gender in digital game competition for female players. Cyberpsychol. Behav. Soc. Netw. **17**(5), 303–309 (2014)

24. Ruotsalainen, M., Friman, U.: "There Are No Women and They All Play Mercy": understanding and explaining (the lack of) women's presence in esports and competitive gaming. In: Proceedings of Nordic DiGRA 2018 (2018)

25. Kasumovic, M.M., Kuznekoff, J.H.: Insights into sexism: male status and performance moderates female-directed hostile and amicable behaviour. PloS one **10**(7) (2015)

26. Ramler, I., Lee, C.-S., Strong, S.: Investigating match performance differences between genders of league of legends champions. In: Fowler, A. (ed.) The 16th International Conference on the Foundations of Digital Games (FDG) 2021, pp. 1–11. ACM, New York (2021)

27. Gestos, M., Smith-Merry, J., Campbell, A.J.: Representation of women in video games: a systematic review of literature in consideration of adult female wellbeing. Cyberpsychol. Behav. Soc. Netw. **21**(9), 535–541 (2018)

28. UNITY: Toxicity in Multiplayer Games Report (2021). https://web.archive.org/web/202021 1201092228/https:/create.unity.com/toxicity-in-multiplayer-games-report

29. Takahashi, D.: How Riot Games will ensure that Valorant's esports stars include women.. VentureBeat (2021). https://venturebeat.com/games/how-riot-games-wants-to-ensure-that-valorants-esports-stars-include-women/. Accessed 14 June 2021

30. Milella, V.: Valorant Rank Distribution and players percentage – June 2023 (2023). https://www.esportstales.com/valorant/rank-distribution-and-percentage-of-players-by-tier

31. Dresing, Th., Pehl, Th.: Praxisbuch Interview, Transkription & Analyse. Anleitungen und Regelsysteme für qualitativ Forschende. 8th ed. Marburg: Self-Published (2018)

32. Tang, W.Y.: Sexual harassment in online videogames: What we found so far.. Game Developer (2016). https://www.gamedeveloper.com/business/sexual-harassment-in-online-videogames-what-we-found-so-far Accessed 18Apr 2016

33. Baur, N., Blasius, J. (eds.): Handbuch Methoden der empirischen Sozialforschung. Springer, Wiesbaden (2014)

34. Breuer, M., Görlich, D.: E-sport. In: Zimmermann, O., Falk, F. (eds.): Handbuch Gameskultur – Über die Kulturwelten von Games. Deutscher Kulturrat, pp. 165–170 (2020)

35. Milella, V.: Overwatch Competitive Rank Distribution: PC and Console (2019). https://www.esportstales.com/overwatch/competitive-rank-distribution-pc-and-console

36. Fox, J., Tang, W.Y.: Sexism in online video games: the role of conformity to masculine norms and social dominance orientation. Comput. Human Behav. **33**, 314–320 (2014)

37. Vergel, P., La parra-Casado, D., Vives-Cases, C.: Examining cybersexism in online gaming communities: a scoping review. Trauma Viol. Abuse **25**(2), 1201–1218 (2024)

38. De Letter, J., van Rooij, T., Van Looy, J.: Determinants of harassment in online multiplayer games. In: 67th ICA Conference: Interventions: Communication Research and Practice (2017)

39. Breuer, M., Görlich, D. (eds.): eSport: Status quo und Entwicklungspotenziale. Springer-Gabler (2020)

Now You See Me: Recognizing the Player's Arousal Changes in the Game Through Game Footage Videos and Game Context Features

Yi Xia[1]([✉])(iD), Xiaoxu Li[1](iD), Siyuan Chen[1](iD), and Ruck Thawonmas[2](iD)

[1] Graduate School of Information Science and Engineering, Ritsumeikan University, Kyoto, Japan
`{gr0666ih,gr0557hs,gr0634hi}@ed.ritsumei.ac.jp`
[2] College of Information Science and Engineering, Ritsumeikan University, 2-150 Iwakura-cho, Ibaraki, Osaka 567-8570, Japan
`ruck@is.ritsumei.ac.jp`

Abstract. This paper proposes an approach that utilizes non-intrusive and non-restrictive multimodal data—game footage videos and game context features—to recognize the player's arousal changes in the game. In recent years, affect modeling in games from a subject-agnostic perspective has emerged due to hardware limitations and ethical considerations. However, evaluation results of these approaches across various games indicate that their effectiveness is weaker in some games compared to other games. Design patterns in such games make it difficult for their methods to accurately capture the context of the games, thus making the task more challenging. Focusing on one of these games, we utilize a new preprocessing method to generate more samples from the game data in The Arousal video Game AnnotatIoN (AGAIN) dataset. In addition, we validate our hypothesis and evaluate the effectiveness of our proposed approach. We hypothesize that the information required to recognize the player's arousal changes is embedded in the game footage videos and the game context features, and that this information can be more effectively learned by utilizing transfer learning with a model pre-trained on a large human action dataset, such as Kinetics-400. Experimental results demonstrate that our approach achieves an accuracy of 79.96% on the test set, which shows a significant improvement over existing methods on the AGAIN dataset. This suggests that our approach can be a valuable tool for affect modeling in games.

Keywords: Arousal Modelling · Video Games · Preference Learning

1 Introduction

Despite recent advances in the field of Affective Computing (AC) in games [15], reliably transferring affect modeling methods trained on laboratory data to real-world (in the wild) scenarios remains challenging. In real-world scenarios, some

M. Hartisch et al. (Eds.): CG 2024, LNCS 15550, pp. 159–169, 2025.
https://doi.org/10.1007/978-3-031-86585-5_13

major hardware limitations are that several of the sensors used in the laboratory can be invasive, impractical, or even impossible to use [15]. Ethics is another aspect to consider. For example, collecting facial data in real-world environments involves very sensitive personal privacy issues. These hardware limitations and ethical considerations are factors that mainly contribute to the challenge.

To overcome these factors, we apply AC to games only through game footage videos (GFV) and game context features (GCF), which is inspired by findings in the studies by Makantasis et al. [7,8]. However, when evaluating affect modeling based on non-intrusive data across different games, both approaches in [8,9] showed significantly lower performance in some games due to their game design patterns, compared to the game with the best performance. Our work targets such games. We hypothesize that the information required to recognize the player's arousal changes, embedded in GFV and GCF, can be more effectively learned by leveraging transfer learning with a pre-trained model based on a large human action dataset.

In this paper, we propose a novel approach to recognize the player's arousal changes in video games through GFV and GCF. We use a different data preprocessing approach than those in [8] and [9] to obtain more samples and mitigate the data loss caused by their approaches. Furthermore, we validate our hypothesis and the effectiveness of our approach on a publicly available dataset.

The contributions of the paper are summarized as follows. First, we propose a multimodal deep learning model that utilizes non-intrusive and non-restrictive multimodal data—GFV and GCF modalities—to recognize the player's arousal changes in the game. Second, we introduce a data preprocessing method to generate more samples from data in the task of affect modeling in games, which we target. Third, we validate the hypothesis that transferring knowledge from a pre-trained transformer-based model, trained on a large human action dataset, is effective for the target task.

2   Related Work

2.1   Models of Affect Based on Multimodal Information

Many studies have focused on developing machine learning models to recognize emotions using various modalities such as facial expressions, body language, speech, text, and physiological signals [1,5,13,16]. However, sensing this subject-related modality information in the wild will face some hardware limitations and ethical considerations [15]. Our proposed approach performs affect modeling only through GFV and GCF, without relying on subject-related modalities.

2.2   Preference Learning in Game Affect Modeling

Extensive studies within the domain of affect modeling in games indicate that preference learning is a superior supervised learning method for player affect modeling [15]. Recognizing the player's arousal changes can be viewed as preference learning via pairwise comparisons between the data in two adjacent time windows [14]. A threshold parameter is used to determine if the absolute difference between the mean arousal values of two consecutive segments is significant enough for them to be considered as a preference pair [8–10]. Setting the threshold to a considerable positive value can improve the prediction accuracy [8], but this also results in a larger volume of data loss, leading to a less accurate approximation of the ground truth of player experience. In this paper, we employ an alternative transformation approach and set the threshold to 0 to increase the sample size and minimize such data loss.

2.3 Video Vision Transformer

The Video Vision Transformer (ViViT) [2] is an extension of the Vision Transformer (ViT) for video classification, leveraging the success of transformer architectures in image processing. ViViT captures both spatial and temporal information from video data, representing a significant advancement in video classification. A ViViT model utilized in our approach was trained by Google based on the Kinetics-400 dataset [3]. The dataset contains 400 human action categories with at least 400 video clips for each category. The model is often used in action recognition tasks [17] due to the nature of its training dataset. In this paper, we explore its potential for our affect modeling task.

3 Method

This section describes the main elements of our approach. We begin by describing the data we use. We then introduce our new data preprocessing approach and highlight the differences between our approach and the existing approach. Finally, we present the details of the modeling methods used for mapping GFV and GCF to the player's arousal changes.

3.1 Dataset

We explore our affect modeling approach based on the data from the "Solid" driving game (henceforth, Solid), which is part of The Arousal Video Game AnnotatIoN (AGAIN) dataset [9]. In Solid, players take control of a rally car from a first-person perspective and compete against three other rally cars in a race (see Fig. 1). The race ends when the player completes three laps or when the time reaches two minutes. Additionally, Solid offers more realistic handling, with the player viewing the track from the driver's seat. The approaches proposed in [8,9] both perform worse in this game compared to the game with the best performance. The design patterns in this game hinder their methods from accurately capturing the game's context, thereby making the task more challenging than in the game with the best performance. For this reason, we select this game.

The data from the Solid section of the AGAIN dataset consists of 109 human play sessions (after data cleaning), each associated with player-annotated arousal

Fig. 1. Game footage view in the Solid Rally racing game.

traces [9]. In the AGAIN dataset, each play session consists of more than 480 250-millisecond time windows with the data for telemetry game features. These features cover basic game attributes, including spatial attributes such as rotation, speed, and collision status of the player and opponent cars, as well as event attributes such as score, number of keystrokes pressed during the period, and number of opponent cars in the field of view. Arousal traces are annotated and collected in a continuous, unbounded manner. All features (except qualitative features) and arousal annotations are then normalized to values between zero and one in the dataset.

3.2 Data Preprocessing

Before training our model, we apply a new data preprocessing approach to the clean Solid dataset in the AGAIN dataset. Melhart et al. showed that using a 3-second window size is effective for capturing changes in arousal, and affective data processed at this granularity can lead to better model performance [9]. We follow this window size setting and calculate the average arousal value within each window as the arousal value for that window. In contrast to their method of directly segmenting annotation traces into 3-second time windows, our approach extracts time windows using a one-second sliding step. Doing this enables the collection of a more nuanced and extensive set of time window samples.

We treat arousal modeling based on the Solid dataset as a preference learning task [14]. Our task focuses on predicting an arousal change of the player between the previous window and the next window, over six seconds. We, therefore, create a new dataset representation through pairwise transformation. In each human play session, each sample pair contains two windows, starting at time t and $t+3$ (for $t = 0, \ldots, n-6$, n is the last second in the session). In this way, changes in arousal can be described as differences in arousal values between the two windows in each pair. This new representation reformulates the preference learning problem as a ternary classification problem (arousal increasing, decreasing, or unchanging). As a result of the processing, there were a total of 12,800 sample pairs in the Solid data, of which 6,520 pairs are classified as 'arousal increasing,' 4,333 pairs as 'arousal decreasing,' and 1,947 pairs as 'arousal unchanging.'

There are two additional differences between our data preprocessing method and that proposed by Melhart et al. [9]. In their method, features absent from a game are assigned zero-variance values (zeroes or ones, depending on the feature), and these zero-variance features are removed during data preprocessing for each game. Instead, we keep all features in the AGAIN dataset, but only remove the non-numeric features, because we want to be able to extend and evaluate our approach to other games in future research. The other difference is that we reformulate our task as a ternary classification task, while they reformulate this task as a binary classification task (arousal increasing or decreasing). Thereby, they omit all window pairs in which the arousal change is less than 10% of the maximum amplitude of the session's arousal value. We do not use such a threshold but label arousal unchanging for the sample pairs in which the arousal values of two respective windows are equal; the other sample pairs are labeled either arousal increasing or arousal decreasing depending on the sign of the difference in arousal value between the two windows within those pairs. The latter difference makes our task more complex than theirs, but it also allows us to obtain a more accurate approximation of the ground truth of player experience.

Another necessary data preprocessing step for each sample pair is the extraction of frames from GFV. To utilize the feature representations of a pre-trained model more efficiently and to initially examine the performance of the pre-trained model used as part of our approach in this task, we chose the same number of input frames as the pre-trained model. In each sample pair, we uniformly extract 32 frames from the GFV of the corresponding period as the GFV input for that sample pair.

3.3 Model of Affect

An overview of the architecture of our approach utilizing both modalities is depicted in Fig. 2.(a). Our approach receives both GFV frames and GCF as its input and fuses these two streams of information. We first perform representation learning to obtain two encoders. Each encoder projects high-dimensional data for each modality into a lower-dimensional latent space, respectively, by which two high-level representations of the input data from both modalities are obtained [4] [11]. Then, by concatenating the outputs of the two encoders as the input of a classifier, shown on top, we train this classifier to obtain the classification results. Each classifier used in this study (shown on top of Fig. 2.(a, b, d)) is a linear layer with softmax loss. The rest of the section presents the details of the main components used in our modeling approach.

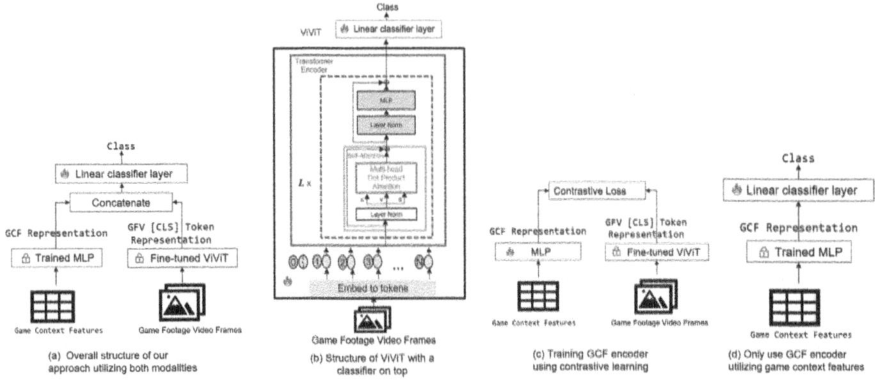

Fig. 2. Structures of the model used in our approach for recognizing arousal changes. Fire and lock symbols indicate parts where the parameters are trained and frozen, respectively.

We fine-tune all the trainable parameters of the selected ViViT model, consisting of the encoder part and the classifier part. The structure of this ViViT is shown in Fig. 2.(b). The ViViT model automatically resizes the input frames to 224×224 pixels. After that, it extracts non-overlapping, spatio-temporal tubelets from the input and then linearly projects these tubelets into tokens [2]. We use our preprocessed GFV data to fine-tune the vivit-b-16x2-kinetic400 pre-trained model. In this model notation, 'b-16x2' denotes that the model uses a ViT-Base (ViT-B, L=12, N_H=12, d=768) backbone with a tubelet size of $h \times w \times t = 16 \times 16 \times 2$ [2], L represents the number of transformer layers, N_H is the number of the attention heads, d is the dimension of the hidden layers, and h, w, and t denote the height, width, and temporal length of the tubelet, respectively. Upon completion of fine-tuning, the remaining part of the fine-tuned ViViT model after removing the classifier is frozen to serve as the encoder for the GFV modality.

For the GCF modality, we use contrastive learning to train a multilayer perceptron (MLP) as its encoder, shown in Fig. 2.(c). Affect information can be fused with the latent space through contrastive learning to produce more robust representations [11]. Inspired by the Contrastive Language-Image Pre-training in the study by Radford et al. [12], we train this encoder using the following contrastive loss function, which includes the outputs of both encoders.

$$\mathcal{L}_{gcf \to gfv} = -\frac{1}{N} \sum_{i=1}^{N} \log \frac{\exp\left(\left(e_{gcf}^i \cdot e_{gfv}^i\right)/\tau\right)}{\sum_{j=1}^{N} \exp\left(\left(e_{gcf}^i \cdot e_{gfv}^j\right)/\tau\right)} \tag{1}$$

$$\mathcal{L}_{gfv\rightarrow gcf} = -\frac{1}{N}\sum_{i=1}^{N}\log\frac{\exp\left(\left(e_{gfv}^{i}\cdot e_{gcf}^{i}\right)/\tau\right)}{\sum_{j=1}^{N}\exp\left(\left(e_{gfv}^{i}\cdot e_{gcf}^{j}\right)/\tau\right)} \tag{2}$$

$$\mathcal{L}_{total} = \frac{1}{2}\mathcal{L}_{gfv\rightarrow gcf} + \frac{1}{2}\mathcal{L}_{gcf\rightarrow gfv} \tag{3}$$

where $\mathcal{L}_{gcf\rightarrow gfv}$ represents the loss when aligning GCF to GFV, $\mathcal{L}_{gfv\rightarrow gcf}$ represents the loss when aligning GFV to GCF, and N is the number of samples in the batch. In addition, e_{gfv}^{i} and e_{gcf}^{i} are sample i's hidden representations from the GFV and GCF encoders, respectively. Finally, τ is a learnable temperature parameter. As shown in Fig. 2.(d), we also train a classifier exclusively on top of the trained GCF encoder to evaluate the effectiveness in recognizing the player's arousal changes when using only this encoder.

To reduce the computational cost of training and evaluating the learning model, we use the classification (CLS) token representation in the output of the GFV encoder as the GFV representation. Thereby, we set the structure of the GCF encoder in the following. It consists of an input layer with 24*112 neurons, followed by a hidden layer with 1024 neurons, another hidden layer with 512 neurons, and an output layer. Each hidden layer uses the ReLU activation function. The output layer, where the linear activation function is applied, consists of 768 neurons, which matches the dimension of the CLS token representation from the GFV encoder.

4   Experiment

In our experiment, after the data preprocessing mentioned in Sect. 3.1, the dataset is randomly split into 80% for training and 20% for testing. To fairly compare multiple model variants, we apply the same setting to each of them. Namely, during training, we maintain a constant initial learning rate of 5×10^{-5}, use the AdamW optimizer [6], and run 10 epochs for each variant. The training was conducted on a machine equipped with an Intel Core i9-9980XE CPU and an NVIDIA Quadro GV100 GPU, running Ubuntu 20.04. Each trained model variant is then employed to predict outcomes on the testing set. We also compare them against a baseline provided in the previous work [9] that uses a *Random Forest Classifier*, for which we maintain the same training setup described in the previous work.

Furthermore, with respect to the GCF modality, we train both an encoder and a classifier from scratch using supervised learning to compare this variant with the one shown in Fig. 2.(d), where its encoder is trained using contrastive learning (Fig. 2.(c)). Additionally, we compare the performance of the fine-tuned ViViT model across different epochs. These comparisons help us explore the potential of the ViViT model and validate our hypothesis. We make all source code and data publicly available[1].

---

[1] https://github.com/Yi-Xia-2010/Recognize-Player-Arousal-Changes/tree/main.

5   Results and Discussion

Table 1. Performance of each method or variant on the preprocessed Solid Testing Dataset

Methods Used	Accuracy
Random Forest Classifier (baseline)	63.36%
ViViT-b-16x2-kinetic400 (without fine-tuning)	34.49%
Fine-tuned ViViT 1 (5 epochs)	73.52%
Fine-tuned ViViT 2 (10 epochs)	76.52%
Fine-tuned ViViT 3 (15 epochs)	79.57%
GCF encoder 1 (contrastive learning)	50.78%
GCF encoder 2 (supervised learning)	-
Fine-tuned ViViT 2 + GCF encoder 1	79.61%
Fine-tuned ViViT 3 + GCF encoder 1	**79.96%**

The performance of each method is shown in Table 1. In Table 1, Fine-tuned ViViT 1, 2, and 3 denote the models obtained by fine-tuning ViViT-b-16x2-kinetic400 for 5, 10, and 15 epochs, respectively. GCF encoder 1 indicates the GCF encoder trained using contrastive learning, and GCF encoder 2 denotes the GCF encoder trained from scratch using supervised learning.

Our proposed approach achieved an accuracy of 79.96%, which is 16.6% higher than the baseline for our preprocessed dataset. While the accuracy of the baseline approach is about 68% in [9], it decreases to 63.36% in our preprocess dataset. This is expected due to our preprocessing methods, which increase the complexity of the task while retaining more data. In addition, the preprocessing methods used in [9] require determining that the player has a change in arousal before applying their methods to recognize whether arousal is increased or decreased, as they omit the unchanged pairs that account for 75.17% of total pairs. This means their methods only allow predicting arousal increase or decrease. On the contrary, based on our preprocessing approach, our model can directly recognize changes in the player's arousal state, making it more suitable for applications during gameplay. The results indicate that our approach can obtain a more accurate approximation of the ground truth of player experience in the target task and improve the prediction accuracy.

The results show that the variant utilizing both modalities performs better than utilizing unimodal. The GFV modality plays a significant role in the accuracy of model predictions. We believe this is because the GFV modality contains far richer information related to arousal changes than the GCF modality. The GCF modality, on the other hand, contains some of the most important abstractions of the game context. The GCF modality can be used to supplement and emphasize the patterns in the GVF when the GVF encoder fails to recognize them well, thus improving the model's performance to a certain extent. Although the improvement is relatively small when the GVF encoder is well-trained compared to the prediction accuracy of using only the GFV modality, utilizing bi-modalities simultaneously does improve the model's prediction accuracy.

When training both a GCF encoder and a classifier from scratch using supervised learning, despite trying different training settings, the training loss remains extremely high and is difficult to reduce over a certain number of epochs. Consequently, we terminate the training of this encoder, and its result is not included in Table 1. We posit that this is because, for our challenging task, it is difficult to directly train a model that is complex enough to better fit the mapping between the GCF modality's representations and the player's arousal changes using a small amount of data in this way. The GCF encoder trained in a contrastive learning manner that utilizes only this modality is less accurate than the baseline, indicating that using the GCF encoder alone is unsuitable for our task. One reason for this result is that the GCF modality loses a lot of relevant information, making it ineffective for training a classification model based on the GCF encoder. We also suggest the subpar performance of this GCF encoder may stem from the small batch size of 4 used during contrastive learning. Although the GCF modality does not perform well on its own, it can be used to improve overall performance when the GVF encoder is not performing well enough.

When fine-tuning the ViViT model for no more than 15 epochs, its accuracy on the test set improves with more epochs. The actions in the Kinetics-400 dataset cover a broad range of human-object interactions, including driving a car. The ViViT model, trained on this dataset, learns features related to these interactions. During fine-tuning, this knowledge can be transferred to our task. Based on these, we argue that some of the knowledge ViViT learned from the kinetic400 dataset can be transferred to our task by fine-tuning the ViViT model using our dataset and training the GCF encoder using contrastive learning.

6   Conclusion

In this paper, we proposed a non-intrusive and non-restrictive multimodal deep learning model for recognizing the player's arousal changes in the game. In a more challenging task caused by the preprocessing approach we introduce in this study, our model shows state-of-the-art performance with 79.96% test accuracy on the Solid game data in the AGAIN dataset. Our results validate that the transformer-based model can improve prediction accuracy in such affect modeling tasks. This study also indicates that the knowledge embedded in a pre-trained transformer-based model, which was trained on a large human action dataset, can be transferred to the tasks of affect modeling in games.

As this is an initial exploratory study, some limitations need to be further explored in future research. First, we focus only on Solid game data in the AGAIN dataset in this paper. Second, we evaluate the relative performance of the model variants under the same training settings, which means we do not explore the optimal performance of some variants that require different training settings, such as varying batch sizes, to fully utilize their potential. Last, we do not discuss the impact of input frame resolution and explore other fusion methods for the two modalities on the performance of the model. Therefore, in future work, we will investigate the effectiveness of our approach in other games and game genres, as well as explore the topics mentioned in the last two limitations.

References

1. Ahmed, N., Aghbari, Z.A., Girija, S.: A systematic survey on multimodal emotion recognition using learning algorithms. Intell. Syst. Appl. **17**, 200171 (2023). https://doi.org/10.1016/j.iswa.2022.200171, https://www.sciencedirect.com/science/article/pii/S2667305322001089
2. Arnab, A., Dehghani, M., Heigold, G., Sun, C., Lučić, M., Schmid, C.: Vivit: A video vision transformer. In: Proceedings of the IEEE/CVF International Conference on Computer Vision (ICCV), pp. 6836–6846 (October 2021)
3. Kay, Wet al.: The kinetics human action video dataset. arXiv preprint arXiv:1705.06950 (2017)
4. Khosla, P., et al.: Supervised contrastive learning. In: Larochelle, H., Ranzato, M., Hadsell, R., Balcan, M., Lin, H. (eds.) Advances in Neural Information Processing Systems, vol. 33, pp. 18661–18673. Curran Associates, Inc. (2020)
5. Li, J., Peng, J.: End-to-end multimodal emotion recognition based on facial expressions and remote photoplethysmography signals. IEEE J. Biomed. Health Inform. 1–10 (2024). https://doi.org/10.1109/JBHI.2024.3430310
6. Loshchilov, I., Hutter, F.: Fixing weight decay regularization in adam. CoRR **abs/1711.05101** (2017). http://arxiv.org/abs/1711.05101
7. Makantasis, K., Liapis, A., Yannakakis, G.N.: From pixels to affect: a study on games and player experience. In: 2019 8th International Conference on Affective Computing and Intelligent Interaction (ACII), pp. 1–7 (2019). https://doi.org/10.1109/ACII.2019.8925493
8. Makantasis, K., Liapis, A., Yannakakis, G.N.: The pixels and sounds of emotion: General-purpose representations of arousal in games. IEEE Trans. Affect. Comput. **14**(1), 680–693 (2023). https://doi.org/10.1109/TAFFC.2021.3060877
9. Melhart, D., Liapis, A., Yannakakis, G.N.: The arousal video game annotation (again) dataset. IEEE Trans. Affect. Comput. **13**(4), 2171–2184 (2022)
10. Melhart, D., Sfikas, K., Giannakakis, G., Liapis, G.Y.A.: A study on affect model validity: Nominal vs ordinal labels. In: Hsu, W., Yates, H. (eds.) Proceedings of IJCAI 2018 2nd Workshop on Artificial Intelligence in Affective Computing. Proceedings of Machine Learning Research, vol. 86, pp. 27–34. PMLR (15 Jul 2020), http://proceedings.mlr.press/v86/melhart20a.html
11. Pinitas, K., Makantasis, K., Liapis, A., Yannakakis, G.N.: Supervised contrastive learning for affect modelling. In: Proceedings of the 2022 International Conference on Multimodal Interaction, pp. 531-539. ICMI '22, Association for Computing Machinery, New York, NY, USA (2022). https://doi.org/10.1145/3536221.3556584
12. Radford, A., et al.: Learning transferable visual models from natural language supervision. In: Meila, M., Zhang, T. (eds.) Proceedings of the 38th International Conference on Machine Learning. Proceedings of Machine Learning Research, vol. 139, pp. 8748–8763. PMLR (18–24 Jul 2021). https://proceedings.mlr.press/v139/radford21a.html

13. Wei, Q., Huang, X., Zhang, Y.: Fv2es: a fully end2end multimodal system for fast yet effective video emotion recognition inference. IEEE Trans. Broadcast. **69**(1), 10–20 (2023). https://doi.org/10.1109/TBC.2022.3215245
14. Yannakakis, G.N., Cowie, R., Busso, C.: The ordinal nature of emotions: an emerging approach. IEEE Trans. Affect. Comput. **12**(1), 16–35 (2021). https://doi.org/10.1109/TAFFC.2018.2879512
15. Yannakakis, G.N., Melhart, D.: Affective game computing: a survey. Proc. IEEE **111**(10), 1423–1444 (2023). https://doi.org/10.1109/JPROC.2023.3315689
16. Zhang, S., et al.: Eeg-svrec: An eeg dataset with user multidimensional affective engagement labels in short video recommendation. In: Proceedings of the 47th International ACM SIGIR Conference on Research and Development in Information Retrieval, pp. 698–708. SIGIR '24, Association for Computing Machinery, New York, NY, USA (2024). https://doi.org/10.1145/3626772.3657890
17. Zhou, X., Arnab, A., Sun, C., Schmid, C.: How can objects help action recognition? In: Proceedings of the IEEE/CVF Conference on Computer Vision and Pattern Recognition (CVPR), pp. 2353–2362 (June 2023)

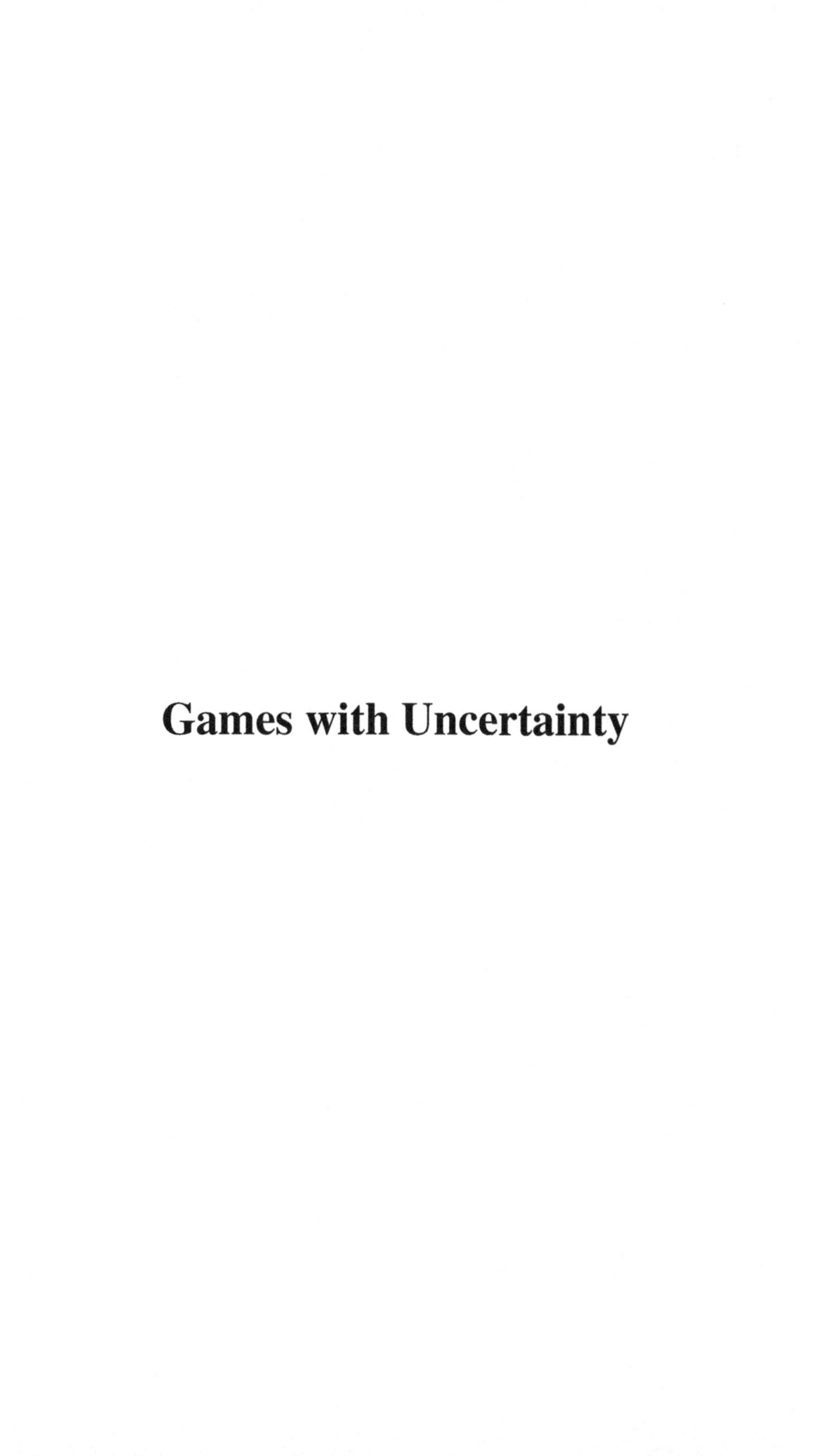

Games with Uncertainty

Belief Stochastic Game: A Model for Imperfect-Information Games with Known Positions

Achille Morenville$^{(\boxtimes)}$ and Éric Piette

ICTEAM, UCLouvain, Ottignies-Louvain-la-Neuve, Belgium
{achille.morenville,eric.piette}@uclouvain.be

Abstract. Imperfect-information games present significant challenges for General Game Playing (GGP) agents. Traditional models have limitations that hinder their applicability in this domain. These models require agents to construct and maintain estimates about the game state, a process that is often game-specific and can unintentionally introduce domain-specific knowledge. Furthermore, this specificity undermines the core goal of GGP to generate domain-independent strategies.

To overcome these challenges, we propose the Belief Stochastic Game model. This novel framework shifts the responsibility of state estimation from the agent to the game model itself, allowing agents to focus solely on strategy development. This externalisation of the state estimation process is enabled by the exploitation of the common structures found in many imperfect-information games. The new model facilitates the development of more general agents that can adapt to a wide range of games.

Keywords: General Game Playing · Imperfect-Information Games · Knowledge Representation

1 Introduction

Imperfect-information games pose a major challenge in Artificial Intelligence and Game Theory. Unlike perfect-information games, where all players know the full game state, these games involve hidden information that players must infer to make optimal decisions. The complexity of this hidden information complicates the development of general strategies and agents.

Traditional models, such as Extensive Form Games (EFG) [16], and more recent ones like Factored-Observation Stochastic Games (FOSG) [11], have been instrumental in representing and analysing imperfect-information games. However, their limitations hinder their use in General Game Playing (GGP). EFG, for example, doesn't differentiate between public and private information, and both EFG and FOSG rely on handcrafted, game-specific state estimation methods. This has led to agents tailored to individual games, making it difficult to generalise strategies across different games.

© The Author(s), under exclusive license to Springer Nature Switzerland AG 2025
M. Hartisch et al. (Eds.): CG 2024, LNCS 15550, pp. 173–184, 2025.
https://doi.org/10.1007/978-3-031-86585-5_14

In this paper, we introduce the Belief Stochastic Game (Belief-SG) model, a novel framework that addresses the limitations of existing models. Belief-SG externalises state estimation, enabling agents to focus entirely on strategy development. By leveraging common structures found in many imperfect-information games, Belief-SG offers a more generalised and standardised approach to reasoning about these games. As a result, it allows the development of agents that can more easily adapt to a wide range of games. This has the potential for many interdisciplinary applications. For example, it could enable historians to simulate and study a wide variety of historical card games, providing new insights into game strategies and decisions [3].

The remainder of this paper is structured as follows: Sect. 2 provides background and related work, Sect. 3 introduces the Belief-SG model, Sect. 5 presents an example and prototype implementation, and we conclude by discussing the implications and future extensions.

2 Background and Related Work

The problems under consideration in this study are imperfect information games. Formally, many models exist to represent a game G. The oldest and most used model is Extensive Form Games (EFG). EFG formalises game states as histories, where a history h is the sequence of actions taken by the players since the beginning of a game. Since some information is hidden from the players, some histories are indistinguishable to them. For example, in poker, players don't know the cards of their opponents, so the histories where the opponents have different cards are indistinguishable. EFG groups these indistinguishable histories into information sets, which are partitions of the possible histories $\mathcal{H}$.

However, this method of representing hidden information overlooks important concepts that are valuable for agents. To play optimally, an agent must consider the available actions of its opponents. In imperfect information games, these actions depend on the knowledge of the opponents, which is not captured by the information sets. Additionally, EFG does not distinguish between publicly available information and information that is private to each player. This distinction, along with the understanding of who knows what, is essential for effective decision making and search strategies in imperfect information games. Furthermore, while there are some works that extend EFG to extract these concepts [4], they rely on hand-crafted solutions that are specific to the games. Moreover, it has been shown that these concepts cannot be extracted in general [12], making EFG unsuitable for general imperfect information games.

In order to address the limitations of EFG, Kovařík et al. proposed a model called Factored-Observation Stochastic Games (FOSG) [11]. This model, a generalisation of the Partially Observable Stochastic Games (POSG) [7], is based on the concept of observation. In FOSG, the agents don't interact directly with the underlying state of the environment. Instead, they receive observations describing the perceivable part of the state. In addition, FOSG divides the observations into private and public parts, allowing agents to reason about what others know. This model can be formalised as a tuple $G = (\mathcal{N}, \mathcal{S}, s_0, \boldsymbol{A}, T, \boldsymbol{\mathcal{O}}, O, \boldsymbol{R})$ where:

- $\mathcal{N} = \{1, \ldots, N\}$ is a set of N players.
- $\mathcal{S}$ is a set of states and $s_0 \in \mathcal{S}$ is the initial state.
- $\boldsymbol{\mathcal{A}} = \mathcal{A}_1 \times \ldots \times \mathcal{A}_N$ is the joint action space, where $\mathcal{A}_i$ being the set of actions of player i.
    - $\mathcal{A}_i(s) \subseteq \mathcal{A}_i$ is the set of legal actions for player i in state s.
    - A state s where $\mathcal{A}_i(s)$ is empty for all players $i \in \mathcal{N}$ is a terminal state.
- $T \colon \mathcal{S} \times \boldsymbol{\mathcal{A}} \to \Delta(\mathcal{S})$ is the transition function. After taking a joint action $\boldsymbol{a}$ in state s, the game transitions to a new state $s' \sim T(s, \boldsymbol{a})$.
- $\boldsymbol{\mathcal{O}} = (\mathcal{O}_{priv(1)} \times \ldots \times \mathcal{O}_{priv(N)} \times \mathcal{O}_{pub})$ is the joint observation set. Each player i has a private observation set $\mathcal{O}_{priv(i)}$ and there is a public observation set $\mathcal{O}_{pub}$.
- $O \colon \mathcal{S} \times \boldsymbol{\mathcal{A}} \to \Delta(\boldsymbol{\mathcal{O}})$ is the observation function. After taking a joint action $\boldsymbol{a}$ and transitioning to a state s', the observations are sampled according to the observation function $\boldsymbol{o} \sim O(s', \boldsymbol{a})$.
- $\boldsymbol{R} = (R_1, \ldots, R_N)$ is the reward functions where $R_i \colon \mathcal{S} \times \boldsymbol{\mathcal{A}} \to \mathbb{R}$ is the reward of player i in a state after a joint action is applied to it.

The game starts in the state s_0. At each turn, each player simultaneously selects a legal action $a_i \in \mathcal{A}_i(s)$ to apply to the current state. The game then transitions to a new state s', sampled according to the transition function $T(s, \boldsymbol{a})$, where $\boldsymbol{a} = (a_1, \ldots, a_N)$ is the joint action. Each player receives a private observation $o_{priv(i)} \in \mathcal{O}_{priv(i)}$ and all players receive a public observation $o_{pub} \in \mathcal{O}_{pub}$ according to the observation function $O(s', \boldsymbol{a})$. The agents also receive a reward based on their reward functions $R_i(s, \boldsymbol{a})$. The game continues until a terminal state is reached. While this formulation is suited to simultaneous games, it can be adapted to sequential games by adding a noop action to the legal actions of players who are not active in the current turn.

Although FOSG provides all the information needed for sound search in imperfect information games, it has limitations that hinder its use in GGP. In FOSG, agents receive only partial observations about the game state, requiring them to construct and maintain state estimates. This often results in handcrafted state estimation tailored to specific games, making it difficult to generalise developments across different games.

The limitations of EFG and FOSG result in the development of agents that are specific to a single game or a small subset of games. For example, Libratus [2], an agent developed for Heads-Up No-Limit Texas Hold'em Poker (HUNL), uses hard-coded abstraction levels designed specifically for HUNL to reduce the state space. This specificity makes it difficult to adapt Libratus's methods to other games. Similarly, DeepStack [14], another HUNL agent, has a state representation tailored to games similar to poker.

While most agents are designed for specific games, some research has taken a GGP approach. One example is Student of Games [20], which has demonstrated strong performance in perfect information games and has outperformed state-of-the-art agents in several imperfect information games. However, this agent is hard-coded to select different architectures based on the game, which restricts its general applicability.

Several systems have been developed to describe and model a wide variety of games. The Stanford General Description Language (S-GDL) [6] is foundational for GGP research, allowing formal game descriptions. Its extension, GDL-II [22], supports imperfect information games but is cumbersome and leaves state estimation to the agent. Ludii [18] simplifies game descriptions, resulting in a large library of games. Although it has been proven that the Ludii language can describe any game [21], its focus on perfect information games limits its application to imperfect information games. Our previous work suggests an extension to Ludii that includes hidden information, aligns more closely with reinforcement learning formalism, and optimises search algorithms to leverage the game description. This approach could enhance Ludii's applicability to general game play in imperfect information settings, broadening its utility beyond perfect information games [15]. While ReCYCLE, with the CardStock simulation engine [1], does support imperfect information games, its design is tailored to classic card games, making it less adaptable for board games like Stratego.

The systems mentioned above are all based on game description languages, but other frameworks use general programming languages to describe games. The most notable is OpenSpiel [13], designed as a flexible framework for reinforcement learning in games. It has a large library of games and is widely used by researchers. However, OpenSpiel is not intended for GGP, as many specific methods must be developed for each game, which introduces domain knowledge. In addition, OpenSpiel still leaves the state estimation to the agent.

3   Model

Although EFG and FOSG offer a strong foundation for reasoning about imperfect information games, their dependence on internal state estimation and representation constrains their applicability in GGP. To overcome these limitations, we introduce a new model, the Belief Stochastic Game, which leverages the structure of games commonly played by humans. By removing the burden of state estimation from the agents, Belief-SG aims to provide a more generalised and standardised framework for reasoning about imperfect information games.

3.1   State Estimation and Representation

The state estimation process in EFG and FOSG is tasked with constructing and updating an estimate of the game state. In imperfect information games, some states are indistinguishable to the agents. To represent this indistinguishability, the estimate, known as the belief state, can be formalised as a probability distribution over all possible game states. A belief state b assigns a probability $b(s)$ to each possible state s, reflecting the likelihood that the game is currently in state s according to the agent's belief.

While it is impractical to find a universal representation of belief states that applies to all games, many games played by humans share common structures that can simplify this challenge. These games often involve different types of pieces such as stones, cards, or other components, which are placed or moved within a defined playable area, such as a board, players' hands, or other regions. In common imperfect information games, hidden information typically originates from two primary sources:

- the unknown position of the pieces within the playable area (e.g., Battleship, the Kriegspiel variant of Chess, ...).
- the unknown value or identity of the pieces (e.g., the color and suit of a card in Poker, or the rank of a piece in Stratego, ...).

In this paper we focus on the largest category of commonly played games with hidden information, where only the type or identity of the pieces is unknown. Most games involving cards fall into this category, as do board games where all positions are visible, such as Stratego.

Similar to how the state of a game can be described, the belief state must include several key elements: the set of pieces; the playable area, which includes all places where pieces can be placed, such as the board, players' hands, the deck, and other relevant zones; the position of the pieces within this area; the current agents; and any game variables that can change over time, such as an agent's money or the pot in poker. Although it may seem unusual to include the playable area in the state, certain rules or actions in a game can change this area.

In the class of imperfect information games considered here, hidden information arises solely from uncertainty regarding the values of the pieces. Consequently, belief states must also encode probability distributions over the possible values for each piece.

We describe a belief state as a tuple $b = (\mathcal{P},\ \mathcal{T},\ \mathcal{V},\ \theta,\ \omega,\ \phi,\ \Gamma)$ where:

- $\mathcal{P}$ is the set of pieces.
- $\mathcal{T}$ is the set of types that pieces can be.
- $\mathcal{V}$ is the set of all possible values for all types.
  - $\mathcal{V} = \bigcup_{t \in \mathcal{T}} \mathcal{V}_t$, where $\mathcal{V}_t \subseteq \mathcal{V}$ is the set of possible values associated with a type $t \in \mathcal{T}$.
- $\theta \colon \mathcal{P} \to \mathcal{T}$ is a function that associates each piece with its type.
- $\omega \colon \mathcal{P} \to 2^{\mathcal{N}}$ is a function that associates each piece with a subset of agents who own it.
- $\phi \colon \mathcal{P} \times \mathcal{V} \to [0, 1]$ is the probability function that associates each piece with a probability distribution over all possible values:
  - Since each piece can only take on values consistent with its type $\phi(p, v) = 0$ for $v \notin \mathcal{V}_{\theta(p)}$.
  - For a valid probability distribution, we require that $\sum_{v \in \mathcal{V}_{\theta(p)}} \phi(p, v) = 1$ for each piece $p \in \mathcal{P}$.
- Γ is a tuple containing additional elements essential for representing the game state, specifically:
  - The playable area of the game, modeled as a graph.
  - A position function, which maps each piece in $\mathcal{P}$ to a specific location within the playable area.

- The current set of acting players.
- A mapping of variable names to their current values, representing any additional game-specific parameter.

During the game, the action, or their outcomes may reveal information about the hidden values of the pieces, requiring the belief state to be updated to reflect this information. The update process follows the steps outlined in Algorithm 1.

Algorithm 1: Belief State Update

Input: A belief state b, a piece $p^* \in \mathcal{P}$, a value $v^* \in \mathcal{V}_{\theta(p^*)}$, and a target probability $\phi^* \in [0, 1]$

Result: Set $\phi(p^*, v^*)$ to ϕ^* and propagate this update to other probabilities.

$\delta^* \leftarrow \phi^* - \phi(p^*, v^*)$
$r^* \leftarrow 1 - \phi(p^*, v^*)$
$updated\_values = \emptyset$
forall $v \in \mathcal{V}_{\theta(p^*)} \setminus \{v^*\}$ **do**
    $u \leftarrow \delta^* \cdot \phi(p^*, v)/r^*$
    if $u > 0$ **then**
        $updated\_values \leftarrow updated\_values \cup \{v\}$
        $\phi(p^*, v) \leftarrow \phi(p^*, v) - u$

$\phi(p^*, v^*) \leftarrow \phi^*$
$r_g \leftarrow 0$
forall $p \in \mathcal{P} \setminus \{p^*\}$ **do**
    if $\omega(p^*) = \omega(p)$ **and** $\theta(p^*) = \theta(p)$ **then**
        $r_g \leftarrow r_g + \phi(p, v^*)$

forall $p \in \mathcal{P} \setminus \{p^*\}$ **do**
    if $\omega(p) \neq \omega(p^*)$ **or** $\theta(p^*) \neq \theta(p)$ **then**
        continue
    $\delta_p \leftarrow -\delta^* \cdot \phi(p, v^*)/r_g$
    $r_p \leftarrow \sum_{v \in updated\_values \setminus \{v^*\}} \phi(p, v)$
    forall $v \in updated\_values \setminus \{v^*\}$ **do**
        $\phi(p, v) \leftarrow \phi(p, v) - \delta_p \cdot \phi(p, v)/r_p$
    $\phi(p, v^*) \leftarrow \phi(p, v^*) + \delta_p$

The algorithm takes as input the belief state b, a target piece $p^* \in \mathcal{P}$, the specific value $v^* \in \mathcal{V}_{\theta(p^*)}$ for which we want to update the probability, and the new probability ϕ^*. The algorithm first adjusts the probability distribution of p^* by setting the probability of v^* to ϕ^* and proportionally updating the probabilities of all other possible values of p^*. Next, the algorithm propagates the change to other pieces that share the same owner and type as p^*. For each of these pieces, the algorithm adjusts the probability distribution over the possible values to remain consistent with the new information about p^*. This propagation step ensures coherence across the belief state, maintaining updated likelihoods for all relevant pieces, taking into account the new information.

Although it may seem that the game master will arbitrarily assign ϕ^*, in practice, updates to piece probabilities occur only when a piece is revealed or when a value becomes impossible. Consequently, the procedure is usually called with ϕ^* set to either 0 or 1, and rarely with other values.

This representation enables encoding belief states across a wide variety of games and different point of view using a unified format, with updates handled by the same procedure. By standardising this process, the state estimation can be shifted from the agent to the game model itself.

3.2 Belief Stochastic Game

Using the previously described belief state representation, we introduce a new model called Belief Stochastic Game (Belief-SG). In this model, the focus shifts from actual states to belief states, as it now handles state estimation. Since each player has different knowledge of the game, the belief states must account for all perspectives. Inspired by the factorisation in FOSG, Belief-SG tracks these viewpoints using three distinct types of belief states:

- The world belief state, b_w, represents the game as if all players had complete information, effectively encoding the actual state of the game. In this belief state, the values of all pieces are fully determined.
- The private belief states, $b_{priv(i)}$ $\forall i \in \mathcal{N}$, represent player i's individual perspective of the game state, based solely on what that player has observed.
- The public belief state, b_{pub}, represents the shared public perspective, containing only information visible to an external spectator.

Formally, we describe a Belief-SG as a tuple $G = (\mathcal{N}, \mathcal{B}, \boldsymbol{B}_0, \boldsymbol{\mathcal{A}}, \tau, \boldsymbol{\rho})$ where:

- $\mathcal{N} = \{1, \ldots, N\}$ is a set of N agents.
- $\mathcal{B}$ is a set of belief states.
- $\boldsymbol{B}_0 = (b_w, b_{priv(1)}, \ldots, b_{priv(N)}, b_{pub}) \subseteq \mathcal{B}$ is a tuple of the initial belief states, where:
    - b_w is the world belief state.
    - $b_{priv(i)}$ represents the private belief state of agent i.
    - b_{pub} represents the public belief state.
- $\boldsymbol{\mathcal{A}} = \mathcal{A}_1 \times \ldots \times \mathcal{A}_N$ is the joint action space, where:
    - $\mathcal{A}_i$ being the set of actions of player i.
    - $A_i \colon \mathcal{B} \to \Delta(\mathcal{A}_i)$ is the legal actions function for player i which gives the probability distribution over the actions of player i, encoding its legal actions in a belief state.
- $\tau \colon \mathcal{B} \times \boldsymbol{\mathcal{A}} \to \Delta(\mathcal{B})$ is the transition function that returns a probability distribution over the belief states based on the joint action taken.
- $\boldsymbol{\rho} = (\rho_1, \ldots, \rho_N)$ is the reward functions, where $\rho_i \colon \mathcal{B} \times \boldsymbol{\mathcal{A}} \to \mathbb{R}$ is the reward of player i in a belief state after a joint action is applied to it.

Unlike the FOSG and EFG models, the available actions for each player in a belief state are not fully determined. The legal action function must return a probability distribution over possible actions, as the opponents' piece types-and thus their actions-are uncertain. However, as a player knows the values of his own pieces, the legal actions in his private belief state are fully determined and remain identical to those in the actual game state.

The game unfolds in a manner similar to FOSG. A key difference is that the agent only receives its private state $b_{priv(i)}$ along with the public state b_{pub}, rather than observations. Agents also have access to the transition and legal action functions. In addition, when an agent takes an action, all the belief states stored in the game are updated. Since only the global belief state represents the actual state of the game, for each private belief state and the public belief state, the transition that is most consistent with the global belief state is preserved.

The Belief-SG model can be derived from an original FOSG model, similar to the derivation of Belief-MDP from a POMDP [8], ensuring that work designed for FOSG can be applied to Belief-SG. To simplify notations, let $O(o\,|\,s',a)$ denote the probability of observing o given the world state s' and the joint action a in the original FOSG. Similarly, let $T(s'\,|\,s,a)$ represent the probability of transitioning to s' given the world state s and the joint action a, and $b(s)$ represent the probability of the world state s in the belief state b. The joint action space $\mathcal{A}$ is the same in both models. The transition probability $\tau(b'\,|\,b,a)$ in the Belief-SG model can be defined as follows:

$$\tau(b'\,|\,b,a) = \sum_{o \in \mathcal{O}} P(b'\,|\,b,a,o)P(o\,|\,b,a),$$

where:

$$P(o\,|\,b,a) = \sum_{s' \in \mathcal{S}} O(o\,|\,s',a) \sum_{s \in S} T(s'\,|\,s,a)b(s),$$

$$P(b'\,|\,b,a,o) = \begin{cases} 1 & \text{if } \forall s' \in S\colon b'(s') = P(s'\,|\,b,a,o) \\ 0 & \text{otherwise} \end{cases},$$

$$P(s'\,|\,b,a,o) = \frac{O(o\,|\,s',a) \sum_{s \in S} T(s'\,|\,s,a)b(s)}{P(o\,|\,b,a)}.$$

And the reward function $\rho_i(b,a)$ in the Belief-SG model can be defined as $\sum_{s \in S} R_i(s,a)b(s)$.

The Belief-SG model offers a more general and unified framework for reasoning about imperfect information games within the GGP domain. By externalising the state estimation process, it enables agents to focus solely on strategy development, addressing key limitations that have previously impeded the advancement of general agents.

4   Example

To illustrate the Belief-SG model, we consider a miniature version of Stratego. We will outline the initial setup and demonstrate how belief states are initialised and updated, showcasing state estimation, transition function, legal actions, and terminal functions.

The game is played by 2 players on a 5×5 board, with each player having 5 pieces: a flag, a bomb, a miner, and two sergeants. The rules are similar to Stratego[1]: capturing the flag wins the game, the bomb kills any attacking piece, the miner defuses the bomb, sergeants capture any piece except the bomb, and only the miner and sergeants can move one square orthogonally. Each player starts with all pieces in their hand.

To initialise the game, the world belief state, private states and public states are created. Each state includes the playing area graph, which in this case is a 5×5 grid of orthogonally connected nodes, plus two additional nodes representing the players' hands, connected to their respective home rows. The pieces are initially placed in the players' hands, and player 0 is set as the starting player. In these belief states, the probability distributions over a player's pieces are uniform if the player is not an observer for that state, while observers fully know their own pieces.

To demonstrate how the game functions, consider the scenario depicted in Fig. 1, where each player has already positioned their pieces on the board and made three moves. The red player has already captured a blue piece.

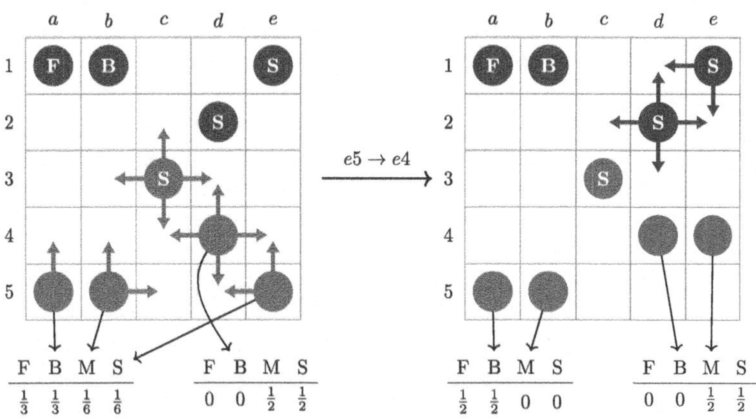

Fig. 1. Belief states in a miniature version of Stratego from the blue player's perspective. Probability distributions over piece types are shown, with known types displayed on the pieces. Legal actions for the respective players are represented by coloured arrows. The transition due to the red player's action $e5 \to e4$ is illustrated. (Color figure online)

During the setup phase, legal actions involve placing pieces from the hand onto the player's home row. Once the game begins, legal actions consist of possible moves by miners and sergeants. For pieces that could potentially be a miner or sergeant, legal actions are generated with a probability based on the likelihood

---

[1] https://boardgamegeek.com/boardgame/1917/stratego.

of the piece being that type. The set of available actions and their associated probabilities in a specific game state are shown in Fig. 1.

The transition function updates belief states based on actions taken. It first applies the action to the pieces, their positions, the graph or the variables, and then updates the probabilities on the values of the pieces. For example, if a piece is moved after the setup phase, the transition function eliminates the possibility that the piece is a flag or a bomb, and also propagates this information to other pieces, as shown in Fig. 1.

After each action, the terminal function is called. In this example, a belief state is considered terminal when a player has no piece that could potentially be a flag, or when the acting player has no more valid actions. If the belief state is terminal, the return function awards $+1$ to the winner and -1 to the other player.

A prototype of the Belief-SG has been implemented in C++ and is freely available[2]. The implementation allows for defining games and agents, is easily extensible, and includes a miniature version of Stratego.

5   Discussion

Externalising the state estimation process from the agent has several important advantages. One major benefit is that it allows the agent to focus entirely on strategy development, without the need to track or estimate hidden information. This streamlines the agent's role, allowing it to focus on maximising rewards based on the knowledge available. In fact, agents are no longer tied to specific game environments or user-defined state estimation, making it easier to apply them to different games and scenarios. This effectively removes the limitations of the EFG and FOSG models and facilitates the development of more versatile agents that can adapt to a wide range of games.

Moreover, by managing imperfect information within the model itself, the agent's perspective is more closely related to that of a model designed for perfect information games. This similarity simplifies the adaptation of methods typically conceived for perfect information games, facilitating their adaptation to apply to games with hidden information.

Another important advantage is that this approach separates the agent's strategic decision-making from its estimation of hidden states. By isolating the policy computation from state estimation, the focus remains on evaluating the quality of policies and strategies. This results in a more objective assessment of agent performance and ensures a fairer comparison between agents.

However, this approach is not without its limitations. The generalisation comes at the cost of increased computational complexity. Since state estimation is handled within the model itself, the complexity of the transition function grows, potentially leading to slower performance when calculating state transitions. This can, in turn, slow down the policy search process, especially in

---

[2] https://github.com/AchilleMorenville/Belief-SG.

large or complex environments. Additionally, the model is currently suited only for games where hidden information arises from the unknown identities of the pieces. While this encompasses many popular games, it does not generalise to all games with hidden information.

6   Conclusion

This paper introduced the Belief Stochastic Game (Belief-SG) model, a framework for reasoning about imperfect information games in the GGP domain. By externalising state estimation, the model allows agents to focus purely on strategy development, addressing limitations that have hindered the development of general agents capable of performing well across diverse games. We also presented a prototype implementation of the Belief-SG model, showcasing its application through a simplified version of Stratego.

Future work will aim to extend the Belief-SG model to address additional sources of hidden information, such as unknown piece positions. We also plan to apply the model to a broader range of games and scenarios, integrating it into existing GGP systems to evaluate its performance and scalability. One promising avenue is to integrate it with Ludii by extending its ludemic game description language with concepts specific to games with imperfect information [19]. In addition, this integration will provide access to a large database of games [5], enabling the interdisciplinary study of historical card games. We will also investigate combining the model with constraint-based methods from perfect-information GGP [9,10] to evaluate their effectiveness in games with imperfect information.

Acknowledgments. This article is based on the work of COST Action CA22145 - GameTable [17], supported by COST (European Cooperation in Science and Technology).

References

1. Bell, C., Goadrich, M.: Automated playtesting with recycled cardstock. Game & Puzzle Design **2**(1) (2016)
2. Brown, N., Sandholm, T.: Superhuman AI for heads-up no-limit poker: libratus beats top professionals. Science **359**(6374), 418–424 (2017)
3. Browne, C., et al.: Foundations of Digital Archæoludology. Tech. rep, Schloss Dagstuhl Research Meeting, Germany (2019)
4. Burch, N., Johanson, M., Bowling, M.: Solving imperfect information games using decomposition. In: Proceedings of the AAAI Conference on Artificial Intelligence, vol. 28 (2014)
5. Crist, W., Stephenson, M., Piette, É., Browne, C.: The ludii games database: A resource for computational and cultural research on traditional board games (2024)
6. Genesereth, M.R., Love, N., Pell, B.: General game playing: overview of the AAAI competition. AI Mag. **26**(2), 62–72 (2005)
7. Hansen, E.A., Bernstein, D.S., Zilberstein, S.: Dynamic programming for partially observable stochastic games. In: AAAI. vol. 4, pp. 709–715 (2004)

8. Kaelbling, L.P., Littman, M.L., Cassandra, A.R.: Planning and acting in partially observable stochastic domains. Artif. Intell. **101**(1–2), 99–134 (1998)

9. Koriche, F., Lagrue, S., Piette, É., Tabary, S.: Constraint-based symmetry detection in general game playing. In: Proceedings of the Twenty-Sixth International Joint Conference on Artificial Intelligence, IJCAI-17, pp. 280–287 (2017)

10. Koriche, F., Lagrue, S., Piette, É., Tabary, S.: WoodstockâĂŕ: Un programme-joueur générique dirigé par les contraintes stochastiques. Revue D'Intelligence Artificielle (RIA) **31**(3), 307–336 (2017)

11. Kovařík, V., Schmid, M., Burch, N., Bowling, M., Lisỳ, V.: Rethinking formal models of partially observable multiagent decision making. Artif. Intell. **303**, 103645 (2022)

12. Kovařík, V., Lisỳ, V.: Problems with the efg formalism: a solution attempt using observations. arXiv preprint arXiv:1906.06291 (2019)

13. Lanctot, M., et al.: OpenSpiel: A framework for reinforcement learning in games. CoRR **abs/1908.09453** (2019). http://arxiv.org/abs/1908.09453

14. Moravčík, M., et al.: Deepstack: expert-level artificial intelligence in heads-up no-limit poker. Science **356**(6337), 508–513 (2017)

15. Morenville, A., Piette, É.: Vers une approche polyvalente pour les jeux à information imparfaite sans connaissance de domaine. In: RJCIA (2024)

16. von Neumann, J., Morgenstern, O.: Theory of Games and Economic Behavior. Princeton University Press, Princeton, NJ, USA (1944)

17. Piette, É., et al.: Gametable cost action: Kickoff report. ICGA J. **46**(1), 1–17 (2024)

18. Piette, É., Soemers, D., Stephenson, M., Sironi, C.F., Winands, M., Browne, C.: Ludii – the ludemic general game system. In: Proceedings of the 24th European Conference on Artificial Intelligence (ECAI 2020). vol. 325, pp. 411–418 (2020)

19. Piette, É., Stephenson, M., Soemers, D.J.N.J., Browne, C.: General board game concepts. In: Proceedings of the 2021 IEEE Conference on Games (CoG), pp. 932–939. IEEE (2021)

20. Schmid, M., Moravčík, M., et al.: Student of games: a unified learning algorithm for both perfect and imperfect information games. Sci. Adv.s **9**(46), eadg3256 (2023)

21. Soemers, D.J., Piette, É., Stephenson, M., Browne, C.: The ludii game description language is universal. In: 2024 IEEE Conference on Games (CoG), pp. 1–8. IEEE (2024)

22. Thielscher, M.: A general game description language for incomplete information games. In: Proceedings of the Twenty-Fourth AAAI Conference on Artificial Intelligence, pp. 994–999. AAAI (2010)

A Mathematical Analysis of PLACEIT: A Game of Perfect Online Sorting

Pablo Ruiz Cuevas$^{(\boxtimes)}$, Casey Chock , and Bernardo Subercaseaux

Carnegie Mellon University, Pittsburgh, USA
`pablo.r.c@live.com, bersub@cmu.edu`

Abstract. In the single-player game of PLACEIT, a player must sort a random sequence of numbers in an *online* fashion. The game begins by sampling a sequence $S = (s_1, \ldots, s_{20})$ of numbers uniformly at random from $\{1, \ldots, 999\}$ without replacement. The elements of S are presented one by one to the player. Upon seeing an element s_i, a player must try to guess its *rank*, that is, the number n such that s_i is the nth smallest number in S. For example, if $s_1 = 496$, the player might reasonably guess that s_1 will be the 10th smallest number in S. The player must guess the rank of all 20 numbers of S correctly to win the game. Additionally, the game requires each guess to be *consistent* with previous guesses, so if the player guessed the rank of $s_1 = 240$ to be 6, and then $s_2 = 316$ is presented, the player is forced to guess a rank larger than 6 for s_2. If at any point the player cannot make a consistent guess, they lose immediately. Once a rank has been assigned, it cannot be changed. This article presents a mathematical analysis of PLACEIT, in which we prove that the optimal strategy wins with probability close to 0.0001335. We then extend our analysis to a continuous variant of the game.

Keywords: PlaceIt · Online Ranking · Online Sorting · Games

1 Introduction

Simple games can lead to mathematically rich theories, as shown for instance by Nim (leading to Sprague-Grundy theorems in combinatorial game theory [10]), Conway's Game of Life (and its long-lasting impact on the theory of cellular automata [11]), or Hex (and its equivalence to Brouwer Fixed-Point Theorem [6]). In this article, we analyze a very simple game that leads to several interesting mathematical and computational questions related to online algorithms, some of which we manage to answer, and some of which we leave as open challenges for future research. Before diving into a formal description of the game of PLACEIT, we encourage the reader to try playing it at https:// dae314.github.io/placeit-game/.

PLACEIT is a web-game based on a *TikTok* trend that started around February 2023 [8]. We were unable to verify the origin of the trend, but the creator,

---

P. R. Cuevas and C. Chock: Independent Researcher.

M. Hartisch et al. (Eds.): CG 2024, LNCS 15550, pp. 185–196, 2025.
https://doi.org/10.1007/978-3-031-86585-5_15

Fig. 1. Original interface of the PLACEIT game. In this case, $s_9 = 539$, and the only valid guesses are $13, 14, 15, 16$, underlined with green in the game's interface. (Color figure online)

@_nickvogel, has some of the earliest examples of the challenge, which he called the 20-number challenge. He also published variations of the challenge with fewer required slots to fill. On *TikTok*-a platform similar to *YouTube* for sharing short form videos-creators use the *"EffectHouse Randomizer 2D"* effect to pick random numbers from 0 to 999, which they would then need to sort into 20 slots. The trend took off, and by March 2023, there were over 856 thousand videos with "20-number challenge" in their name [9].

The game of PLACEIT differs slightly compared to the original *TikTok* version, and it is parameterized by two positive integers, M and N, which in the original game has values $M = 999$ and $N = 20$. A game of PLACEIT(M, N) starts by sampling a sequence of numbers $S = (s_1, \ldots, s_N)$, uniformly at random and without replacement, from the set $\{1, \ldots, M\}$. Let $\bar{S}$ be the sequence obtained by sorting S increasingly. For each element s_i, its *rank* $r_i \in \{1, \ldots, N\}$ is defined as the position of s_i in the sorted sequence $\bar{S}$. The goal of the player is to progressively fill an array A of size N, initialized with values $\bot$ (representing an empty position), so that at the end of the game $A = \bar{S}$. The game proceeds by rounds: in the i-th round, the number s_i is presented to the player, who must make a guess $\widehat{r_i} \in \{1, \ldots, N\}$ for the rank of s_i, and set $A[\widehat{r_i}] = s_i$. For a guess $\widehat{r_i}$ to be *consistent* (with the previous guesses), it must preserve the invariant that the non-empty positions of A are sorted increasingly. Concretely, after a consistent guess it holds that $A[i] < A[j]$ for every pair of indices $i < j$ such that $A[i] \neq \bot \neq A[j]$. Let us say a consistent guess $\widehat{r_i}$ is *valid* if at time i it holds that $A[\widehat{r_i}] = \bot$. If at some round the player has no valid guess to make, they immediately lose the game. On the other hand, the player wins if and only if all their guesses are correct, i.e., $\widehat{r_i} = r_i$ for all i. Figure 1 shows the original interface of the game, where $M = 999, N = 20$.

1.1 Summary of Results

We begin Section 2, by calculating the probability of winning the original version of PLACEIT, where $M = 999$ and $N = 20$ using the best possible strategy.

Theorem 1. *The maximum probability of winning* PLACEIT*(999, 20) is approximately* 0.0001335. *The maximum probability of winning a game of* PLACEIT(M, N) *can be computed in time* $O(M^2 \cdot N)$.

We will then generalize the analysis to a continuous version of PLACEIT in Section 3, where N numbers are sampled uniformly at random from the continuous $[0, 1]$ interval. Our code, containing both the discrete and continuous solutions, is publicly available at the following url: https://github.com/PabloRuizCuevas/probability-sorting/tree/main.

> *Example 1.* Consider $N = 5$, and $M = 10$. The sequence $S = (3, 1, 5, 7, 4)$ is sampled, and thus $\bar{S} = (1, 3, 4, 5, 7)$. In the first round, the player receives $s_1 = 3$. The player guesses $\hat{r}_1 = 2$, leading to $A = [\perp, 3, \perp, \perp, \perp]$. Then, $s_2 = 1$ is presented, and the player chooses $\hat{r}_2 = 1$, resulting in $A = [1, 3, \perp, \perp, \perp]$. Next, $s_3 = 5$, and the player guesses $\hat{r}_3 = 3$, leading to $A = [1, 3, 5, \perp, \perp]$. Then, $s_4 = 7$, and the player guesses $\hat{r}_4 = 4$, resulting in $A = [1, 3, 5, 7, \perp]$. Finally, $s_5 = 4$, no valid guess is possible and player loses in the round 4.

2 Solving the Original PLACEIT

First, let us introduce, as a tool for our analysis a variant of the game that we call *Delayed*-PLACEIT, in which whenever the player does not have any valid guesses for an element s_i, instead of losing immediately, the element is just skipped and $s_{i+1}, \ldots, s_N$ are presented next, but the player is declared to lose at the end nonetheless. In other words, the winning condition for *Delayed*-PLACEIT is whether $A[i] \neq \perp, \forall i \in \{1, \ldots, N\}$ at the end of round N. Note immediately that the optimal probability of winning a game of *Delayed*-PLACEIT over (M, N) is exactly the same as over a game of PLACEIT since any deterministic strategy wins a game of *Delayed*-PLACEIT after S has been sampled if and only if that same deterministic strategy wins the game of PLACEIT over the same sequence S. General strategies, that are distributions over deterministic strategies, will naturally have the same probability of winning both variants of the game, since they are distributions over strategies that have the same probability of winning. We therefore continue this section analyzing *Delayed*-PLACEIT.

Let us call $h_i := (s_1, \hat{r}_1, \ldots, s_{i-1}, \widehat{r_{i-1}})$ the *history* of the game up to round $i - 1$, and using the convention $\hat{r}_j = \perp$ if there was no valid guess for s_j. Then, a deterministic strategy σ_d for *Delayed* $-$ PLACEIT(M, N) is a function that maps the history of the game up to round $i - 1$, together with the number s_i revealed in round i, into a valid guess $\hat{r}_i$. Concretely, $\sigma_d(h_i, s_i) = \hat{r}_i$. Naturally, a general strategy σ is a distribution over deterministic strategies, implying that $\sigma(h_i, s_i)$ is a random variable over the space of valid guesses $\hat{r}_i$ (or $\perp$). We can thus define our objective in terms of the probability that $\sigma(h_i, s_i) := \widehat{r_i}$ matches the true answer r_i for every $i \in \{1, \ldots, N\}$.

Definition 1. *The optimal probability of winning* $\textsc{PlaceIt}(M, N)$*, or equivalently,* Delayed-$\textsc{PlaceIt}(M, N)$*, denoted by* $\mathcal{P}(M, N)$*, is defined as*

$$\mathcal{P}(M, N) := \sup_{\sigma} \Pr_{S, \sigma} \left[\bigcap_{i=1}^{N} \sigma(h_i, s_i) = r_i \right]$$

Let us state immediately that no randomized strategy can beat the best deterministic strategy in *Delayed*-$\textsc{PlaceIt}$. To do so, note that for any strategy σ that must make a guess on element s_i with a history h_i, there is a set of valid guesses for s_i which we will denote V_i.

Lemma 1 (Optimality of a Deterministic Strategy). *Let* $\sigma^\star$ *denote a deterministic strategy that guesses* $\sigma^\star(h_i, s_i) = \arg\max_{j \in V_i} \Pr_S[r_i = j]$*, breaking ties arbitrarily. Then,* $\mathcal{P}(M, N) = \Pr_S \left[\bigcap_{i=1}^{N} \sigma^\star(h_i, s_i) = r_i \right]$

This lemma is a direct corollary of [7, Proposition 2.3], as in general all single-player games with perfect recall (i.e., the player does not forget previously learned information) have optimal deterministic strategies. In a nutshell, $\sigma^\star$, the optimal strategy for $\textsc{PlaceIt}$ can be computed efficiently through dynamic programming according to the next lemma.

Lemma 2. *Provided that* $M \geq N \geq 1$*, the function* $\mathcal{P}$ *satisfies the following recursive equation*

$$\mathcal{P}(M, N) = \frac{1}{M} \sum_{i=1}^{M} \max_{1 \leq j \leq N} \mathcal{P}(i - 1, j - 1)\mathcal{P}(M - i, N - j)\frac{\binom{i-1}{j-1}\binom{M-i}{N-j}}{\binom{M-1}{N-1}}$$

with the convention that $\mathcal{P}(0, b) = \mathcal{P}(1, b) = 1$ *for any* $b \geq 1$*, as well as* $\mathcal{P}(a, b) = 0$ *for any* $1 < a < b$*.*

Before a formal proof, let us present the intuition behind Lemma 2. Consider first the following example that we will generalize afterward.

Example 2. Consider $M = 8, N = 5$, and $S = (4, 5, 2, 1, 7)$. Assume the player guesses $\widehat{r_1} = 3$ upon seeing $s_1 = 4$. The state is thus $A = [\perp, \perp, 4, \perp, \perp]$. Note now that the upcoming values (s_2, s_3, s_4, s_5) can be partitioned according to whether they are greater or less than s_1 in A. Namely, $(s_3, s_4) = (2, 1)$ must be placed to the left of s_1, that is, in A_1 or A_2, and $(s_2, s_5) = (5, 7)$ must be placed to the right of s_1, that is in A_4 or A_5. This partitioning creates two independent "sub-games": a left sub-game with values $(2, 1)$ and a right sub-game with values $(5, 7)$. From the player's perspective without knowledge of S, the possible values for the right sub-game are $\{5, 6, 7, 8\}$. As there are four possible values for the right sub-game, and two empty positions (A_4, A_5), the right sub-game is analogous to a game of PLACEIT$(4, 2)$ (proved formally later on). Similarly, the left sub-game has $\{1, 2, 3\}$ as possible values, and two empty positions (A_4, A_5). So it will be analogous to a game of PLACEIT$(3, 2)$. Finally, for the player to win after having guessed $\widehat{r_1} = 3$, they require exactly 2 of the 4 remaining values in S be smaller than $s_1 = 4$. What are the odds that exactly 2 out of 4 values chosen uniformly at random and without replacement from $\{1, \ldots, 8\} \setminus \{4\}$ are smaller than 4? The answer is $\frac{18}{35}$, and in general this can be modeled by a hypergeometric distribution. Putting these facts together, we have that given $s_1 = 4$ the probability of winning the game is $\mathcal{P}(3, 2) \cdot \mathcal{P}(4, 2) \cdot \frac{18}{35}$. Naturally, Lemma 2 does not assume $s_1 = 4$ but rather takes the average over all possibilities for s_1.

To generalize Example 2, let us focus on the first guess of the game. Let $\mathcal{P}(M, N \mid s_1 = i)$ be the optimal probability of winning the game conditioned on $s_1 = i$, for any $i \in \{1, \ldots, M\}$. Namely,

$$\mathcal{P}(M, N \mid s_1 = i) := \sup_\sigma \Pr\left[\bigcap_{j=1}^{N} \sigma(h_j, s_j) = r_j \mid s_1 = i\right]$$

By the law of total probability, we have

$$\mathcal{P}(M, N) = \sum_{i=1}^{M} \mathcal{P}(M, N \mid s_1 = i) \Pr[s_1 = i] = \frac{1}{M} \sum_{i=1}^{M} \mathcal{P}(M, N \mid s_1 = i) \tag{1}$$

After the first guess has been made, every future number $s_j, j > 1$ is either (i) smaller than s_1, in which case it must be placed in $A[1, \ldots, \widehat{r_1} - 1]$, or (ii) larger than s_1, in which case it must be placed in $A[\widehat{r_1} + 1, \ldots, N]$. Let the random variable L denote the number of values $s_j, j > 1$ that are smaller than s_1, and R the random variable corresponding to the number of values $s_j, j > 1$ larger than s_1. For strategy σ to win the game, the following three conditions must be fulfilled:

(a) $L = \widehat{r_1} - 1$ and $R = N - \widehat{r_1}$.
(b) σ correctly places all L values that are smaller than s_1 in $A[1, \ldots, \widehat{r_1} - 1]$.
(c) σ correctly places all R values that are larger than s_1 in $A[\widehat{r_1} + 1, \ldots, N]$.

The probability of condition (a) is given by a hypergeometric distribution; after s_1 was drawn, there are $N-1$ draws without replacement remaining from $\{1, \ldots, M\} \setminus \{s_1\}$, and the condition asserts that exactly $\widehat{r_1} - 1$ of them will be smaller than s_1. It is thus standard that $\Pr[L = \widehat{r_1} - 1] = \frac{\binom{s_1-1}{\widehat{r_1}-1}\binom{M-s_1}{N-\widehat{r_1}}}{\binom{M-1}{N-1}}$, and naturally the event $L = \widehat{r_1} - 1$ is equivalent to $R = N - \widehat{r_1}$, since $L + R + 1 = N$. Note as well that the first guess being correct is equivalent to the event $L = \widehat{r_1} - 1$. Therefore, if $s_1 = i$, and $\sigma(s_1) = j$, the probability of this first guess being correct is exactly $\frac{\binom{i-1}{j-1}\binom{M-i}{N-j}}{\binom{M-1}{N-1}}$.

To analyze the probabilities of conditions (b) and (c) being fulfilled, we will need a couple of additional lemmas. Let $\mathcal{L} := \{j \mid s_j < s_1\}$, so $|\mathcal{L}| = L$, and $\mathcal{R} := \{j \mid s_j > s_1\}$, $|\mathcal{R}| = R$. Then, we define the events

$$W_{\mathcal{L}} := \bigcap_{j \in \mathcal{L}} \sigma(h_j, s_j) = r_j \quad \text{and} \quad W_{\mathcal{R}} := \bigcap_{j \in \mathcal{R}} \sigma(h_j, s_j) = r_j$$

Unfortunately, for any fixed strategy σ, the events $W_{\mathcal{L}}, W_{\mathcal{R}}$ are not independent since losing in an arbitrary round, where an element s_j of e.g., $\mathcal{L}$ is presented, prevents σ from guessing the rank of any future elements of $\mathcal{R}$. Nonetheless, the game can be analyzed as if these events were independent, as we show next.

We now prove that in *Delayed*-PlaceIt we can indeed assert that $W_{\mathcal{L}}$ and $W_{\mathcal{R}}$ are independent in a precise way. Let *Grouped-Delayed*-PlaceIt be a variant of *Delayed*-PlaceIt with the guarantee that all elements $s_j, j > 1$ such that $s_j < s_1$ appear before all elements $s_j > s_1$. In other words, all elements of $\mathcal{L}$ are presented before any element of $\mathcal{R}$. For instance, $S = (3, 4, 5, 1, 2)$ is a valid sequence for *Delayed*-PlaceIt, which can be transformed into a sequence $S' = (3, 1, 2, 4, 5)$ for *Grouped-Delayed*-PlaceIt. Formally, the sequence S for a game of *Grouped-Delayed*-PlaceIt(M, N) is drawn uniformly at random from the set of length N sequences of $\{1, \ldots, M\}$ where all elements smaller than the first one come before any element larger than the first one.

Lemma 3 (Grouped Invariance). *The optimal probability of winning a game of* Grouped-Delayed-PlaceIt(M, N) *is exactly* $\mathcal{P}(M, N)$.

Proof. As we already argued that the optimal probability of winning a game of *Delayed*-PlaceIt(M, N) is exactly $\mathcal{P}(M, N)$, we need to prove that the optimal probability of winning a game of *Delayed*-PlaceIt(M, N) is the same as that of winning a game of *Grouped-Delayed*-PlaceIt(M, N) The same argument of Lemma 1 shows that $\sigma^\star$ is an optimal strategy for both *Delayed*-PlaceIt(M, N) and *Grouped-Delayed*-PlaceIt(M, N). Let f be the function that maps every sequence S of N elements of $\{1, \ldots, M\}$ to a valid sequence for *Grouped-Delayed*-PlaceIt without changing the relative order of elements in $\mathcal{L}$ nor in $\mathcal{R}$. For example, $f((3, 4, 5, 1, 2)) = (3, 1, 2, 4, 5)$. Thus, to conclude the lemma we will prove that $\sigma^\star$ wins in a game of *Delayed*-PlaceIt over a sequence S if and only if it wins over $f(S)$ in a game of *Grouped-Delayed*-PlaceIt. To see this, note that for each element $s_i \in S$ presented in *Delayed*-PLACEIT, its corresponding set of valid guesses V_i is exactly the same as its set of valid guesses when that element is presented to σ^* in *Grouped-Delayed*-PLACEIT.   □

Let us now prove that it does not matter whether numbers are drawn from $\{1, \ldots, M\}$ or any other set of size M.

Lemma 4 (Translational Invariance). *The optimal probability of winning a game of* PLACEIT *in which N numbers are drawn uniformly at random and without replacement from a set $X \subseteq \mathbb{N}$ with $|X| = M$ is also $\mathcal{P}(M, N)$.*

Proof. Let us denote by $\mathcal{P}(X, N)$ the optimal probability of winning the game stated in Lemma 4. Then, we can prove both that $\mathcal{P}(X, N) \geq \mathcal{P}(M, N)$ and $\mathcal{P}(M, N) \geq \mathcal{P}(X, N)$. It suffices to show that for any strategy over the game with numbers drawn from X, we can construct an associated strategy with the same probability of winning when numbers are drawn from $\{1, \ldots, M\}$, and vice-versa. Consider the bijective map $f : X \to \{1, \ldots, M\}$ that maps the i-th smallest element of X to i, for $i \in \{1, \ldots, M\}$. Then, we can take a strategy σ_1 for the game over the set $\{1, \ldots, M\}$ and define its equivalent counterpart σ_2 over the set X as follows

$$\Pr\left[\sigma_2\left(s_1, \widehat{r_1}, \ldots, s_{i-1}, \widehat{r_{i-1}}; s_i\right)\right] := \Pr\left[\sigma_1\left(f(s_1), \widehat{r_1}, \ldots, f(s_{i-1}), \widehat{r_{i-1}}; f(s_i)\right)\right]$$

It follows that σ_2 has the same probability of winning as σ_1, since to each sequence $S_1 = (s_1, \ldots, s_N)$ drawn from $\{1, \ldots, M\}$ we can bijectively associate a sequence $S_2 := (f(s_1), \ldots, f(s_N))$ drawn from X, and the ranks r_i are the same for both S_1 and S_2. We thus conclude that $\mathcal{P}(X, N) \geq \mathcal{P}(M, N)$. As the presented mappings are bijective, by considering f^{-1} instead of f we get the opposite inequality, and thus finish the proof.   □

We are now ready to prove Lemma 2.

Proof (of Lemma 2). We have

$$\mathcal{P}(M, N \mid s_1 = i) = \sup_{\sigma} \Pr\left[\bigcap_{j=1}^{N} \sigma(h_j, s_j) = r_j \mid s_1 = i\right]$$

$$= \sup_{\sigma} \Pr\left[\sigma(i) = r_1 \cap W_{\mathcal{L}} \cap W_{\mathcal{R}}\right]$$

$$= \sup_{\sigma} \Pr\left[\sigma(i) = r_1\right] \Pr\left[W_{\mathcal{L}} \cap W_{\mathcal{R}} \mid \sigma(i) = r_1\right]$$

$$= \max_{j=1}^{N} \frac{\binom{i-1}{j-1}\binom{M-i}{N-j}}{\binom{M-1}{N-1}} \sup_{\sigma} \Pr\left[W_{\mathcal{L}} \cap W_{\mathcal{R}} \mid \sigma(i) = r_1\right]$$

Then, note that

$$\Pr\left[W_{\mathcal{L}} \cap W_{\mathcal{R}} \mid \sigma(i) = r_1\right] = \Pr\left[W_{\mathcal{R}} \mid W_{\mathcal{L}} \cap \sigma(i) = r_1\right] \Pr[W_{\mathcal{L}} \mid \sigma(i) = r_1]$$

Combining Lemmas 3 and 4 we have that $\Pr[W_{\mathcal{L}} \mid \sigma(i) = r_1] = \mathcal{P}(i - 1, j - 1)$ and $\Pr\left[W_{\mathcal{R}} \mid W_{\mathcal{L}} \cap \sigma(i) = r_1\right] = \mathcal{P}(M - i, N - j)$, from where we conclude the proof after using Eq. (1).   □

We can now easily prove Theorem 1. Algorithm 1 presents the concrete algorithm, which uses two tricks to achieve a runtime of $O(M^2N)$. First, it takes constant time to compute the hypergeometric probabilities (assuming constant time arithmetic operations) by precomputing the binomial coefficients. Second, it uses Knuth's *monotonicity* trick [3] (cf. lines 12, 14-19 of Algorithm 1) to reduce the complexity from $O(M^2N^2)$ down to $O(M^2N)$ since the probabilities of winning after guessing $\widehat{r}_i = j$ are *unimodal*; namely, if the best guess for $s_1 = i$ is j, then the best guess for $s_1 = i' > i$ must be some $j' \geq j$. Our C++ implementation solves the game for $M = 999, N = 20$ in 0.2 seconds on a personal computer (MacBook Pro M1, 8GB RAM). Figure 2 shows how the probabilities of winning are affected by the parameters M and N.

Algorithm 1: Dynamic Programming Algorithm

Input: M, N
Output: Table $\text{opt}[0..M][0..N]$ where $\text{opt}[m][n] = \mathcal{P}(m, n)$

```
/* Precompute binomial coefficients (a choose b) into global table C[a][b].  */
```

1 **Function** hypergeometricProbability(N, K, n, k):
2   **return** $(\texttt{C}[K][k] \cdot \texttt{C}[N - K][n - k]) / \texttt{C}[N][n]$;

3 **for** $m \leftarrow 0$ **to** M **do**
4   **for** $n \leftarrow 0$ **to** N **do**
5   **if** $n \leq 1$ **then**
6           $\text{opt}[m][n] \leftarrow 1.0$;
7   **continue**
8   **end**
9        $\text{sum} \leftarrow 0.0$, $\text{best\_}j \leftarrow 1$;
10   **for** $i \leftarrow 1$ **to** m **do**
11           $\text{max} \leftarrow 0.0$, $\text{prev} \leftarrow 0.0$;
12   **for** $j \leftarrow \text{best\_}j$ **to** n **do**
13              $p \leftarrow \text{opt}[i - 1][j - 1] \cdot \text{opt}[m - i][n - j] \cdot$ hypergeometricProbability(*m-1, i-1, n-1, j-1*);
14   **if** $p < \text{prev}$ **then**
15   **break**
16   **end**
17   **if** $p \geq \text{max}$ **then**
18                 $\text{max} \leftarrow p$;
19                 $\text{best\_}j \leftarrow j$;
20   **end**
21              $\text{prev} \leftarrow p$;
22   **end**
23           $\text{sum} \leftarrow \text{sum} + \text{max}$;
24   **end**
25        $\text{opt}[m][n] \leftarrow \text{sum}/m$;
26   **end**
27 **end**

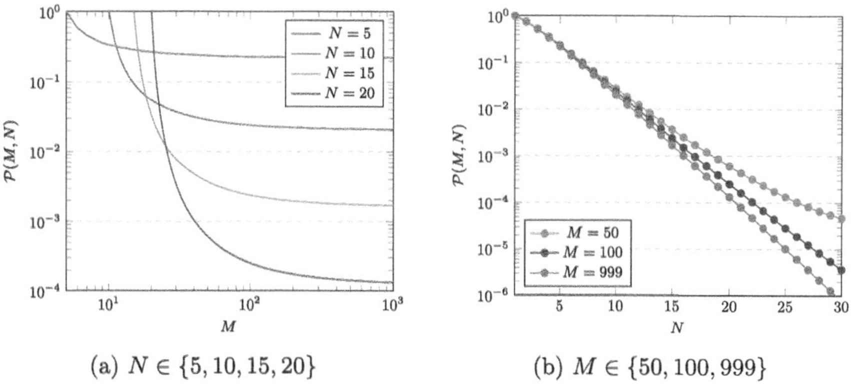

(a) $N \in \{5, 10, 15, 20\}$ (b) $M \in \{50, 100, 999\}$

Fig. 2. Optimal probability of winning for different values of M and N.

3   The Continuous Version of PlaceIt

We now study a version of the game where the sequence S is sampled from a continuous range $[a, b]$. As we will demonstrate, the analysis carried out in the discrete version can be readily adapted to the continuous variant.

Indeed, using an argument analogous to Lemma 4, we can establish an even stronger symmetry for the continuous case, where all continuous intervals $[a, b]$ lead to the same probabilities, and thus we can choose the range $[0, 1]$ for simplicity. Let us denote by $\mathcal{P}_c$ the optimal probability of winning over a game with N slots over the range $[0, 1]$, as this choice will simplify later calculations.

Theorem 1. *The optimal probability of winning a game of continuous Pla-ceIt is given by:*

$$\mathcal{P}_c(N) = \int_0^1 \max_{1 \leq i \leq N} \mathcal{P}_c(i)\mathcal{P}_c(N - 1 - i)B(i, s_1)\,\mathrm{d}s_1$$

where $B(i, s_1) := \binom{N-1}{i}s_1^i(1 - s_1)^{N-i-1}$ is the probability that exactly i out of $N - 1$ draws will be smaller than s_1.

Interestingly, $\mathcal{P}_c$ can be computed in practice as we show next. Note first that, after fixing N, for each possible value of s_1 there is an optimal value i that the max in Theorem 2 takes. Furthermore, we can define $b_{i,N}$ as the range of values for s_1 such that i is the value that the max in Theorem 2 takes. For example, if $N = 2$, then $b_{1,N} = [0, 0.5]$, $b_{2,N} = [0.5, 1]$. In general, we have

$$\mathcal{P}_c(N) = \sum_{i=1}^{N} \int_{b_{i,N}} \mathcal{P}_c(i)\mathcal{P}_c(N - 1 - i)B(i, s_1)\,\mathrm{d}s_1 \tag{2}$$

$$= \sum_{i=1}^{N} \mathcal{P}_c(i)\mathcal{P}_c(N - 1 - i) \int_{b_{i,N}} B(i, s_1)\,\mathrm{d}s_1. \tag{3}$$

To compute the ranges $b_{i,N}$, it suffices to identify the values of s_1 at which the optimal solution is indifferent between placing s_1 in $A[i]$ or $A[i+1]$. Namely, the cut-off between range $b_{i,N}$ and $b_{(i+1),N}$ occurs precisely at the value s_1 for which

$$\mathcal{P}_c(i)\mathcal{P}_c(N-1-i)B(i,s_1) = \mathcal{P}_c(i+1)\mathcal{P}_c(N-i)B(i+1,s_1). \tag{4}$$

Assuming inductively that we have already computed $\mathcal{P}_c(n)$ for every value $n < N$, then the previous equation reduces to

$$\alpha_i \cdot B(i,s_1) = \alpha_{i+1} \cdot B(i+1,s_1)$$

with $\alpha_i := \mathcal{P}_c(i)\mathcal{P}_c(N-1-i), \alpha_{i+1} := \mathcal{P}_c(i+1)\mathcal{P}_c(N-i)$ being known constants.

Then, by expanding the binomials $B(i,s_1)$ and $B(i+1,s_1)$ we obtain the following expression for s_1:

$$s_1 = \left(\frac{\alpha_{i+1}(n-1)}{\alpha_i(i+1)} + 1\right)^{-1}. \tag{5}$$

Naturally, the lower bound of the range $b_{1,N}$ is 0 and the upper bounds of $b_{N-1,N}$ is 1. We thank the anonymous reviewers for noticing this simplification. Figure 3 illustrates this for $N = 6$.

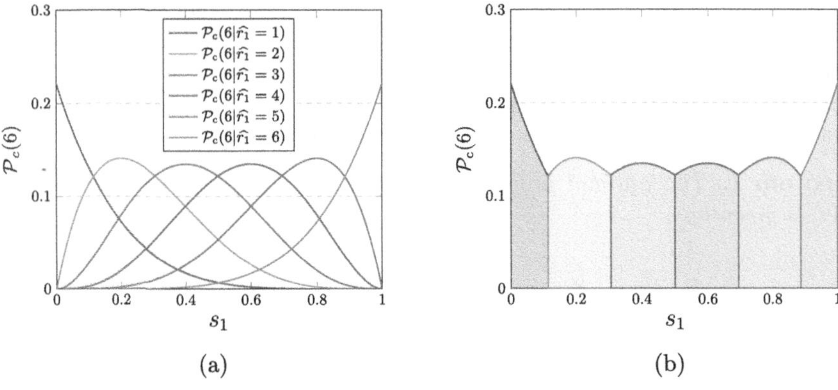

(a)   (b)

Fig. 3. Analysis of continuous PLACEIT with $N = 6$. Figure 3a presents the curves for the probability of winning according to the different possible guesses for s_1. Figure 3b depicts how the points at which the curves in Fig. 3a intersect define the ranges $b_{i,6}$, as per Eq. (4). Moreover, the total area under the curve (i.e., adding the area of all 6 ranges) is precisely $\mathcal{P}_c(6)$.

It is worth noting that Fig. 3a and 3b showcase the symmetry of the problem around $s_1 = 0.5$, which can be also used to speed up the calculation. Moreover, note that the integral in Eq. (3) features only constants (the $\mathcal{P}_c(\cdot)$ terms that can be computed recursively) and the binomial terms, which are polynomials in s_1 and thus their integral is easy to compute exactly without any need for numerical methods.

4   Related Work

The game of PLACEIT represents an interesting combination of the widely studied *secretary problem* [4] and *online sorting* [1], a problem that has recently received significant attention in the online-algorithms community. The secretary problem appeared for the first time in 1960, and it can be described as follows:

> *A total of N candidates for a secretary position interview one by one; after each interview, the candidate must be either immediately hired, or immediately rejected (in which case the next candidate is interviewed). When a candidate is interviewed, the interviewer evaluates how that candidate compares to all previously interviewed candidates. The goal is to maximize the probability of hiring the candidate with the highest evaluation.*

Interestingly, the simple strategy "reject the first N/e candidates, and hire the first candidate better than all the previous ones" results in the asymptotically optimal probability of success, $1/e \approx 0.368$. The secretary problem has been widely studied in a variety of settings [5], and it holds an interesting relationship with PLACEIT: it can be seen as a particular case in which one only focuses on getting $A[N]$ right, without requiring other guesses to be valid.

On the other hand, the online sorting problem was introduced in 2021 by Aamand et al. [1], and it roughly consists of receiving a stream of real numbers between 0 and 1, which must be placed irrevocably in an array A, with the goal of making A as closed to sorted as possible, which can be formalized in terms of minimizing $\sum_{i=1}^{N-1} |A[i+1] - A[i]|$. The state-of-the-art is due to Abrahamsen et al. [2], who showed a competitive ratio of roughly $N^{1/4}$ when N numbers are drawn uniformly at random from $[0, 1]$. The main difference between online sorting and the game of PLACEIT is that the former tries to optimize for the *"sortnedess"* of A, whereas in PLACEIT that sortnedess is a hard restriction, and the goal is to maximize the probability of winning or the expected number of rounds before losing. Hence, PLACEIT is a game about *"perfect"* online sorting. In general, the applications for the analysis of PLACEIT are similar to those of online sorting: ranking inputs that are revealed online in scenarios where changing the ranking of an input after the initial ranking guess is either impossible or too expensive.

5   Conclusion

We have analyzed the game PLACEIT and proved that the probability of winning the original game with the optimal strategy is close to 0.0001335. Furthermore, we proposed and analyzed a continuous version of PLACEIT, showing how the optimal probability of winning can be computed. Our analysis can be extended to other distributions over $\mathbb{R}$; if numbers are drawn from a distribution X whose CDF is $f(x) := \Pr[X \leq x]$, then it suffices to replace $B(i, s_1)$ by $B(i, f(s_1))$ in Eq.

(3). We leave open some questions of interest that are not covered by our work: analyzing the maximum expected number of rounds that any strategy can attain, and providing asymptotic bounds on the probability of winning according to the optimal strategy described by Theorem 1. With respect to the implementation in the discrete case, one potential avenue for improvement is to obtain an equation analogous to Eq. (5) for finding the cut-off points of two scaled hyper-geometrical distributions, which may speed up the original implementation.

References

1. Aamand, A., Abrahamsen, M., Beretta, L., Kleist, L.: Online sorting and translational packing of convex polygons (2024). https://arxiv.org/abs/2112.03791
2. Abrahamsen, M., Bercea, I.O., Beretta, L., Klausen, J., Kozma, L.: Online sorting and online tsp: randomized, stochastic, and high-dimensional (2024). https://arxiv.org/abs/2406.19257
3. Bein, W., Golin, M.J., Larmore, L.L., Zhang, Y.: The Knuth-Yao quadrangle-inequality speedup is a consequence of total monotonicity. ACM Trans. Algorithms **6**(1) (dec 2010). https://doi.org/10.1145/1644015.1644032
4. Ferguson, T.S.: Who solved the secretary problem? Statistical Science **4**(3), 282–289 (8 1989). https://doi.org/10.1214/ss/1177012493
5. Freeman, P.R.: The secretary problem and its extensions: a review. Int. Stat. Rev./Revue Internationale de Statistique **51**(2), 189–206 (1983). https://doi.org/10.2307/1402748
6. Gale, D.: The game of hex and the Brouwer fixed-point theorem. Am. Math. Mon. **86**(10), 818–827 (1979). https://doi.org/10.2307/2320146
7. Koller, D., Megiddo, N.: The complexity of two-person zero-sum games in extensive form. Games Econom. Behav. **4**(4), 528–552 (1992). https://doi.org/10.1016/0899-8256(92)90035-Q
8. @_nickvogel: We're doing 20 numbers today. https://www.tiktok.com/@_nickvogel/video/7200799424015027499 (2023). Accessed 11 Nov 2024
9. Nirjara: '20 Number'- New TikTok challenge?. https://hashtaghyena.com/tiktok/tiktok-challenges/20-number-new-tiktok-challenge/ (2023). Accessed 11 Nov 2024
10. Siegel, A.N.: Combinatorial game theory, vol. 146. American Mathematical Society (2023)
11. Toffoli, T., Margolus, N.: Cellular automata machines: a new environment for modeling. The MIT Press (1987). https://doi.org/10.7551/mitpress/1763.003.0004

Optimal Play of the All Yellow Zombie Dice Game

Todd W. Neller[✉], John C. Llano, Minh Q. Vu Dinh,
and Clifton G. M. Presser

Department of Computer Science, Gettysburg College, Gettysburg, USA
tneller@gettysburg.edu

Abstract. In this paper, we solve and visualize optimal play for All Yellow Zombie Dice, a simplification of the Zombie Dice jeopardy dice game by Steve Jackson [1] where we assume that all dice have the same outcome distribution. We present a spectrum of All Yellow Zombie Dice human-playable strategies that trade off greater play complexity for better performance, and collectively clarify key considerations for excellent play.

1 Introduction

Zombie Dice is a dice game first published in 2010 by Steve Jackson [1]. It is a jeopardy dice game [4, Ch. 6] in the Ten Thousand dice game family [2]. In this paper, we analyze a simplified variant, All Yellow Zombie Dice, computing optimal play as well as providing additional insights to gameplay.

We begin by describing the rules of Zombie Dice, and a variant thereof, All Yellow Zombie Dice. We define 2-player optimality equations for All Yellow Zombie Dice and our method for solving them. After visualizing the optimal play policy, we share observations on the optimal roll/hold boundary. We then present an array of human-playable policies we have devised along with their performances against the optimal policy. The policies demonstrate different design trade-offs of greater complexity for greater win rates, and highlight key play policy considerations. Finally, we discuss future work and summarize our conclusions.

2 Rules

Zombie Dice (ZD) is a dice game for two or more players using 13 nonstandard six-sided dice described in Fig. 1.

A *turn* consists of a sequence of player dice rolls where rolled brains and shotguns are set aside. The turn ends when, after rolling, the player either decides to *hold* (i.e. stop rolling) and score the total number of brains rolled, or has rolled three or more shotguns, ending the turn and scoring 0 points.

At the beginning of the turn, three of the supply of 13 dice are drawn at random and rolled. Any rolled brains and shotguns are then set aside. If 3 or

M. Hartisch et al. (Eds.): CG 2024, LNCS 15550, pp. 197–206, 2025.
https://doi.org/10.1007/978-3-031-86585-5_16

Color	Number of Dice	Brain Sides	Shotgun Sides	Footprint Sides
Green	6	3	1	2
Yellow	4	2	2	2
Red	3	1	3	2

Fig. 1. Zombie Dice outcome distributions

more shotguns are set aside, the turn ends scoring 0 points. Otherwise, the player chooses either to hold, scoring the number of brains and ending their turn, or to roll again. To roll again, dice are drawn at random and added to any rolled footprints until there are three dice to roll. (If there are no dice to draw, keep track of the number of brains set aside, and add all rolled brain dice back into the dice supply, and continue drawing dice at random.) Then those three dice are rolled, any brains and shotguns are again set aside, and we repeat the process described above.

A *round* consists of each player taking one turn in sequence. When a round ends with any player having 13 or more points, a player having the most points wins. If two or more players are tied with the most points (13 or more), another round is played between those players only. In this paper, we will focus on the two-player ZD game, so we can say that a 2-player game ends when a round concludes with a single winner having the most points with 13 or more points.

We will denote red, yellow, and green dice as R, Y, and G, respectively, with brain, shotgun, and footprint rolls denoted as B, S, and F, respectively. We denote a brain roll of a green die as BG. Consider this example round of two-player play:

- Player 1 draws G, G, and Y dice and rolls FG, FG, and SY. SY is set aside. We have zero (fewer than three) S set aside, so the player can hold (scoring zero B) or roll. The player chooses to roll, drawing a third random die to join the two FG dice. A G is drawn and the three G are rolled as BG, SG, and FG. BG and SG are set aside. We have two S set aside, so the player can hold (scoring one B) or roll. The player chooses to roll, drawing two R dice at random, and rerolling FG with these to get BG, SR and SR. All three B/S dice are set aside, totaling four S. With three or more S, the turn ends with no score change. (All dice are returned to the supply at the end of a turn.)
- Player 2 draws three G dice and rolls BG, BG, and FG. The two BG dice are set aside. Player 2 with no S set aside chooses to roll, draws a G and Y, and rerolls the FG with these to get BG, BY, and FG. The two B dice are set aside for a total of four B dice. Player 2 with no S chooses to roll, draws Y and R dice, and rerolls the FG with these to get BY, SG, and SR. These are all set aside for a total of five B and two S dice set aside. Although player 2 could roll again with less than three S set aside, player 2 decides to hold, scoring five points, one for each B set aside, ending the round.

The game thus consists of roll/hold risk assessments in a race to achieve a unique top score of 13 or more points, playing additional tie-breaker rounds with tied leaders as necessary. Given the player scores, the numbers of colored B and S dice set aside, and the current locations of non-S dice of different colors, should the current player roll or hold so as to maximize the probability of winning?

2.1 All Yellow Zombie Dice (AYZD)

It can often be insightful to first analyze a simplification of a game. In this case, we create a 2-player variant we call All Yellow Zombie Dice (AYZD), where all 13 dice are yellow with two B, two S, and two F sides. The three roll outcomes are equiprobable for all dice and we need not include dice colors nor their locations as part of our state description for this simplified game.

3 AYZD Optimality Equations and Solution Method

We here define optimality equations for the AYZD two-player game.

Nonterminal states are described as the 5-tuple (p, i, j, b, s), where p is the current player number (1 or 2), i is the current player score, j is the opponent score, b is the turn total (number of brains set aside), and s is the number of rolled shotguns set aside. $P(p, i, j, b, s)$ will denote the probability of player p winning in state (p, i, j, b, s) under the assumption of optimal play, i.e. each player plays so as to maximize one's own expected win probability.

Terminal states consist of a player 1 win or player 2 win. (Draws are not allowed, as tie-breaker rounds are mandated.) Player 1 wins at the beginning of their turn ($p = 1, b = 0$) when player 1 has achieved the goal score ($i \geq g$ where $g = 13$) and player 2 ended their turn with a lesser score ($j < i$). Player 2 wins on their turn ($p = 2$) when player 2's score plus their turn total exceed both the goal score and player 1's score ($i \geq 13$ and $i > j$), at which point player 2 can and should hold, winning the game.

Let $P_{\text{roll}}(b, s)$ be the probability of rolling b brains and s shotguns (and thus $3 - b - s$ footprints) on a roll of 3 dice:

$$P_{\text{roll}}(b, s) = \frac{\binom{3}{b}\binom{3-b}{s}}{3^3} = \frac{2}{9 b! s! (3 - b - s)!}$$

The probability of winning with a roll $P_{\text{roll}}(p, i, j, b, s)$ under the assumption of optimal play thereafter is:

$$P_{\text{roll}}(p, i, j, b, s) = \sum_{s^+=0}^{2-s} \sum_{b^+=0}^{3-s^+} (P_{\text{roll}}(b^+, s^+) P(p, i, j, b + b^+, s + s^+))$$
$$+ \sum_{s^+=3-s}^{3} \sum_{b^+=0}^{3-s^+} (P_{\text{roll}}(b^+, s^+)(1 - P(3 - p, j, i, 0, 0)))$$

where b^+ and s^+ denote the number of additional brains and shotguns rolled.

The probability of winning with a hold $P_{\text{hold}}(p, i, j, b, s)$ under the assumption of optimal play thereafter is:

$$P_{\text{hold}}(p, i, j, b, s) = (1 - P(3 - p, j, i + b, 0, \ 0))$$

Then the probability of winning $P(p, i, j, b, s)$ under the assumption of optimal play is:

$$P(p, i, j, b, s) = \max(P_{\text{roll}}(p, i, j, b, s), P_{\text{hold}}(p, i, j, b, \ s))$$

Players can tie at or above the goal, requiring a tiebreaker round. Players can tie within a tiebreaker round as well, requiring another tiebreaker round. Since there is no limit to tiebreaker rounds and no limit to the turn total, we must create an artificial upper limit for computational purposes. We have chosen twice the goal score ($M = 2g = 26$) as this bound, and observe that computational results do not change for $M = 3g$, $4g$, or $5g$, assuring us that we capture optimal play behavior within such bounds.

Having bounded our nonterminal state space representation such that $p \in \{1, 2\}, 0 \le i, j, b \le M, s \in \{0, 1, 2\}$, we apply value iteration as in [5] until the maximum probability change of an iteration is less than $\epsilon = 10^{-14}$.

4 AYZD Optimal Policy

The optimal roll/hold boundaries of AYZD are shown in Fig. 2. Each subfigure depicts a 3-dimensional (i, j, b) roll/hold boundary for each possible pair of player p and rolled s. Axes are player score i, opponent score j, and turn total b. Given a current state inside or outside of the appropriate solid, an optimal player should roll or hold, respectively.

We first observe a few expected similarities between these roll/hold solids. First, the $i + b = 13$ diagonal plane indicating a rolling for the goal score appears in situations where player(s) are close to the end of the game or have little to risk with many dice to roll. Player 2 should exceed ($s < 2$) or meet ($s = 2$) player 1's score when player 1 has reached the goal score, so the planes $i + b = j$ or $i + b = j + 1$ are also a prominent hold planes. As a player has fewer dice to roll, play becomes more conservative.

There are some interesting differences and subtleties to observe as well. Player 1 plays more aggressively than player 2 with higher minimum hold values with all other state variables being equal. Also, there are interesting nonlinearities when player 1 seeks to not just reach 13 points, but to far enough exceed 13 so as to make it unlikely that player 2 will exceed their final score. Player 2, having the opportunity to exceed player 1's final score, has an advantage and generally plays so as to keep within striking distance of player 1's score.

Most interesting and complex are the roll/hold boundaries when a player has rolled one shotgun. Here we observe nonlinearities in the roll/hold surface for both players. Whereas one might approximate player with no shotguns or two shotguns as "always roll" and "hold at 1", respectively, the roll/hold surface

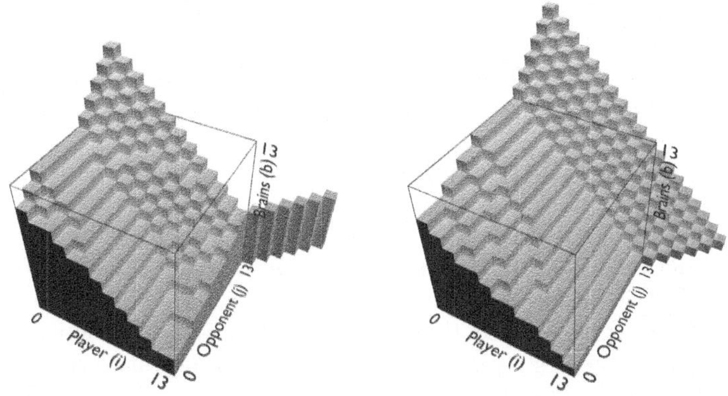

(a) Player 1 with no shotguns rolled (b) Player 2 with no shotguns rolled

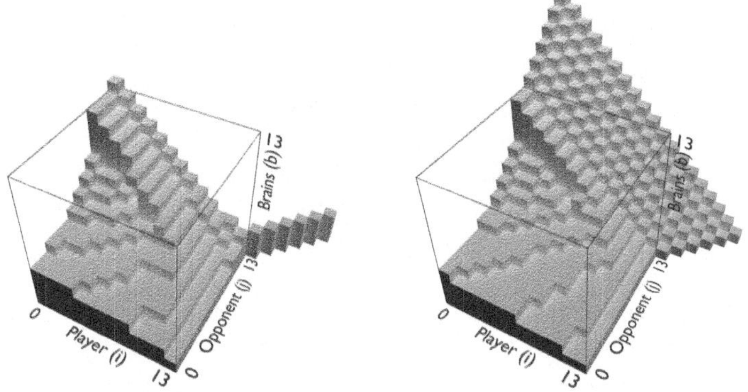

(c) Player 1 with one shotgun rolled (d) Player 2 with one shotgun rolled

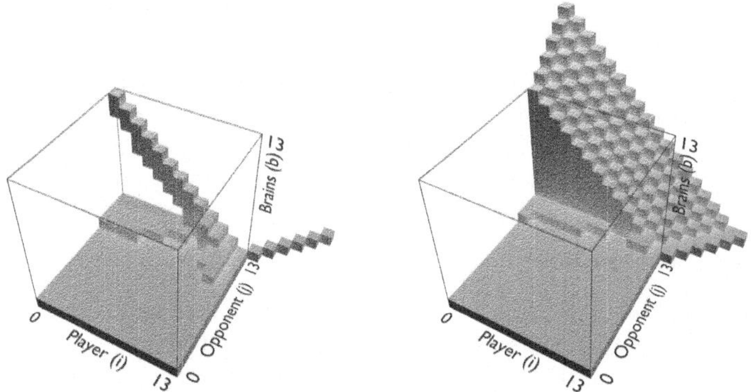

(e) Player 1 with two shotguns rolled (f) Player 2 with two shotguns rolled

Fig. 2. AYZD optimal play visualization. A player in a state inside or outside the gray solid should roll or hold, respectively. Subfigures are by p, s cases, and axes follow i, j, b state variables.

shape is relatively complex when the current player has rolled one shotgun and player scores are not close to the goal.

We also observe that, during tiebreaker rounds, player 1 should hold at 6/3/1 when 0/1/2 shotgun(s) have been rolled, respectively.

5   Human-Playable Policies

In this section, we present a range of human-playable policies mapping states to roll/hold actions that trade off greater complexity for greater win rate. By *human-playable*, we mean that all roll/hold decisions may be made through simple mental math. As we will see, these policies range from extremely simple rules to very-complex sub-cases requiring memorization of several constants in order to approximate roll/hold surfaces.

Each policy is evaluated against the optimal policy with each having equal probability of playing first. Policy evaluation follows the same value-iteration-style algorithm of [6]. The performance of each is summarized in Fig. 3.

Policy	Difference
Fixed Hold-At	-0.0274
Minh Cases	-0.0133
Llano Cases	-0.0118
Neller Cases	-0.0100

Fig. 3. Differences between human-playable and optimal policy win rates

We present each policy as a method that returns whether or not to roll in the given state.

5.1   Fixed Hold-At Policy

First, we consider a Fixed Hold-At Policy (Algorithm 1) where we need only remember a few turn total thresholds.

Requiring memorization of only a few cases and two hold-at constants (4 and 1), Algorithm 1 reduces the optimal play gap to ~2.74%.

5.2   Minh Cases Policy

The Minh Cases Policy (Algorithm 2) elaborates the Fixed Hold-At Policy (Algorithm 1) for situations where a player has rolled 1 shotgun.

In this situation, if the opponent's score is greater than or equal to 8, the current player will aim for the winning score of 13 or try to exceed the opponent's score by 3 brains if the opponent has reached 10 or more. This policy results in an optimal play gap of ~1.33%.

The policy relies on four non-goal score constants to keep in mind (8, 3, 4, and 1) which is relatively simple but still provides a close approximation to optimal play.

Algorithm 1: Fixed Hold-At Policy

Input   : player p, player score i, opponent score j, turn total b, shotguns rolled s

Output: whether or not to roll

```
1  if p = 2 ∧ j ≥ 13 ∧ i + b < j then       // When player 2 with j ≥ goal...
2  |   return true                          // and holding would lose, roll.
3  else if s = 0 then                       // Keep rolling with 0 shotguns.
4  |   return true
5  else if s = 1 then                                // Hold at 4 with 1 shotgun.
6  |   return b < 4
7  else                                              // Hold at 1 with 2 shotguns.
8  |   return b < 1
9  end if
```

Algorithm 2: Minh Cases Policy

Input   : player p, player score i, opponent score j, turn total b, shotguns rolled s

Output: whether or not to roll

```
1   if p = 2 ∧ j ≥ 13 ∧ i + b < j then        // When player 2 with j ≥ goal...
2   |   return true                            // and holding would lose, roll.
3   else if s = 0 then                         // Keep rolling with 0 shotguns.
4   |   return true
5   else if s = 1 then                                  // With 1 shotgun,
6   |   if j ≥ 8 then                          // if opponent's score j ≥ 8,
7   |   |   return i + b < max(13, j + 3)      // win (with lead of 3 if j ≥ 10),
8   |   else                                                // else hold at 4.
9   |   |   return b < 4
10  |   end if
11  else                                               // Hold at 1 with 2 shotguns.
12  |   return b < 1
13  end if
```

5.3 Llano Cases Policy

Algorithm 3, "Llano Cases Policy", breaks down cases by player p and number of shotguns rolled s. Policies for each player are near identical, with a minor difference for zero shotguns rolled.

Though not as computationally simple as the previous policies, this policy requires the memorization of few constants when playing below the goal score and allows the player to play nearly the same each game, regardless of whether they went first or second. The main differences arise from playing beyond the goal score with zero shotguns rolled as player 1, and the added condition of either player being at or above 10 in order to go for the goal with 1 shotgun rolled. Also, specific strategy has been determined for play when either player is

---

Algorithm 3: Llano Cases Policy

Input : player p, player score i, opponent score j, turn total b, shotguns rolled s

Output: whether or not to roll

```
 1  i' ← i + b                                        // i': score after holding
 2  h = {6, 3, 1}    // h: tiebreaker hold values indexed by shotguns rolled
 3  if i ≥ 13 ∨ j ≥ 13 then       // If either player reached/exceeded goal...
 4  │   if i = j then                            // if the scores are even...
 5  │   │   if p = 1 then   // player 1 holds at the appropriate turn score.
 6  │   │   │   return b < h[s]
 7  │   │   else                           // Player 2 holds when b reaches 1.
 8  │   │   │   return b < 1
 9  │   │   end if
10  │   else if p = 2 ∧ i < j then               // If player 2 is trailing...
11  │   │   return (s < 2 ∧ i' ≤ j) ∨ (s = 2 ∧ i' < j) // match the opponent with
12  │   │       2 shotguns, exceed by 1 otherwise.
12  │   end if
13  │   return false                                      // Otherwise hold.
14  else                         // If both players are below goal score...
15  │   if s = 0 then                              // if 0 shotguns rolled...
16  │   │   if p = 1 then   // player 1 goes for the higher of goal or j + 9.
17  │   │   │   return i' < max(13, j + 9)
18  │   │   else                             // Player 2 goes for the goal.
19  │   │   │   return i' < 13
20  │   │   end if
21  │   else if s = 1 then                         // If 1 shotgun rolled...
22  │   │   if i ≥ 10 ∧ j ≥ 10 then    // and either player has at least 10...
23  │   │   │   return i' < 13                            // go for the goal.
24  │   │   else
25  │   │   │   return b < 4                      // Otherwise, hold at 4.
26  │   │   end if
27  │   else                                      // If 2 shotguns rolled...
28  │   │   return b < 1                                   // Hold at 1.
29  │   end if
30  end if
```

---

above the goal score, involving the memorization of a few constants for player 1, and playing to catch or slightly exceed their opponent in the case of player 2.

5.4   Neller Cases Policy

Algorithm 4, "Neller Cases Policy", also breaks down cases by player p and number of shotguns rolled s.

This policy is similar in complexity and decisions to Algorithm 3, organizing and handling endgame and 0 shotgun cases differently. It also has player 1 and 2 treating 8 and 10 as different end-game score thresholds, respectively. However,

---

Algorithm 4: Neller Cases Policy

    Input   : player p, player score i, opponent score j, turn total b, shotguns rolled s

    Output: whether or not to roll

1 $i' \leftarrow i + b$ `// i': score after holding`

2 $h = \{6, 3, 1\}$ `// h: tiebreaker hold values indexed by shotguns rolled`

3 **if** $p = 1$ **then**   `// If player 1, ...`

4   **if** $i \geq 13 \wedge i = j$ **then**   `// if tied at/above 13, hold at h values.`

5 | **return** $b < h[s]$

6   **else if** $s = 0$ **then**   `// If 0 shotguns, hold at ≥ 13 with ≥ 8 lead.`

7 | **return** $i' < \max(13, j + 8)$

8   **end if**

9     $e \leftarrow 8$ `// Set player 1 end-game score threshold e to 8.`

10 **else**   `// Else if player 2, ...`

11   **if** $j \geq 13$ **then**   `// if player 1 has achieved the goal score, ...`

12 | **return** $(s < 2 \wedge i' \leq j) \vee (s = 2 \wedge i' < j)$ `// exceed/meet player 1's score with under/exactly 2 shotguns, respectively.`

13   **else if** $i \geq 13 \wedge i > j$ **then**   `// If holding wins, hold.`

14 | **return** *false*

15   **else if** $s = 0$ **then**   `// Always roll with no shotguns.`

16 | **return** *true*

17   **end if**

18    $e \leftarrow 10$ `// Set player 2 end-game score threshold e to 10.`

19 **end if**

20 **if** $s = 1$ **then**   `// If 1 shotgun rolled, ...`

21   **if** $i \geq e \vee j \geq e$ **then**   `// hold at 13 if score(s) ≥ e.`

22 | **return** $i' < 13$

23   **else**   `// Otherwise, hold at 4.`

24 | **return** $b < 4$

25   **end if**

26 **else if** $s = 2$ **then**   `// If 2 shotguns rolled, hold at 1.`

27 | **return** $b < 1$

28 **end if**

---

this better approximates optimal play performance, closing the optimal play gap to ∼1.00%.

Through these algorithms, we see that key play considerations (beyond trivial decisions regarding immediate win/loss) could be approximately summarized as follows: With 0 shotguns, keep rolling. With 1 shotgun, get at least 4 points, but close to the game end, try to win with a lead as player 1, and just win as player 2. With 2 shotguns, get at least 1 point. For tiebreaker rounds, player 1 rolls for 6/3/1 points with 0/1/2 shotguns, whereas player 2 tries to exceed/match player 1's score with under/exactly 2 shotguns.

6   Future Work

Recall that our AYZD simplification to Zombie Dice treats all dice as having the average (i.e. yellow) distribution of brains, shotguns, and footprints. In the full game, we have the distribution of dice and dice outcomes shown in Sect. 2.

Our next step will be to compute optimal play for the full complexity of 2-player Zombie Dice. We will then compare performance of both the optimal and human-playable AYZD policies against optimal Zombie Dice play to see how much dice color distribution matters for play performance.

7   Conclusions

In this paper, we have computed and visualized optimal play for the 2-player case of the All Yellow Zombie Dice game, a simplification of the regular Zombie Dice game. Prior work has determined optimal turn scoring strategy [3], but this is the first step towards understanding optimal game winning strategy. To maximize expectation of score gain per turn is not to maximize expectation of winning probability. We have determined that player 2 has a slight informational advantage due to the fact that the game will always end with player 2's turn.

In addition, we presented a variety of human-playable strategies, trading off simplicity for performance against optimal play, with optimal play performance gaps ranging from ~2.74% to ~1.00%. For casual play, we recommend the Minh Cases Policy (Algorithm 2) with an optimal play performance gap of only ~1.33%.

The All Yellow Zombie Dice game has a fairly complex optimal roll-hold policy boundary (Fig. 2), yet relatively simple human-playable policies offer decent performance against optimal play, revealing some of the key considerations for excellent play.

References

1. Zombie dice. https://boardgamegeek.com/boardgame/62871/zombie-dice Accessed 24 May 2023
2. Busche, M., Neller, T.W.: Optimal play of the Farkle dice game. In: Advances in Computer Games: 15th International Conferences, ACG 2017, Leiden, The Netherlands, July 3–5, 2017, Revised Selected Papers 15, pp. 63–72. Springer (2017). https://doi.org/10.1007/978-3-319-71649-7_6
3. Cook, H.L., Taylor, D.G.: Zombie dice: An optimal play strategy (2014). https://arxiv.org/abs/1406.0351
4. Knizia, R.: Dice Games Properly Explained. Elliot Right-Way Books, Brighton Road, Lower Kingswood, Tadworth, Surrey, KT20 6TD U.K. (1999)
5. Neller, T.W., Presser, C.G.: Optimal play of the dice game pig. UMAP J. **25**(1), 25–47 (2004)
6. Neller, T.W., Presser, C.G.: Practical play of the dice game pig. UMAP J. **31**(1), 5–19 (2010)

Zweistein: A Dynamic Programming Evaluation Function for Einstein Würfelt Nicht!

Wei-Lin Hsueh[1] and Tsan-sheng Hsu[2]

[1] Department of Computer Science and Information Engineering,
National Taiwan University, Taipei 106319, Taiwan
b08902034@ntu.edu.tw
[2] Institute of Information Science, Academia Sinica, Taipei 115201, Taiwan
tshsu@iis.sinica.edu.tw
https://homepage.iis.sinica.edu.tw/pages/tshsu

Abstract. This paper introduces Zweistein, a dynamic programming evaluation function for Einstein Würfelt Nicht! (EWN). Instead of relying on human knowledge to craft an evaluation function, Zweistein uses a data-centric approach that eliminates the need for parameter tuning. The idea is to use a vector recording the distance to the corner of all pieces. This distance vector captures the essence of EWN. It not only outperforms many traditional EWN evaluation functions but also won first place in the TCGA 2023 competition.

Keywords: Einstein Würfelt Nicht! · Evaluation Function · Table Lookup

1 Introduction

EinStein würfelt nicht! (abbr. EWN) is a two-player stochastic game with perfect information [5], played on a 5×5 board. Pieces are red or blue and labeled 1 to 6. Red starts in the top left, blue in the bottom right. The board's initial placement is usually symmetrical (see Fig.1).

Players roll dice to move pieces. A piece can only move if its label matches the dice roll; otherwise, the player can move a piece with the next higher or lower number. Red pieces move right, down, or diagonally right-down, while blue pieces move left, up, or diagonally left-up. Pieces capture any piece at their destination, regardless of color.

Taking Fig. 2 as an example, the red side has pieces 1, 2, and 6. With a dice roll of 4, piece 4 is unavailable. Thus, the movable pieces are 6 (next higher) and 2 (next lower). Moving piece 6 to the right captures piece 2, as shown in Fig. 3. In the next move, with a dice roll of 1, the blue side must move piece 1. The available moves for blue are also depicted in Fig. 3.

© The Author(s), under exclusive license to Springer Nature Switzerland AG 2025
M. Hartisch et al. (Eds.): CG 2024, LNCS 15550, pp. 207–218, 2025.
https://doi.org/10.1007/978-3-031-86585-5_17

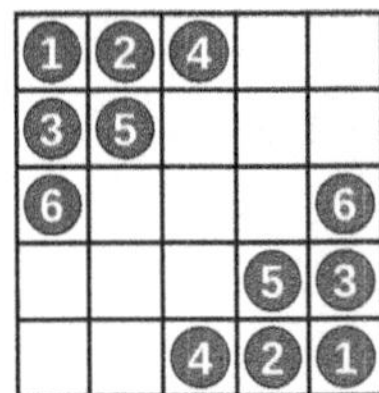

Fig. 1. The initial board.

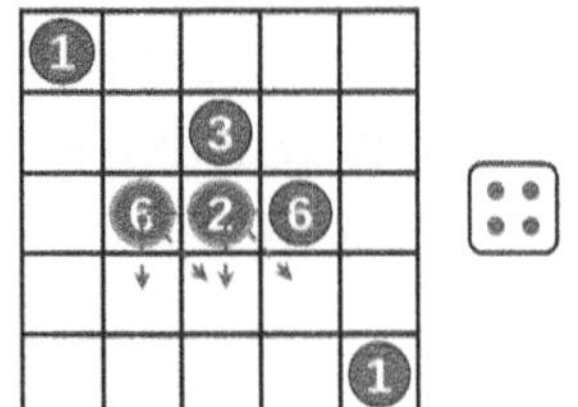

Fig. 2. An example showing the piece selection and movement

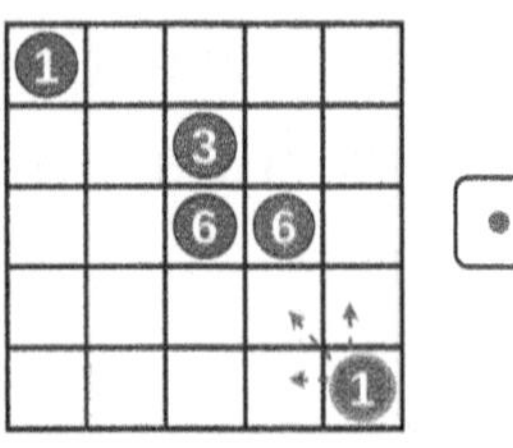

Fig. 3. Another example showing the piece selection and movement

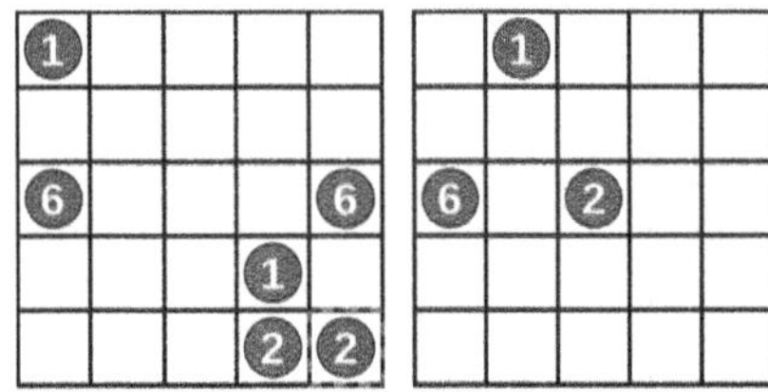

Fig. 4. An example showing the win conditions. On the left side, red reaches the corner and wins. On the right side, red captures all blue pieces and wins. (Color figure online)

The game ends when one side captures all opponent pieces or a piece reaches the opponent's corner square (bottom right for red, top left for blue), with no draws possible.

Despite the game's simple rules, designing an AI for EWN is challenging due to its inherent randomness and the strategic balance between defense and attack.

Traditional minimax tree search methods are less common in modern EWN contests. Instead, Monte Carlo tree search or machine learning techniques are more commonly used. However, this does not mean minimax search is inferior to other methods. This paper introduces a novel dynamic programming evaluation function that bypasses the need for human-crafted parameters, just like Monte Carlo methods or machine learning. Its effectiveness was demonstrated in the TCGA 2023 competition, where it secured first place against contestants who had previously won ICGA tournaments using machine learning and Monte Carlo methods [8] (Fig. 4).

2 Background

2.1 Motivation

Evaluation functions are essential in computer gaming programs. Claude E. Shannon recognized this as early as the 1940s [1], noting that an ideal evaluation function should correlate positively with the quality of a game position.

Achieving an ideal evaluation function, however, is equivalent to solving the game, which is infeasible for most popular games, including EWN. In practice, evaluation functions are approximations. Using Minimax search can reduce errors and strengthen the computer program.

Designing an effective evaluation function often requires extensive human knowledge, with no standardized method. For games like chess, abundant human insight makes creating a strong evaluation function easier, as demonstrated by IBM's Deep Blue [11], which defeated top human players.

For newly invented or complex games with limited human knowledge, designing evaluation functions can be time-consuming. Go, for example, requires fine-tuning numerous parameters. While GnuGo [2] was a strong program in the early 2000 s, it still could not defeat top players.

Recent methods, such as Monte Carlo tree search and reinforcement learning, minimize reliance on human knowledge. AlphaGo [3] used these techniques to beat the best Go players, showing that avoiding human expertise may be more effective for games with limited knowledge.

However, these methods do not provide insights that help players improve. Therefore, we introduce a dynamic programming approach to construct an evaluation function that requires no manual fine-tuning and offers a human-understandable heuristic.

2.2   Related Works

EWN, being a game with only 20 years of history, has limited human knowledge available. Consequently, designing an evaluation function for EWN is challenging and complex. Most researchers have focused on using Monte Carlo tree search techniques to develop EWN programs [5–8].

Several attempts have also been made to craft evaluation functions for EWN, often focusing on balancing attacking and defending power through parameter tuning [9,10].

In the experiments section, we will compare the performance of Zweistein with these existing functions.

3   Methods

This section primarily discusses the details of implementing Zweistein, which represents the win rate of EWN-simple, introduced below.

3.1   EWN-Simple

Zweistein employs a new concept from EWN-simple. While this new game resembles the original EWN rules, EWN-simple simplifies the win rate calculation significantly. The main difference between EWN-simple and vanilla EWN is the elimination of piece-capturing rules. Some adjustments were necessary to account for the removal of these rules.

First, since EWN-simple does not allow piece capturing, two different pieces can overlap when they move to the same space.

Second, EWN-simple introduces a special rule. Without the piece-capturing rule, each piece cannot interfere with others, there is no reason for a player to go along a longer path to the corner. Meaning players will always move their pieces toward the goal along the shortest path. To simplify the calculation, players are restricted to moving only along the shortest path, ensuring that the Chebyshev distance to the goal corner decreases by 1 with every move. The table of Chebyshev distance to the corner is shown in Fig. 5.

4	4	4	4	4	goal	1	2	3	4
4	3	3	3	3	1	1	2	3	4
4	3	2	2	2	2	2	2	3	4
4	3	2	1	1	3	3	3	3	4
4	3	2	1	goal	4	4	4	4	4

Fig. 5. The first table shows the Chebyshev distance to the goal corner from the red side's perspective. The second table provides a similar view from the blue side's perspective. (Color figure online)

3.2 Collapse an EWN-Simple Board Into a Distance Array

This section is the core of Zweistein. The reason for removing the piece-capturing rules in EWN-simple is that it creates numerous isomorphic boards, allowing us to collapse all isomorphic boards into a single array form. This significantly reduces the space complexity.

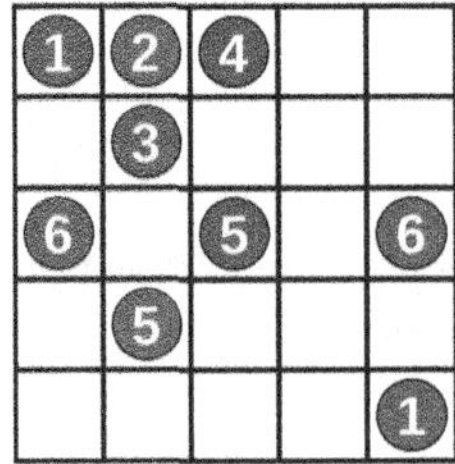

Fig. 6. An example board

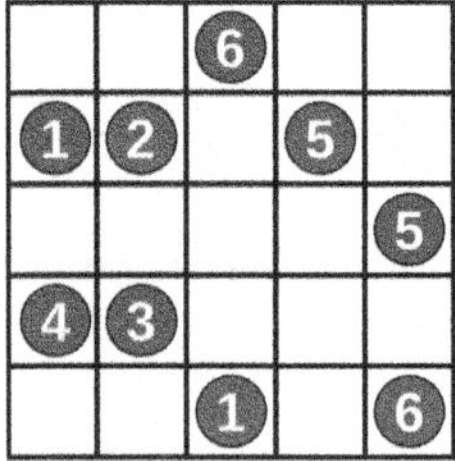

Fig. 7. An isomorphic board for Fig. 6

Take Fig. 6 for example. We can use an array to describe the distance each piece has to the corner. For instance, according to Fig. 5, red piece 1 has a distance of 4, red piece 2 has been captured, red piece 3 has a distance of 3, and so on. Finally, the array for the red side and the blue side will look like Fig. 8.

When collapsing the example in Fig. 7 to an array, the result will be the same as the array shown in Fig. 8. Therefore, Fig. 6 and Fig. 7 have the same distance array.

Fig. 8. The distance array for the Fig. 6 and Fig. 7

When two boards have the same distance array, they are considered isomorphic. In EWN-simple, each move decreases the distance to the corner by 1, meaning that pieces with the same distance to the corner exhibit the same behavior in playing.

3.3 Building a Database for EWN-Simple

To save more space, Zweistein does not directly store the win rate for every possible game position. Instead, it employs some techniques to further reduce space complexity.

Viewing a Player as a Random Variable. The first technique is to model a player as a random variable representing the number of steps required for any piece to reach the corner. To simplify this term, the number of steps required for any piece to reach the corner will be abbreviated as DTC (distance to corner).

For example, let X be a random variable that describes a player's behavior. The probability that the player's DTC is equal to d is given by:

$$P(X = d) \tag{1}$$

The range of DTC is [1, 19]. When DTC is 0, there is no need to calculate the evaluation function because the game has ended. The upper limit of 19 comes from the worst-case scenario: in this scenario, all 6 pieces initially have a distance of 4. They all move to a position where the distance is reduced to 1, which takes 18 steps. Finally, in the next step, one piece must reach the goal, adding up to a total of 19 steps.

Calculate Win Rate of EWN-Simple Using DTC Comparison. Because there is no piece-capturing rule in EWN-simple, the only way to win an EWN-simple game is to reach the corner. Therefore, the win rate of our side is the probability that our DTC is less than our opponent's DTC.

Even if our side has the same DTC as the opponent, it is still considered a loss. When evaluating a game position, we have already completed our move, and the opponent will move next. Therefore, having the same DTC as the opponent is not sufficient for our side to win.

To express this mathematically, let the DTC random variable of our side be denoted as X, and the DTC random variable of our opponent as Y. The probability that our DTC is less than our opponent's DTC can be written as:

$$P(X < Y) \tag{2}$$

However, the value of this probability cannot be directly calculated. The formula should be split by the value of DTC, which ranges from 1 to 19.

$$P(X \leq 0)P(Y = 1) + P(X \leq 1)P(Y = 2) + \\ \dots + P(X \leq 18)P(Y = 19) \tag{3}$$

The summation form for (3) is thus:

$$\sum_{i=1}^{19} P(X \leq i - 1)P(Y = i) \tag{4}$$

Equation (4) shows that using a probability density function (abbr. pdf) and a cumulative density function (abbr. cdf) database of a DTC random variable is sufficient to calculate Zweistein, which represents the win rate in EWN-simple. The pseudo-code for utilizing the pdf and cdf database to compute Zweistein is provided in Algorithm 1.

Algorithm 1. Calculate Zweistein from pdf and cdf database

Require: pdf and cdf database: PDF_VAL[15625][20],CDF_VAL[15625][20]
Require: our distance array and the opponent's distance array
   our_index=ENCODE(our dist array)
   $oppo\_index$=ENCODE(opponent dist array)
   $sum = 0$
   for $i = 1, 2, ..., 19$ **do**
      sum+=CDF_VAL[our_index][i-1]*PDF_VAL[$oppo\_index$][i]
   end for
   return sum

As discussed in Sect. 3.2, calculating Zweistein requires collapsing the game into a distance array. Since there are only $5^6 = 15625$ different distance arrays for each side, we can use any encoding function to map a distance array to an index in the range $[0, 15624]$. This index can then be used to query the pdf and cdf database to determine the win rate.

Building the Pdf Database. Since constructing a cdf from a pdf is a straightforward programming task, this paper will focus on demonstrating how to build a DTC pdf database.

Algorithm 2 is the pseudo-code for constructing the DTC pdf database. It follows a process similar to building an endgame database: perform a tree search for every game position and store the results after calculation. Because the database is very small, the entire building process takes less than a second to complete.

There is a GitHub repository [12] that implements this algorithm in C, available for anyone interested in using this evaluation function.

4   Experiments

4.1   Comparison with Other Functions

In Sect. 2.2, we mentioned some previous attempts to craft an evaluation function for EWN. In this section, we will compare Zweistein with those earlier approaches.

All of the experiments were conducted on a computer equipped with dual AMD EPYC 9354 32-core processors, with the program written in C++. For each searching depth, Zweistein played with the other function 100,000 times.

The first function we will compare is called ODEMA [10]. This function combines the attacking power, threat power, and blocking power with the formula:

$$attack\_factor \times Attack + Block - threat\_factor \times Threat \qquad (5)$$

For our experiment, we used the parameters provided in the original paper: $attack\_factor = 2.5$, $threat\_factor = 0.05$. Although the value of parameter N was not specified in the paper, it is necessary to calculate $Block$. So we use $N = 2$ for the experiment.

Table 1. The win rate of Zweistein when playing with ODEMA

searching depth	1	2	3	4	5	6	7
Win rate of Zweistein	0.47284	0.59492	0.55789	0.62252	0.53955	0.60491	0.52779

The second function is called EWNNY [9]. This function is very complicated and has many parameters, so we used the program written by the author directly for the experiment (Table 2).

Table 2. The win rate of Zweistein when playing with EWNNY

search depth	1	2	3	4	5	6	7
Win rate of Zweistein	0.38912	0.48866	0.45690	0.50192	0.48137	0.49841	0.49362

Algorithm 2. pdf database generator

```
Require: a table that stores all results: PDF_VAL[15625][20]
  procedure CalculateExpectedValueOfDTC(pdf)
      sum=0
      for i = 0, ..., 19 do
          sum += i*pdf[i]
      end for
      return sum
  end procedure
  procedure RightShift(pdf)
      new_pdf[20] = [0,...,0] (20 zeroes)
      for i = 0, 1, 2, ..., 19 do
          new_pdf[i+1] = pdf[i]
      end for
      return new_pdf
  end procedure
  procedure Move(dist array, piece num)
      dist array[piece num]-=1
      return dist array
  end procedure
  procedure TREE_SEARCH(dist array)
      if WIN CONDITION then
          return [1,0,...,0] (1 followed by 19 zeroes)
      end if
      index=ENCODE(dist array)
      if PDF_VAL[index] is visited then
          return PDF_VAL[index]
      else
          sum=[0,...,0] (20 zeroes)
          for dice = 1, 2, ..., 6 do
              min_exp = ∞,min_pdf=[]
              for num = all movable piece number do
                  child array=Move(a copy of dist array, num)
                  child_pdf=TREE_SEARCH(child array)
                  expval=CalculateExpectedValueOfDTC(child_pdf)
                  if expval < min_exp then
                      min_exp = expval
                      min_pdf=child pdf
                  end if
              end for
              sum+=min_pdf
          end for
          PDF_VAL[index]=RightShift(sum/6)
          mark PDF_VAL[index] as visited
      end if
  end procedure
  for index = 1, 2, ..., 15624 do
      dist array=DECODE(index)
      TREE_SEARCH(dist array)
  end for
  return PDF_VAL
```

In Table 1, Zweistein appears weak during a depth-1 search, primarily due to the absence of piece-capturing rules. However, since piece captures are possible during the tree search, this process naturally compensates for Zweistein's blind spot. As a result, the function's performance improves rapidly with increasing search depth when playing against ODEMA. The win rate never drops below

50% when the depth is greater than 1. Notably, ODEMA only showed better performance when the search depth was an odd number, indicating that this function lacks stable performance across different search depths.

In the second table, Zweistein's performance closely mirrors that of EWNNY when the search depth is greater than 4. Despite the similarity in performance, Zweistein stands out for being simpler and faster, with a speed advantage of 52.4% over EWNNY. Table 3 shows that Zweistein takes an average of 16.53 ns per call, while EWNNY takes an average of 25.20 ns.

Table 3. Time analysis between Zweistein and EWNNY on AMD EPYC 9354

function type	Zweistein	EWNNY
Time spend after executing 10^8 times	1.653 s	2.520 s

Although Zweistein is faster than EWNNY, it is still insufficient for an additional search layer. However, the increased speed provides greater flexibility in time management, making Zweistein stronger than EWNNY when the total time is fixed.

An experiment was conducted to support this statement. We used dynamic time control to set the time limit for each move. The dynamic time control formula we used is as follows:

$$time\_limit\_each\_step = \frac{remaining\_time}{max((15 - number\_of\_steps\_taken), 3)} \quad (6)$$

Table 4 shows the win rate between EWNNY and Zweistein at various fixed total times. Each cell represents the win rate over 100,000 games. We observe that when the total time exceeds 5 s, Zweistein achieves a higher win rate than EWNNY.

Table 4. The win rate of Zweistein when playing with EWNNY in various fixed total times

total time (in seconds)	1	2	3	4	5
Win rate of Zweistein	0.496050	0.499440	0.499060	0.498910	0.502150
total time (in seconds)	6	7	8	9	10
Win rate of Zweistein	0.502710	0.501050	0.500350	0.501000	0.502430

4.2 Comparison with Exact Win Rate

In this section, we use simple boards for which the exact win rate can be calculated by brute force. We then compare the exact win rate and evaluation values of Zweistein. Since Zweistein does not include piece-capturing rules, when each piece is separated from the others and capture is not possible on the next move, Zweistein's evaluation value closely approximates the exact win rate. For example, in Fig. 9, if the blue side moves first, the exact win rate for the red side is 0.564142, while Zweistein's value is 0.588791.

On the other hand, when piece-capturing has a significant impact on the win rate, Zweistein's value becomes inaccurate. For example, in Fig. 10, the blue side can avoid losing the game by capturing red 2, but Zweistein does not take this into consideration. If the blue side moves first, the exact win rate for the red side is 0.659595, while Zweistein's value is 0.954475.

However, by performing a depth-1 search, the influence of piece capture can be detected by the search algorithm, making the depth-1 Zweistein value 0.608869, which is more accurate than the original version. This is the primary reason why Zweistein performs poorly at lower search depths but performs better at higher search depths.

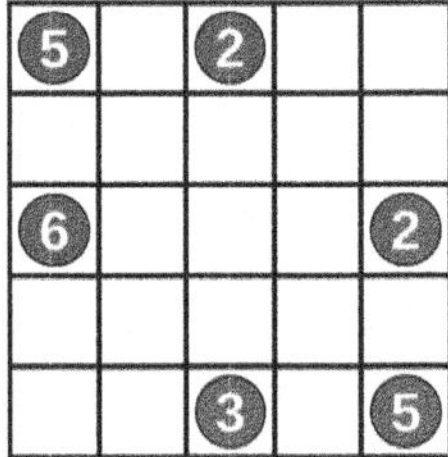

Fig. 9. An example board that Zweistein is accurate

Fig. 10. Another example board that Zweistein is not accurate

5   Computer Tournaments

Zweistein participated in the TCGA 2023 tournament and secured first place among 8 contestants. Table 5 provides the contest record, demonstrating the strength and effectiveness of this evaluation function.

Table 5. The record of TCGA2023

No.	rounds	1		2		3		4		5		6		7		result	
		opp	win	opp	win	opp	win	opp	win	opp	win	opp	win	opp	win	sum	rank
1	EWN_AI	6	37	2	39	3	59	4	50	5	68	8	76	7	53	382	4
2	Zweistein	5	57	1	61	7	53	6	53	8	83	3	73	4	49	429	1
3	Reinstein	4	35	5	48	1	41	7	33	6	32	2	27	8	74	290	7
4	Monte_Alpha	3	65	8	73	5	66	1	50	7	50	6	46	2	51	401	3
5	EWN_Alpha	2	43	3	52	4	34	8	62	1	32	7	46	6	38	307	6
6	deku_Ein	1	63	7	52	8	68	2	47	3	68	4	54	5	62	414	2
7	ssunoo	8	66	6	48	2	47	3	67	4	50	5	54	1	47	379	5
8	MuMu	7	34	4	27	6	32	5	38	2	17	1	24	3	26	198	8

6   Concluding Remarks and Future Work

In this paper, we introduced a novel approach to designing an EWN evaluation function by simplifying the game rules and constructing a database based on these simplified rules. This resulted in a simple, yet powerful, evaluation function that requires no parameter tuning. It also acts as a strong and simple baseline when crafting a stronger EWN evaluation function.

Although experiments demonstrate that it is possible to construct an evaluation function with performance similar to Zweistein using traditional methods, these functions typically require parameter tuning and are significantly more computationally expensive to develop. Additionally, the potential for improving traditional evaluation functions is limited. Due to the curse of dimensionality [13], adding a new parameter to the function exponentially multiplies the time complexity of grid search.

For example, EWNNY [9] requires an extensive grid search to acquire an optimal set of parameters, with each set of parameters necessitating a $100,000$-round experiment.

The current version of Zweistein requires only a few megabytes of space, which is relatively small by today's standards. This suggests substantial potential for further development and optimization. Expanding the database to include partial rules for piece capturing presents a promising direction for enhancing Zweistein's performance.

Acknowledgments. This research was partially supported by the Ministry of Science and Technology Council (NSTC) of Taiwan under grant numbers 111-2221-E-001-017-MY3. We would also like to express our gratitude to the reviewers for their valuable feedback.

Disclosure of Interests. The authors have no competing interests.

References

1. Shannon, Claude E..: XXII. Programming a computer for playing chess. London, Edinburgh, Dublin Philos. Mag. J. Sci. **41**(314), 256–275 (1950). https://doi.org/10.1080/14786445008521796
2. Fellows, C., Malitsky, Y. and Wojtaszczyk, G.: Exploring GnuGo's Evaluation Function with a SVM. In: AAAI Conference on Artificial Intelligence (2006)
3. Silver, D., et al.: Mastering the game of go with deep neural networks and tree search. Nature **529**(7587), 484–489 (2016)
4. Althöfer, I., Voigt, R.: EinStein würfelt nicht. In: Spiele, Rätsel, Zahlen, pp. 41–47. Springer, Heidelberg (2014). https://doi.org/10.1007/978-3-642-55301-1_4
5. van den Herik, H.J., Plaat, A. (eds.): Advances in Computer Games: 13th International Conference, ACG 2011, Tilburg, The Netherlands, November 20-22, 2011, Revised Selected Papers. Springer Berlin Heidelberg, Berlin, Heidelberg (2012)
6. Chu, Y.J.R., Chen, Y.H., Hsueh, C.H., Wu, I.C.: An agent for EinStein Würfelt Nicht! Using N-Tuple networks. In: 2017 Conference on Technologies and Applications of Artificial Intelligence (TAAI), Taipei, Taiwan, 2017, pp. 184-189, https://doi.org/10.1109/TAAI.2017.32.

7. Li, X., et al.: "A Modification of UCT Algorithm for WTN-EinStein würfelt nicht! Game. In: 2020 IEEE/CIC International Conference on Communications in China (ICCC), Chongqing, China, 2020, pp. 640-644, https://doi.org/10.1109/ICCC49849.2020.9238833.

8. Chen, C.-H.; Chiu, S.-Y.; Lin, S.-S. Design and Implementation of EinStein Würfelt Nicht Program Monte_Alpha. Electronics 2023, 12, 2936. https://doi.org/10.3390/electronics12132936

9. To, S.-T.: In Search of a Heuristic for Einstein Würfelt Nicht!, 2024 Taiwan Computer Games Association conference. National Dong Hwa University. 13-14 June (2024)

10. Li, X., Guang, Y., Wu, L., Zhang, Y.: An offensive and defensive expect minimax algorithm in EinStein Würfelt Nicht!. The 27th Chinese Control and Decision Conference,: CCDC). Qingdao, China **2015**, 5814–5817 (2015). https://doi.org/10.1109/CCDC.2015.7161846

11. Campbell, M., Hoane, A.J., Hsu, F.: Deep Blue. Artif. Intell. **134**(1–2), 57–83 (2002). https://doi.org/10.1016/S0004-3702(01)00129-1

12. W. L. Hsueh, (2024). Zweistein. GitHub repository. https://github.com/weilin97462/Zweistein

13. Richard Ernest Bellman. Dynamic Programming. Courier Dover Publications. 2003 [2012-05-18]. ISBN 978-0-486-42809-3

Author Index

The manufacturer's authorised representative in the EU is Springer
Nature Customer Service Centre GmbH, Europaplatz 3, 69115 Heidelberg,
Germany. If you have any concerns regarding our products, please
contact ProductSafety@springernature.com

Printed and bound by CPI Group (UK) Ltd, Croydon, CR0 4YY

01/07/2026

02153164-0004